Buying, Selling and Letting Property
2004

by
David Hampshire

SURVIVAL BOOKS • LONDON • ENGLAND

First published 2004

Survival Books Limited, 1st Floor,
60 St James's Street, London SW1A 1ZN, United Kingdom
☎ +44 (0)20-7493 4244, ▤ +44 (0)20-7491 0605
✉ info@survivalbooks.net
💻 www.survivalbooks.net
To order books, please refer to page 322.

British Library Cataloguing in Publication Data.
A CIP record for this book is available
from the British Library.
ISBN 1 901130 87 8

Printed and bound in Finland by WS Bookwell Ltd

ACKNOWLEDGEMENTS

My sincere thanks to all those who contributed to the publication of this book, in particular Kerry and Joe Laredo (editing, proof-reading and layout). Diana Tolland (research), Joanna Styles, Grania Rogers, Graeme Chesters, Pat and Ron Scarborough and everyone else who contributed in any way who I have omitted to mention. Also a special thank you to Jim Watson for the superb cover, illustrations and cartoons.

Order forms are on page 322.

WHAT READERS & REVIEWERS

When you buy a model plane for your child, a video recorder, or some new computer gizmo, you get with it a leaflet or booklet pleading 'Read Me First', or bearing large friendly letters or bold type saying 'IMPORTANT - follow the instructions carefully'. This book should be similarly supplied to all those entering France with anything more durable than a 5-day return ticket. It is worth reading even if you are just visiting briefly, or if you have lived here for years and feel totally knowledgeable and secure. But if you need to find out how France works then it is indispensable. Native French people probably have a less thorough understanding of how their country functions. - Where it is most essential, the book is most up to the minute.

LIVING FRANCE

Rarely has a 'survival guide' contained such useful advice. This book dispels doubts for first-time travellers, yet is also useful for seasoned globetrotters - In a word, if you're planning to move to the USA or go there for a long-term stay, then buy this book both for general reading and as a ready-reference.

AMERICAN CITIZENS ABROAD

It is everything you always wanted to ask but didn't for fear of the contemptuous put down - The best English-language guide - Its pages are stuffed with practical information on everyday subjects and are designed to complement the traditional guidebook.

SWISS NEWS

A complete revelation to me - I found it both enlightening and interesting, not to mention amusing.

CAROLE CLARK

Let's say it at once. David Hampshire's ***Living and Working in France*** is the best handbook ever produced for visitors and foreign residents in this country; indeed, my discussion with locals showed that it has much to teach even those born and bred in l'Hexagone. - It is Hampshire's meticulous detail which lifts his work way beyond the range of other books with similar titles. Often you think of a supplementary question and search for the answer in vain. With Hampshire this is rarely the case. - He writes with great clarity (and gives French equivalents of all key terms), a touch of humour and a ready eye for the odd (and often illuminating) fact. - This book is absolutely indispensable.

THE RIVIERA REPORTER

A mine of information - I may have avoided some embarrassments and frights if I had read it prior to my first Swiss encounters - Deserves an honoured place on any newcomer's bookshelf.

ENGLISH TEACHERS ASSOCIATION, SWITZERLAND

Have Said About Survival Books

What a great work, wealth of useful information, well-balanced wording and accuracy in details. My compliments!

Thomas Müller

This handbook has all the practical information one needs to set up home in the UK – The sheer volume of information is almost daunting – Highly recommended for anyone moving to the UK.

American Citizens Abroad

A very good book which has answered so many questions and even some I hadn't thought of – I would certainly recommend it.

Brian Fairman

We would like to congratulate you on this work: it is really super! We hand it out to our expatriates and they read it with great interest and pleasure.

ICI (Switzerland) AG

Covers just about all the things you want to know on the subject – In answer to the desert island question about the one how-to book on France, this book would be it – Almost 500 pages of solid accurate reading – This book is about enjoyment as much as survival.

The Recorder

It's so funny – I love it and definitely need a copy of my own – Thanks very much for having written such a humorous and helpful book.

Heidi Guiliani

A must for all foreigners coming to Switzerland.

Antoinette O'Donoghue

A comprehensive guide to all things French, written in a highly readable and amusing style, for anyone planning to live, work or retire in France.

The Times

A concise, thorough account of the DOs and DON'Ts for a foreigner in Switzerland – Crammed with useful information and lightened with humorous quips which make the facts more readable.

American Citizens Abroad

Covers every conceivable question that may be asked concerning everyday life – I know of no other book that could take the place of this one.

France in Print

Hats off to ***Living and Working in Switzerland***!

Ronnie Almeida

THE AUTHOR

David Hampshire was born in the United Kingdom, where after serving in the Royal Air Force he was employed for many years in the computer industry. He has lived and worked in many countries, including Australia, France, Germany, Malaysia, the Netherlands, Singapore, Switzerland and Spain, where he now resides most of the year. It was while working in Switzerland that he wrote his first book, ***Living and Working in Switzerland***, in 1987. To date David is the author of 15 books, including ***Buying a Home in Britain, Buying a Home in Florida, Buying a Home in France, Buying a Home in Italy, Buying a Home in Portugal, Buying a Home in Spain, Living and Working in France, Living and Working in Spain*** and ***Retiring Abroad***.

Contents

FOR SALE
STONE'S THROW
FROM SCHOOL

Important Note

Readers should note that the laws and regulations regarding buying property are liable to change periodically. **I cannot recommend too strongly that you check with an official and reliable source (not always the same) and take expert legal advice before paying any money or signing any legal documents. Don't, however, believe everything you're told or read, even, dare I say it, herein!**

To help you obtain further information and verify data with official sources, useful addresses and references to other sources of information have been included in all chapters and in **Appendices A** to **C**. Important points have been emphasised throughout the book **in bold print**, some of which it would be expensive or foolish to disregard; **ignore them at your peril or cost.** Unless specifically stated, the reference to any company, organisation, product or publication in this book **doesn't** constitute an endorsement or recommendation.

AUTHOR'S NOTES

- Prices quoted are in pounds (£) sterling and include VAT at 17.5 per cent unless otherwise stated. They should be taken as estimates only, particular property prices which change frequently.
- His/he/him/man/men (etc.) also mean her/she/her/woman/women (no offence ladies!). This is done simply to make life easier for both the reader and (in particular) the author, and **isn't** intended to be sexist.
- Warnings, tips and other important points are printed in **bold** type throughout the book.
- The following abbreviations are used in this book: ☎ (telephone), 🖷 (fax), 🖂 (email) and 💻 (Internet).
- Lists of **Useful Addresses**, **Further Reading** and **Useful Websites** are contained in **Appendices A** to **C** respectively.
- Comprehensive **Checklists for Moving House** are contained in **Appendix D**.
- A list of property, mortgage and other terms used in this book is included in the **Glossary** in **Appendix E**.

INTRODUCTION

Whether you're looking for a cottage or a castle, an apartment or a mansion, this book will help reduce the frustrations and stress, and (hopefully) make it an exciting and rewarding experience. The main aim of ***Buying, Selling & Letting Property 2004*** is to provide you with the information necessary to help you choose the most favourable location and most appropriate home **to satisfy your individual requirements.** Most importantly, it will help you to avoid the potential pitfalls and risks associated with buying a home, which for most people is the largest purchase they will ever make.

Property has always been a good long-term investment and in the last few years it has out-performed the stock market and all forms of savings, and provides both capital growth and income (if you let a property). As a rough rule of thumb, house values in the UK double every seven years, although in recent years property in many areas has doubled in as little as three or four years. In the past, many homeowners dramatically increased the value of their family home by 'trading up' – that is buying a bigger and more expensive home every 'few' years. However, the introduction of buy to let mortgages has encouraged people to buy investment property, and thousands now invest in property, often as an alternative to (or to supplement) a pension. One of the reasons for the huge rise in property values in most regions in the last few years (between 15 and 70 per cent in 2003 alone!) has been the realisation that owing property isn't just about having a roof over your head, but is an excellent long-term investment.

Before buying property you need to decide **exactly** what your motives are; for example are you looking for a principal home, a holiday home or an investment property? How long do you plan to occupy or own a property? Where and what can you afford to buy? How can you maximise your profit when selling? ***Buying, Selling & Letting Property 2004*** will help you answer these and many other questions. It won't, however, tell you where and what to buy or whether having made your decision you will be happy – that part is up to you!

Buying, Selling & Letting Property 2004 contains advice on all aspects of buying a property, including choosing the best location, what sort of home to buy, the buying process, finding the right mortgage, moving house, home improvements, letting and selling. However, it doesn't claim to contain all the answers – most of us don't even know the right questions to ask! What it **will** do is reduce the risk of making an expensive mistake that you may regret later and help you make informed decisions and calculated judgements, rather than costly mistakes and uneducated guesses (forewarned is forearmed!). **Most importantly, it will help you save money and repay your investment many times over.**

Before plunging into the property market and mortgaging yourself up to the hilt, bear in mind that property prices both rise **and** fall, as do interest rates. In the last few decades the property market has gone from boom to bust and back again, and although it has been thriving in the last few years, some analysts believe that it's heading for a downturn in 2004, perhaps fuelled by a rise in interest rates. Nevertheless, property remains one of the best long-term investments and it's certainly one of the most pleasurable. I trust this book will help you avoid the pitfalls and smooth your way to many happy years in your new home, secure in the knowledge that you have made the right decision.

Happy house hunting!

David Hampshire
November 2003

1.

Choosing The Location

The most important thing to consider when buying a home is usually the location – or as the old adage goes, the **three** most important points are **location, location and location!** A property in a reasonable condition in a popular area is likely to be a better investment than an exceptional property in a less attractive location. The wrong decision regarding location is one of the main causes of disenchantment among property buyers. Where you buy a property will depend on a range of factors, including your personal preferences, your financial resources, whether you're buying a principal home, a holiday home or an investment property, and, not least, whether you will be commuting to work. If you've got a job, the location of your home will probably be determined by the proximity to your place of employment or good public transport links. However, if you intend to look for employment or start a business, you must live in an area that allows you the maximum scope (unless you work from home!).

Unless you've good reason to believe otherwise, you'd be foolish to rely on finding employment in a particular area. If, on the other hand, you're looking for a holiday or retirement home, you can live virtually anywhere. When seeking a retirement home, don't be too influenced by where you've spent an enjoyable holiday or two. A town or area that was acceptable for a few weeks holiday may be far from suitable for a retirement home, particularly regarding the proximity to shops, medical facilities and other amenities (a pleasant summer resort may be deserted in winter with most shops and attractions closed).

Bear in mind that the climate, lifestyle and cost of living can vary considerably from region to region.

In autumn 2003, for the first time in many years, as many people were moving from the country to the city as vice-versa.

If you plan to move to an unfamiliar region or city, read as much as you can about the area and spend some time looking around the towns and suburbs of interest. It's necessary to narrow your search area at least to a county or city and preferably to a few towns or a few suburbs of a large city. Before looking at properties it's important to have a good idea of the kind of property you're looking for and the price you wish to pay, and to draw up a shortlist of the areas or towns of interest. If you don't do this, you're likely to be overwhelmed by the number of properties to be viewed. It's advisable to make a list of what you absolutely **must** have and what you definitely **won't** consider, which will help narrow the market considerably.

SURVIVAL TIP
When deciding where you want to live, it also helps to make a list of areas you won't consider at all.

The 'best' area in which to live depends on (not least) your bank balance and lifestyle; a family with children and animals (dogs, horses, etc.) has a very different lifestyle from a young, high-income couple who enjoy shopping, clubbing and 'weekending' abroad! (In an independent survey in 2003, the Chilterns – north-west of London – were named the best area to live in the UK.) When looking for a home, bear in mind travelling times and costs to your place of work, shops and local amenities (such as restaurants and pubs!) – don't believe the times and distances stated in advertisements and by estate agents, but check for yourself. If you buy a remote country property, the distance to local amenities and services could become a problem, particularly if you plan to retire there later. If you live in a remote rural area you will need to be much more self-sufficient than if you live in a town and will need to use the car for everything, which will add significantly to your cost of living (particularly if you've got children who need ferrying to school, friends' houses, sports events, clubs, etc.).

Check a property's exact location on a large-scale map and what is near it. Good points include the following:

- Proximity to a railway station or motorway;
- In a city centre, just outside a town or on the edge of a village;
- Sea or unspoiled country views;
- Close to a golf course and shops.

Bad points include the following:

- Too remote;
- Near a busy sports or entertainment venue such as a pub or discotheque, major road or airport flight path;
- Too close to a railway line or a busy road, next to a factory, milk or bus depot, sewage works, landfill, electricity pylons, radio or telephone mast;
- Near a river with a high risk of flooding or in a flood plain;
- Near a crumbling cliff with a history of erosion!

The positive and negative points of a property's location can dramatically affect its price and investment value and should be taken into account when buying. The table below shows the most common positive and negative features (listed in order of most impact to least), which can effect property prices by up to 15 or 20 per cent:

Positive	**Negative**
Main railway station	Run down/derelict houses
Motorway/dual carriageway link	Airport flight path
Top state school	Derelict land
Open countryside/park	Pungent takeaway
Restaurants/pubs/nightlife	Late licence drink/music venue
Quality food store (e.g. Waitrose/M&S)	Busy road
Good NHS hospital	Waste/refuse station
Sports club/exercise facilities	Poorly-rated comprehensive school
Post office and bank	Local authority housing
Cinema/entertainment	Electricity pylons
	Prison
	Railway line
	Mobile phone/telecom masts

What is the neighbourhood like and the quality of the shops, restaurants and other amenities? Is it an up and coming area or down at heel? What are the neighbouring properties like and does the street and local town look well cared for?

Some areas are said to be 'up and coming', which is estate agent speak for a poor area that may be worth more in future (but don't take their word for it!).

Trying to find the next boom area or hot spot is a lottery and a national pastime. Hot spots are generally very expensive, but if you get in while an area is still only warm you may make a killing.

Hot spots generally have an attractive environment, such as a pretty square or a conservation area in a town, an unspoilt village or a peaceful country location with panoramic views. Generally there must be easy access to a major city and no road, rail or air traffic noise. New public transport links (such as the £10 billion east-west Crossrail railway link in London), fast roads such as motorways and dual carriageways (and other quality infrastructure) can dramatically increase property values – but can also reduce them if they're within earshot! A Local Authority Search costing around £80 will tell you all you need to know about planned developments.

If possible you should visit an area a number of times over a period of a few weeks or months, both on weekdays and at weekends, in order to get a feel for the neighbourhood (walk, don't just drive around!). A property seen on a balmy spring day after a delicious pub lunch and a few glasses of your favourite tipple may not be nearly so attractive on a subsequent visit lacking sunshine and the warm inner glow. If possible, you should also visit an area at different times of the year, e.g. in both summer and winter, as somewhere that's wonderful in summer can be forbidding and inhospitable in winter. If you're unfamiliar with an area, most experts recommend that you rent for a period before deciding to buy.

If you will be commuting, you should obtain a map of the area and decide the maximum distance you wish to travel to work, e.g. by drawing a circle with your workplace in the middle, taking into account local traffic congestion and public transport. If you're prepared to commute, you can save a fortune by buying in the suburbs or up to an hour away from a city by train. You will also get the benefits of the countryside and be relatively close to a city, but you must take into account the extra travelling time and cost of travel, e.g. a rail season ticket (and whether the local rail company has a reputation for punctuality and reliability).

LOCATION CHECKLIST

There are many points to consider regarding the location of a home, which can roughly be divided into the local vicinity, i.e. the immediate surroundings and neighbourhood, and the general area or region. When choosing the location for a home you should take into account the following:

- Check for signs of urban blight. Many once desirable suburbs surrounding major cities are in a crisis of neglect with increasing crime and a breakdown of the community. Indications are unkempt homes, gardens and streets; dumped cars and rubbish; broken streetlights and signs; boarded-up shops and a profusion of second-hand shops; few local services; high crime rates and stagnating property prices.

- If the climate is an important factor in buying a home, you should bear in mind both winter and summer temperatures, the average daily sunshine, the local rainfall, wind conditions and the position of the sun in relation to a property. The orientation or aspect of a building is crucial; if you want morning or afternoon sun (or both) you must ensure that rooms, balconies, patios, terraces and gardens face the right direction. A north-facing house will be cool in summer, but may be damp and chilly in winter, while a south-facing conservatory could be unbearably hot in summer (unless it has air-conditioning).
- Check whether an area is particularly prone to inclement weather and natural disasters such as drought, floods, fog or snow. Despite the UK's high rainfall, some areas are affected by drought and there may be water restrictions during the summer. Floods are a regular occurrence in many parts of the country and north-west Europe's rainfall is expected to increase fivefold by 2100. If a property is located near a coast or waterway, it may be expensive to insure against floods, which are a constant threat in some areas.

The Association of British Insurers' pledge to cover flood-prone properties expired on 31st December 2002 and it's estimated that around 200,000 homes may be uninsurable.

You should be wary of buying a property near a river or in a flood plain. Estate agents must disclose any history of flooding when selling a house and you can also check the occurrence of flooding in the last few decades with the Environment Agency (Floodline – ☎ 0845-988 1188, 🖳 www.environment-agency.gov.uk). Home Check (🖳 www.homecheck.co.uk) will tell you whether a property is at risk from flooding, landslide, subsidence, air or other pollution, radon gas, landfill, waste sites, disused coal mines and so on. The Home Check service is free and all you need do is enter a property's postcode on their website. Enviro Search (🖳 www.home-envirosearch.com) can also tell you whether a property is adversely affected by any environmental factors.

Despite the risks of flooding, properties in flood plains, particularly those with a river frontage or by the sea, are in high demand (most buyers are blasé when it comes to flood risks). It's possible to build impregnable flood defences, although it can be expensive, and you may also be able to raise the ground floor. A relatively cheap solution is the expandable 'Floodgate' (🖳 http://

floodgate.ltd.uk) that fits across doorways and protects homes up to the height of the ground floor windows.

- Noise is a problem, particularly in cities and towns, and millions of people are affected by it (around 40 per cent of the population in some cities). It can be a disaster in apartments (particularly conversions) and in terraced and semi-detached houses. Disputes have increased in recent years and have led to violence and even murder in a number of cases. Much of the problem in cities arises from poor building techniques and the fact that new buildings often don't have the same levels of noise deadening as old buildings. To check the noise level, you should view an apartment in the evening when everyone is at home.

  Although you cannot choose your neighbours, you can at least ensure that a property isn't located next to a busy road, railway line, farm (tractors, dogs, cockerels, etc.), church (with a bell that 'dongs' often), airport, industrial plant, commercial area, discotheque, night club, bar or restaurant, or area with a seedy nightlife and kerb crawlers. Look out for objectionable properties that may be too close to one you're considering and check whether nearby vacant land has been 'zoned' for commercial activities or tower blocks. Be wary of homes near airports, even small private airports. A planned expansion of flight paths for jet aircraft is expected to affect over 1 million homes (unless somebody invents a silent jet engine), with as many as 5,000mi^2 (13,000km^2) affected. The south-east will be particularly badly affected.

- Bear in mind that if you live in a popular tourist area you will be inundated with tourists in summer. They won't just jam the roads and pack the public transport, but may also occupy your favourite table at your local pub or restaurant (heaven forbid!). Although a property on the beach or in a marina development may sound attractive and be ideal for a holiday or investment home, it isn't always the best choice for a permanent home. Many beaches are hopelessly crowded in the high season, streets may be smelly and littered from restaurants and fast food outlets, parking impossible, and services stretched to breaking point – and the incessant noise may drive you crazy!

- Do you wish to be in a town or do you prefer the country? Inland or on the coast? How about living on an island? Bear in mind that if you buy a property in a remote area, you will probably have to tolerate poor public transport (or none at all), long travelling distances to a town of any size, solitude and remoteness. You won't be able to pop along to the local baker for your daily bread, drop into the local pub for a drink with the locals, or have a choice of restaurants on your doorstep. In a town or large village, the market will be just around the corner, the doctor and chemist close at hand, and if you need help or run into any problems, your neighbours will be close by.

In some towns and villages the locals may resent outsiders and if your children don't go to school locally they (and their parents) may find it difficult to make friends.

On the other hand, in the country you will be closer to nature, will have more freedom (e.g. to make as much noise as you wish) and possibly complete privacy, e.g. to sunbathe or swim *au naturel*. Living in a remote area in the country will suit nature lovers looking for solitude who don't want to involve themselves in the 'hustle and bustle' of town life. If you're after peace and quiet, make sure that there isn't a busy road or railway line nearby or local church bells within earshot.

Many people who buy a remote country home find that the peace and quiet of the countryside palls after a time and they yearn for the more exciting city lifestyle.

If you've never lived in the country, it's advisable to rent for six months before buying. Contrary to many town-dwellers' hopes and dreams, it's frequently unpleasantly wet and muddy, smelly and incredibly noisy.

While it's cheaper to buy in a remote or unpopular location, it's usually more difficult to find a buyer when you want to sell.

If you're planning to buy a country property with an extensive garden or plot of land, bear in mind the high cost and amount of work involved in its upkeep. If it's to be a second home, who will look after the house and garden when you're away? Do you want to spend your holidays mowing the lawn and cutting back the undergrowth? Do you want a home with a lot of outbuildings that need constant repairs?

What are you going to do with them? Can you afford to convert them into extra rooms or guest or self-catering accommodation?

- What about your employment and that of your spouse and children (or local employment prospects)? How secure are your jobs or businesses and are you likely to move to another area in the near future? Can you find other work in the same area if necessary? If there's a possibility that you may need to move in a few years' time, you should rent or at least buy a property that will be relatively easy to sell and recoup the cost (hopefully make a profit!).
- What about your children's present and future schooling? What is the quality of local schools? Do they have any places vacant (you may find that they're full and you have to enrol your children in private schools miles away)? Even if your family has no need or plans to use local schools, the value of a home is often influenced by their quality and proximity. The quality of local state schools is one of the most important considerations for parents. Many people pay dearly to live within the catchment area of a good state school, which is a big selling point that can add tens of thousands of pounds to the value of a property. If your children are planning to go on to higher education, could they commute to a local university from home?
- Is the proximity to public transport, e.g. an international airport, ferry port or railway station, or access to a motorway important?

SURVIVAL TIP
Don't believe what you're told about the distance or travelling times to the nearest motorway, railway station, airport, port, beach or town, but check for yourself.

A fast rail link to London and other major cities can increase the value of a property considerably, while a home within earshot of a busy main road or motorway will be greatly devalued. A busy road or bus route running past a property may also devalue it (such as a red route in London).

- If you're planning to buy in a town or city, is there adequate safe parking? In some areas it's important to have secure off-street parking if you value your car. Parking is a nightmare in many towns and cities, where private garages or parking spaces are rare and **very** expensive. Chronic traffic congestion is also a problem in most towns.

Some tradesmen may refuse to work in areas where there's nowhere to park (e.g. in London)!

On the other hand, perhaps you could cope quite well in a city without a car altogether?

- What is the quality of local hospitals and other health services? Do local doctors and dentists have waiting lists for new NHS patients, and if so, can you afford to pay for private treatment? How far is the nearest hospital with an emergency department?
- What shopping facilities are provided in the local neighbourhood? How far is it to the nearest town with good shopping facilities, e.g. a supermarket? How would you get there if your car was off the road or you couldn't drive for health reasons or had lost your licence?

Note that many villages have few shops or facilities and no public transport, and aren't a good choice for a retirement home.

- What is the range and quality of local leisure, sports, community and cultural facilities? What is the proximity to sports facilities such as a gym, beach, golf course or waterway? Is there a local swimming pool and will you be able to use it (at some the membership is full and you need to travel miles to the nearest pool).
- What is the local crime rate? A high incidence of burglaries, housebreaking, stolen cars, muggings, prostitution, drug dealing and crimes of violence will drastically affect property values. Check the crime figures and if prices are low, find out why! Crime rates tend to be higher in areas where property is cheapest and most experts warn against buying in a crime spot, no matter how inexpensive the property. However, areas do change and today's high crime area could become a property hot spot in future.

Professional crooks target isolated rural houses, especially those with expensive (or antique) fixtures, fittings and furniture, that they can strip bare at their leisure.

You're much less likely to be a victim of theft if you live in a village, where crime is usually relatively low. Due to a higher than average crime rate, insurance is higher in major cities and some resort areas.

SURVIVAL TIP
Home contents insurance premiums are a good indication of the local crime rate and it's impossible to obtain insurance at all in some high-crime areas.

- What is the local TV and radio reception like? Can you receive all the terrestrial TV stations? Does an apartment have cable or satellite TV or can you install a satellite dish?

If you live in a conservation area or a listed building, it may be impossible to install a satellite dish (so check whether a property has cable TV).

- Is broadband Internet connection available locally? This may be an important consideration if you're running a business from home or have children who spend hours on the Internet.
- Do houses sell well in the area, e.g. in less than three months? Generally you should avoid neighbourhoods where desirable houses routinely remain on the market for three months or longer (unless the property market is in a severe slump and nothing is selling).

HOUSE PRICES

One of the most important considerations when choosing the location for a home is local property prices, which vary considerably throughout the UK. For example, in 2003 a one-bedroom apartment in central London was sold for £850,000 (which was £250,000 less than the original asking price) – you could buy a few spacious country homes in most regions for less! Prices vary not only from region to region, but also between particular towns and cities and different suburbs of a large city (perhaps divided by a single street, park or golf course). Inevitably you will find that what you want and like is outside your budget and you will have to compromise or be prepared to spend more! When comparing the price of properties, always take into account their overall size (in square feet or square meters), which is a huge factor.

Property prices have risen dramatically throughout the UK in recent years due to high demand and a shortage of homes for sale. Low interest rates have also given rise to rampant speculation (aided by a falling stock market), encouraged by the widespread availability of buy to let mortgages. Predictions of a price collapse in 2003 proved to be groundless and although prices did fall marginally in some regions, they rose considerably in others. This simply goes to illustrate that the UK isn't one market, but a collection of smaller ones that don't necessarily share the same characteristics.

As a rough rule of thumb, property values in the UK double every seven years, although in recent years prices in many areas have doubled in as little as three or four years. Between 1991 and 2001, there were rises of over 200 per cent in some towns and many saw rises of between 100 and 200 per cent, mostly in the south-east, south-west and Northern Ireland. The lowest gains were in Scotland and the north of England, although by autumn 2003 prices in northern England, the Midlands and South Wales had risen by an average of over 20 per cent in the previous 12 months and by up to 70 per cent in some areas (e.g. Northumberland) and towns (e.g. Widnes, Cheshire). Increases in southern and western England were below 15 per cent during the same period and in London they had actually fallen. Surrey has the country's most expensive houses (outside London), where the average price was over £275,000 in autumn 2003.

There are a number of companies and organisations providing monthly or quarterly house price indices, none of which agree entirely. These include the Halifax (💻 www.halifax.co.uk), Nationwide (💻 www.nationwide.co.uk), Right Move (💻 www.rightmove.co.uk), Hometrack (💻 www.hometrack.co.uk) and the Land Registry (💻 www.landreg.gov.uk) – the most accurate, but not the most up-to-date. At the end of the second quarter (July to September) 2003, the average cost of a house in the UK according to the Nationwide Building Society was as follows:

Region	Average Price
London	£213,419
Outer metropolitan	£198,785
Outer south-east	£163,011
South-west	£148,944
East Midlands	£118,028
West Midlands	£126,888
East Anglia	£137,454
North	£93,334
North-west	£109,027
Yorkshire & Humberside	£106,016

Scotland	£88,820
Wales	£101,266
Northern Ireland	£92,999
UK overall	£129,761

The above prices should be taken only as a guide. To obtain up-to-date property prices (and other information) in a particular region or town in England and Wales you can visit websites such as Up My Street (www.upmystreet.com), Provisor (www.proviser.com) and Hometrack (www.hometrack.co.uk), which will also provide a detailed report for £14.95 + VAT.

2.

WHAT TO BUY

After deciding where to buy a home (see **Chapter 1 – Choosing The Location**), your next task will be to decide what sort of home to buy. If you're unsure where and what to buy, the best decision is usually to rent for a period (e.g. six months) in the area where you plan to buy. This will allow you to become familiar with the weather, the amenities and local people, and to investigate the local property market at your leisure.

> **SURVIVAL TIP**
> **The secret of successfully buying a home (at the right price) is research, research and yet more research.**

You may be fortunate and buy the first property you see without doing any homework and live happily ever after. However, a successful purchase is much more likely if you thoroughly investigate the towns in your chosen area and compare the range and prices of homes, and their value for money. It's a wise or lucky person who gets his choice absolutely right first time, but it's much more likely if you do your homework thoroughly.

Before deciding exactly what to buy, you will need to decide exactly what you want and what you plan to do with a property. Ask yourself what you want and what you need – there's usually a huge discrepancy! Most importantly, what can you afford? Another important point may be when to buy, as it could be unwise to buy in a falling market, when interest rates are very high or your long-term finances are uncertain.

Before deciding exactly what to buy, you should ask yourself the following questions:

- Are you looking for a principal home, holiday home or an investment property? If you're buying an investment property, will it be let either permanently or for holiday rentals?
- How long do you plan to keep it? If you plan to sell within a few years you will want to buy a home which will sell easily and hopefully realise a profit. On the other hand, if you plan to stay put indefinitely, investment potential may not be top of your list (but should always be borne in mind, as you may need to sell unexpectedly).
- Do you want to live in a town or in the country?
- Do you want a house or an apartment? If you're looking for a house, must it be detached or would you settle for a semi-detached, terraced or town house? In a large city you may have to settle for an apartment, while in country areas apartments are rare.

- Do you want a new or old house? If you're seeking an old house, must it be of a certain style, e.g. Georgian or Victorian?
- What size must a home be (number of bedrooms and overall space) and what sort of outdoor space (garden, terraces, patio) do you require?
- Do you require off-road parking or a garage? In cities and large towns off-road parking is rare and can be prohibitively expensive. On-street parking is usually available for residents in cities, although it can be difficult to find a space.
- Would you consider a property requiring some work, modernisation or even complete restoration? What about buying a plot of land and building your own home or joining a housing association?
- What is your budget? There is no point in deciding on a particular style of house in a particular town if it will be way above your budget.

This chapter is designed to help you answer the above questions and decide what sort of home to buy. Topics covered include the following:

- Types of homes;
- Research;
- Using an agent;
- Relocation agents;
- First-time buyers;
- Buying a new house;
- Buying an old house;
- Buying an apartment (flat);
- Buying a mobile or park home;
- Buying a retirement home;
- Buying for investment;
- Buying land;
- Building your own home;
- Garages & parking.

TYPES OF HOMES

There's a wealth of different types and styles of property in the UK, which encompass everything from 17th and 18th century period houses to ultra modern, cutting-edge design. However, whatever type of home you choose, it will usually be built to a high standard and be extremely sturdy. Most people prefer older period houses with an abundance of 'charm and character' to 'sterile' modern homes, although you will often find pseudo period features such as beams and open fireplaces in new homes. Some new luxury homes are even built to modern standards using reclaimed materials, thus combining the best of both worlds.

Although new properties may be lacking in character, they're usually well endowed with all mod cons and services, which certainly cannot be taken for granted in older properties. Plumbing, electrical and heating systems in modern houses are more comprehensive and generally of better quality than those found in old houses. Central heating, double (or even triple) glazing and good insulation are standard in new houses and are considered essential by most buyers. In the last few decades, apartment living has become popular in the major cities, many of which are tasteful conversions of old buildings that have been converted into spacious loft apartments. These often come with stainless-steel kitchens, designer bathrooms, and other luxury features such as ducted air-conditioning/heating, multi-room audio systems and broadband (Internet) connections in all rooms.

Old Homes

Old homes usually refers to pre-1940 and homes built before 1914 are generally referred to as period homes, e.g. Georgian or Victorian. Older, larger homes often contain interesting period features such as high ceilings, fireplaces, sash windows, elaborate mouldings such as ceiling roses and cornices, panelled doors, imposing staircases, attics, cellars, alcoves and annexes. Fireplaces are usually a principal feature in old houses, even when central heating is installed, and give a room charm and a focus point as well as allowing the house to breathe. Floors may be made of slate or stone and wooden floors are also common. Most older, smaller homes (e.g. semi-detached and terraced houses) were often built without modern conveniences such as central heating, double glazing, fitted kitchens and proper bathrooms, although most have now been modernised and contain similar mod cons to new homes.

Modern Homes

Modern homes are built in a vast range of styles and sizes, from small studio and one-bedroom apartments and townhouses, to vast 'executive' detached homes on large plots and luxury penthouse apartments. Most new homes in England and Wales (around 60 per cent in Scotland) are built with brick and block cavity walls, and only some 10 per cent are timber frame construction (40 per cent in Scotland). New houses are usually (but not always) built to higher standards than older houses and include thermal insulation, double glazing, central heating and extensive ventilation. They also generally contain a high level of luxury features such as fully-tiled designer kitchens, en-suite bathrooms with power showers, and fitted wardrobes. Modern homes usually have a separate utility room off the kitchen where the washing machine and dryer are stored.

The most common types of homes include the following:

- **Apartment (Flat)** – An apartment (the same as an American condominium or a 'unit' in Australia) is usually located on one floor, although it can be spread over a number of floors.
- **Barn Conversion** – A barn that has been converted into a spacious home with high ceilings, exposed beams and oodles of character.
- **Bed-Sit** – A tiny one-room apartment for living and sleeping, possibly with it's own shower room, but no separate kitchen.
- **Bungalow** – A single-storey detached or semi-detached house. Popular with the elderly as they have no stairs.
- **Cottage** – Traditionally a pretty, quaint house in the country, perhaps with a thatched roof (although the name is often stretched nowadays to encompass almost anything except an apartment). May be detached or terraced.
- **Detached House** – A house that stands alone, usually with its own garden (possibly front and rear) and garage.
- **Houseboat** – These are popular in cities (with waterways!) and modern houseboats are luxurious and spacious. One of the drawbacks is finding a suitable mooring, which costs thousands of pounds a year.
- **Maisonette** – Part of a house or block of apartments comprising separate living accommodation, usually on two floors with its own external entrance.
- **Mews House** – A house that's converted from old stables or carriage houses (usually 17th to 19th century) and is the town equivalent of a genuine cottage. These are common in London and **very** expensive.
- **Mobile (Park) Home** – A pre-fabricated timber-framed home that can be moved to a new site, although most are permanently located on a 'home park'.

- **Period Property** – A property built before 1914 and named after the period in which it was built, e.g. Georgian (1780-1830), Victorian (1810-1901) or Edwardian (1901-1914).
- **Semi-Detached House** – A detached building containing two separate homes joined in the middle by a common party wall.
- **Stately Home** – A grand country mansion or estate, usually a few centuries old, many of which are owned by the UK's oldest titled families and open to the public (the rest are owned by the National Trust!).
- **Studio** – A one-room dwelling (no separate bedroom) plus a bathroom and possibly a small separate kitchen.
- **Terraced House** – Houses built in a row of three or more usually two to five storeys high.
- **Townhouse** – Similar to a terraced house, but more modern and larger, often with an integral garage.

RESEARCH

Don't be in too much of a hurry when buying. Have a good look around in your chosen area (see **Chapter 1 – Choosing The Location**) and obtain an accurate picture of the kinds of property available, the relative prices and what you can expect to get for your money. However, before doing this you should make a comprehensive list of what you want (and don't want) from a home so that you can narrow the field and save time on wild goose chases.

It's sometimes difficult to compare homes in different areas, as they often vary considerably and few houses are exactly comparable. Properties range from period terraced, semi-detached and detached houses, to modern townhouses and apartments with all modern conveniences; from dilapidated country mansions and castles requiring complete renovation to luxury modern executive homes and vast penthouses in converted buildings. You can also buy a plot of land and have an individually designed house built to your own specifications. If, however, after discussing it with your partner one of you insists on a modern luxury apartment in London and the other a crumbling 18th century castle in Scotland, the best solution may be to get a divorce!

Although property in the UK is relatively expensive compared with many other European countries, the fees associated with the purchase of property are among the lowest in Europe and add around 3 to 5 per cent to the cost. To reduce the chances of making an expensive error when buying in an unfamiliar region, it's often prudent to rent a home for a period, taking in the worst part of the year (weather-wise). This allows you to become familiar with the region and weather, and gives you plenty of time to look for a home at your leisure. Wait until you find something you fall head over heels in love with and then think about it for another week or two before rushing headlong to the altar! It's sometimes better to miss the 'opportunity of a lifetime' than end up with an expensive pile of bricks around your neck. However, don't dally too long, as good properties at the right price don't remain on the market for long.

One of the mistakes people make when buying a country property is to buy a house that's much larger than they need with a large plot of land, simply because it offers such comparatively value. Orchards, paddocks and large gardens require a lot of upkeep (work) and machinery, which is compounded if you plan on keeping horses or livestock. Don't, on the other hand, buy a property that's too small, as extra space can easily be swallowed up.

The more research you do before buying a property the better, which should include advice from people who already own a house locally, from whom you may be able to obtain invaluable information (often based on their own mistakes). A huge number of magazines and newspapers (see **Appendix A**) are published for homebuyers and property exhibitions are also staged throughout the year. Property is advertised for sale in all major newspapers (many of which contain property supplements on certain days) and local free newspapers. Information about properties for sale is also available via the Internet and many estate agents also have their own websites (see page 39). Numerous books are published for homebuyers in the UK (see **Appendix B**) and building societies and banks publish free booklets, most of which contain excellent (usually surprisingly unbiased!) advice.

Research Methods

- **Estate Agents** – There are estate agents (see below) in virtually every town in the UK where you can usually register and receive regular information about properties for sale matching your requirements. Most also have websites (see **Appendix C**).
- **Property Shops** – These are located mainly in Scotland where they're often run by solicitors, such as the Glasgow Solicitors' Property Centre (💻 www.gspc.co.uk), Scotland's largest property guide.

- **Search Agencies** – Relocation agents (see page 43) can find your dream home for you and are particularly useful for overseas buyers or when you're buying a luxury home and have special requirements. For information, contact the Association of Relocation Agents (ARA), PO Box 189, Diss, Norfolk IP22 1PE (☎ 01359-251800, 💻 www.relocationagents.com).
- **Internet** – Up to 3 million people or some 60 per cent of house hunters each year use the Internet to find a home. There are numerous websites (see **Appendix C**) where you can enter details of the area or town that you're interested in and the kind of property you seeking, and do a search online. You can register with agents and receive details of properties (over 300,000 are online) matching your requirements by email.
- **Newspapers And Magazines** – Local weekly newspapers are a good source of information about property prices, the types of property for sale and local agents. Most have a property section and free property newspapers are also published in most areas. Property magazines (see **Appendix A**) are good for new homes and usually contain a list of new developments throughout the country. Major daily and Sunday newspapers such as *The Daily Telegraph* (Saturday edition) and *The Sunday Times* contain property or home supplements and are good for up-market properties, as are county magazines.
- **Auctions** – Auction sales (see page 123) are popular in the UK, where they account for an increasing number of sales.
- **Private Sales In Newspapers And On Websites** – Private sales are becoming more popular in the UK through websites and newspapers such as *Loot* (see page 261), although the vast majority of properties are still sold by traditional estate agents.
- **For Sale Boards** – Drive around the areas that you're interested in looking for 'For Sale' boards.

SURVIVAL TIP

Note that properties displaying agents' boards may have an exclusive deal with the agent and you may not be able to buy direct from the vendor and bypass the agent (unless the vendor is permitted to do this in his contract with the agent).

AGENTS

There are three main types of property agents in the UK; estate agents, solicitor agents (Scotland) and relocation agents. There are also letting agents, who find tenants and manage properties. Most property is bought and sold through estate agents, who sell property on commission for owners. In Scotland, most property sales are handled by solicitor agents, whose property centres provide a one-stop shop for buying, selling and conveyancing. Property sold by estate agents and solicitor agents is said to be sold by private treaty, a method of selling a property by agreement between the vendor and the purchaser, either directly or through an estate agent.

Estate Agents

Although there are nation-wide chains of estate agents in the UK, most agents are local and don't have a nation-wide listing of properties in other regions. There's no multiple-listing system in the UK, where agents jealously guard their list of properties from competitors. If you wish to find an agent selling property in a particular town or area, look under estate agents in the local yellow pages or consult the local newspapers or the Internet (see **Appendix C**). Many estate agents produce free newspapers and magazines containing details of both old and new houses, and colour prospectuses for new developments. Some estate agents are also letting and management agents.

Using The Internet

You can search for an agent on the Internet; most agents now have websites (see **Appendix C**) where you can sort properties by location, price, type (e.g. a house or apartment) and the number of bedrooms. It's particularly useful when you're looking for a property in a different area from where you currently live and allows you to peruse property lists at your leisure. Some agents offer virtual viewing, whereby you can take a guided tour around a property via your computer. Many websites aren't dedicated to a single agent, but allow you to search for homes and agents throughout the UK, e.g. by location and price.

Avoiding The Crooks

Estate agents in the UK don't need to be licensed, qualified, trained or have any experience, and aren't required to be members of any professional organisations (although most are – see below). Estate agents have a terrible public image (it's the occupation that dare not speak its name!) and in recent years their reputation has sunk to an all-time low. (It must be said that agents have a much better reputation in Scotland, where the law regarding buying property is different and gazumping is unknown.) There's open warfare between agents in some areas with evidence of sabotage, dirty tricks and rip-offs, with some agents hiring thugs to tear down rivals' 'For Sale' boards. There's very little control over estate agents, some of whom deliberately force up prices, misrepresent properties or have an undisclosed personal financial interest in a property. Other shady or illegal practices include:

- Accepting money from a prospective buyer to 'ring-fence' a property, i.e. not passing on further offers or rejecting higher bids, while at the same time taking legitimate fees from sellers. This often happens when the vendor is elderly and absent, e.g. living abroad or in a hospital or nursing home (it's allegedly widespread in London).
- 'Selling on', where an agent undervalues your home and sells it at a knock-down price to a friend, who makes a fat profit from a quick resale and splits the profit with the agent.

You should be informed in writing if your estate agent or a relative or business partner of the estate agent wants to buy your property.

- Tipping off property developers to undervalued properties owned by naïve sellers in return for a slice of the profit.
- Under-marketing or holding back under-priced, repossessed houses for developers or speculators in return for a bribe.
- Taking a bribe from a developer to reveal the highest bid in a sealed-bid sale (the developer then bids slightly more).
- Discouraging higher offers (particularly if the lower offer is funded by a mortgage through the agent) or keeping the price low by telling buyers how much to offer.
- Lying to buyers about other offers on the table in order to bump up bids.
- Fly-boarding, i.e. putting 'For Sale' signs outside homes that aren't on the market.
- Providing misleading publicity about the ownership, history and associations of a property in order to push up the value.

- Coercing sellers into signing restrictive 'sole agency' or 'sole seller' agreements (this practice is widespread).
- Pushing insurance and mortgage (sometimes promising to put you on the 'priority' list) to cash in on big commissions or through an agent's own financial services division.

In the light of the above catalogue of dirty tricks, it's surprising that the ombudsman for estate agents received **only** 6,000 complaints in 2002!

SURVIVAL TIP
It's advisable to use more than one agent when selling in order to avoid dirty tricks.

Tied Agents & In-House Services

Some estate agents are owned by banks and other financial institutions, and offer only the financial products of their owners, which means that you don't receive independent financial advice and are unlikely to obtain the best mortgage or insurance deal from them. You may receive a better service from the owner-proprietor of a long-established family business than from one of the large chains. Many estate agents offer an in-house conveyancing service, although you may be better off with an independent solicitor or conveyancer, as an agent's services could easily lead to conflicts of interest. You're generally better off obtaining a mortgage or buying insurance through an independent broker or a direct insurer (telephone or Internet), than from an estate agent.

Solicitor Agents

In Scotland, in addition to the usual estate agents, there are also solicitor agents, who are solicitors who also sell property. A solicitor agent isn't tied to any financial institution and is obliged to provide genuine independent financial advice. There are far fewer complaints against agents in Scotland, where the whole process of property buying is quicker and cheaper than in the rest of the UK (see page 126).

PROPERTY DESCRIPTIONS

Most agents provide detailed descriptions of properties, although they may be a bit short on photographs. Generally, the more expensive a property, the better and more comprehensive the information will be, e.g. agents usually produce glossy colour brochures for up-market properties.

Agents aren't permitted to over-elaborate on property descriptions under the Property Misdescriptions Act 1991, before which a garden shed could be (and frequently was) described as a palace in 'agent-speak'. Even so there are many coded terms in agent-speak, such as 'individual' or 'unique' (which usually means that nobody else likes it), 'in need of modernisation' (needs a massive amount of work), 'study/bedroom 4' (a tiny box room), 'cosy' or 'compact' (tiny), bijou (microscopic), individual (quirky, strange), pleasant (boring), well presented (has had a quick paint job), and so on.

When property is advertised the number of bedrooms and bathrooms is always given and possibly other rooms such as a dining room, lounge (living/sitting room), study, breakfast room, drawing room, library, playroom, utility, pantry, cloakroom, cellar and conservatory. More expensive properties often simply list the number of reception rooms (e.g. lounge, dining room, study, drawing room, etc.). The total living area in square feet or square metres is almost never stated in ads or information sheets, although room sizes (in feet and inches) are included (always measure them if you aren't sure).

VIEWING

If you will be travelling a long way to view a property, you should confirm (and reconfirm) that a particular property is still for sale and the price before making plans to see it. Obtain details of as many properties as possible that match your requirements in your chosen area and make a shortlist of those you wish to view. An agent may ask you to sign a document before showing you any properties, which is simply to protect his commission should you obtain details from another source or try to do a deal with the owner behind his back. You're usually shown properties personally by agents and won't be given the keys (particularly to furnished properties) or be expected to deal with tenants or vendors directly. You should make an appointment to see properties, as agents don't like people just turning up. Agents may provide an open day for viewing a particular property when you can view it without an appointment, although this practice isn't common. Agents vary enormously in their efficiency, enthusiasm and professionalism – if an agent shows little interest in finding out exactly what you want you should try someone else.

Although it's important to view sufficient properties to form an accurate assessment of their value for money, quality and features, don't see too many in one day as it's easy to become confused about the merits of each property. If you're shown properties that don't meet your specifications, tell the agent immediately. You can also help an agent narrow the field by telling him exactly what's wrong with the properties you reject. It's advisable to make notes of both the good **and** bad features and take lots of photographs of the properties you like, so that you can compare them later at your leisure – **but keep a record of which photographs are of which house!** The more a property appeals to you, the more you should look for faults and negative points; if you still like it after stressing all the negative points it must have special appeal! It's also advisable to mark each property on a map, so that should you wish to return you can find them without getting lost (too often). You may also wish to make a note of the owner's telephone number so that you can arrange to view a property again at your leisure.

PROFESSIONAL ORGANISATIONS

If possible, always deal with an estate agent who's a member of a professional organisation, such as the National Association of Estate Agents (NAEA, ☎ 01926-496800, 💻 www.naea.co.uk). You should also check whether an agent is a member of the Ombudsman for Estate Agents (OEA) scheme (☎ 01722-333306, 💻 www.oea.co.uk), whose members (indicated by a sticker on an agent's window) must abide by a code of practice and to whom you can complain if you've a problem. The ombudsman can levy fines of up to £25,000, which may explain why only around one-third of agents are members.

RELOCATION AGENTS

If you know what sort of property you want, how much you wish to pay and where you want to buy, but don't have the time to spend looking (or you live in another region or overseas), you can engage a relocation agent or property search company to find a home for you. This can save you considerable time, trouble and money, particularly if you've special or unusual requirements. Many relocation consultants act as buying agents, particularly for overseas buyers, and claim they can negotiate a better deal than private buyers (which could easily save you the cost of their fees). Some specialise in finding exceptional residences costing upwards of £500,000. Agents can usually help and advise with all aspects of house purchase and may conduct negotiations on your behalf, organise finance (including bridging loans), arrange surveys and insurance, and even organise your removal. Most agents can also provide a comprehensive information package for a chosen area comprising information about employment prospects, health services (e.g. doctors and hospitals), local schools (state and private), shopping facilities, public transport, amenities and services, sports and social facilities, and communications.

Agents generally charge a fee of 1.25 to 1.5 per cent of the purchase price (or up to 2 per cent in London) and an up-front retainer of between £500 to £1,000. The retainer is deducted from the fee when a property is purchased, but if no deal is done it's usually non-returnable. To find a relocation agent contact the Association of Relocation Agents (ARA), PO Box 189, Diss, Norfolk IP22 1PE (☎ 08700-737475, 💻 www. relocationagents.com) or look in the yellow pages under 'Relocation Agents'.

FIRST-TIME BUYERS

With the boom in property prices in recent years it has become increasingly difficult for first-time buyers to get on the property ladder and the average age of first-time buyers has increased to 34 (it was 27 less than a decade ago). First-time buyers in rural areas that are popular with holiday-homebuyers have been forced to leave their home towns in order to buy a home. Many villages are dying as the number of absentee owners has soared in recent years, particularly in coastal villages in the south-west of England. Many villages and towns popular with retirees are prohibitively expensive (except among rich pensioners) and in some areas newcomers (second-homeowners, retirees, investors and job relocators) account for up to 75 per cent of sales and can resemble ghosts towns when all the 'weekenders' are out of town.

The booming buy to let market has also meant that most first-time buyers simply cannot match the prices paid by investors. In mid-2003, average house prices in the UK were five times the average salary and much higher in London and the south of England. The average price for a first-time buyer in mid-2003 was just over £60,000 in the north of England rising to almost £200,000 in London. This means that at 3.75 times gross salary, buyers in the north would need to earn just £16,000 to qualify for a mortgage, while in London it's a whopping £53,000! First-time buyers must usually have a deposit of from around £7,000 (Scotland) up to £37,500 (London) to obtain a mortgage (the average is around £22,500), to which must be added extra costs (fees, removals, furnishings, etc.) of around £6,000. Only some 2 per cent of the 3,000 mortgage products available are specifically targeted at first-time buyers.

In the first six months of 2003 the number of first-time buyers fell by over a third compared with the same period a year earlier to around 1,000 per day, the lowest level since records began in 1969. First-time buyers comprise around 30 per cent of all buyers and drive the market at the bottom end. As a result of the slump in the number of first-time buyers, the market slowed considerably in 2003 and was threatening to bring it to a halt. There are, however, a number of ways that first-time buyers can get a toe-hold on the property ladder:

- Some lenders provide special graduate and professional mortgages for young people (with good income prospects) and will lend up to five times their annual salary. Lenders may also waive MIG (see page 136) on graduate mortgages of up to 95 per cent to value. There are also special deals for first-time buyers and 100 per cent mortgages are available – some lenders even offer up to 125 per cent mortgages!
- You may be eligible for a self-certification mortgage (see page 137) where you aren't required to prove your income – these are ideal for the self-employed whose income fluctuates and includes bonuses, commission, etc. Some people lie about their income to qualify for a large (or larger) self-certification mortgage.

If you're tempted to lie you should bear in mind that it's not only fraud (there are custodial sentences for offenders), but you could easily get into payment difficulties and lose your home!

- Pool your resources and buy with relatives or friends – two to four co-buyers can usually afford to buy a home together. (In 2003, the Yorkshire Building Society would lend three times the top co-owner's income, two times the second and one times the remaining two.) Co-buyers don't need to have equal shares and they can be proportionate to the deposit paid and the repayments made. The percentage owned by each co-buyer must be registered on the title deeds and all co-buyers registered as 'tenants in common' rather than 'joint tenants'.

You will need a 'declaration of trust' so that if one person wants to sell, the others have the option of buying them out – if not the property would need to be sold.

- Reduce your mortgage payments by taking in a sharer. To ease the cost of a mortgage you can let out a room in your home, which is tax-free provided the rent is no more than £4,250 per annum (see page 230).

- Obtain a guarantor (for example, your parents) who guarantees your mortgage payments. However, this type of mortgage is difficult to obtain as it usually requires a deposit of at least 25 per cent, although there are lenders that don't require such a high mortgage (try Northern Rock or Scottish Widows). Scottish Widows only require parents to guarantee the part of the mortgage that isn't covered by their child's income. Parents must usually have at least 30 per cent equity in their own home to act as guarantors and can be released from the arrangement as soon as the mortgage holder is earning sufficient income to take on the loan.
- Check whether you're eligible for shared ownership, as offered by housing associations or trusts. These are non-profit organisations designed to enable those on low incomes (who don't qualify for council housing) to buy a home, with priority usually being given to key workers such as NHS staff, teachers and those already in local authority housing. Most schemes involve buying a share of a property and paying rent on the rest, with the option of increasing your share later when you can afford it. To find your nearest housing association or trust, contact the Housing Corporation (☎ 020-7292 4400, 🖳 www.housingcorp.gov.uk), Housing Mobility Exchange (☎ 020-7963 0200, 🖳 www.homes.org.uk/HMSinfo.htm) or your local authority.
- The Housing Corporation (see above) operates a 'starter home' scheme under which key workers in London can borrow up to 30 per cent of the purchase price of a home up to a maximum of £35,000. A similar scheme in the south-east is operated by Key Homebuy (🖳 www.keyhomebuy.com), who will lend up to £50,000. Loans are interest-free and you don't need to repay them until you sell your home.
- Self-build shared ownership is a scheme (usually community-led) which involves helping you build your own home. You're expected to devote around 25 hours a week to the project, usually in the evenings and at weekends, although you aren't required to have any building skills (although they will help!). At the end of the project you will own a percentage of the property and pay rent on the rest, possibly with an option to purchase an additional share with a mortgage. For information, contact the Community Self-Build Agency (☎ 020-7415 7092, 🖳 www.communityselfbuildagency.org.uk) or the Walter Segal Self-Build Trust (☎ 01892-614300, 🖳 www.segalselfbuild.co.uk).

Note that self-build shared ownership isn't for the timid or weak and requires a huge commitment and a lot of work!

- Buying a plot of land (see page 76) and building your own home (see page 78) can also be a relatively inexpensive way to get on the property ladder, depending on where you want to live and what sort of home you wish to you build. For example, you can buy a house in kit form or construct an environment-friendly, earth-sheltered home.
- Move to an area with lower property prices where you qualify for a mortgage.
- Buy a property in a less expensive area that you can afford and let it in order to get a toehold on the property ladder. Provided the rent covers the mortgage you will benefit from the capital growth, which could be considerable.

BUYING A NEW HOUSE

The vast majority (over 80 per cent) of people in the UK live in houses rather than apartments – most people don't like apartment living and want their own detached home with a garden and garage. They prefer more traditional styles and most aren't keen on the more modern high-tech homes favoured by some developers. Houses are also generally better value than apartments and a better investment. However, a major factor may be the size, as homes are getting smaller (particularly apartments) and new homes are a third smaller than 80 years ago. After having decided to buy a house, your next decision will be whether to buy a new or an old home.

The advantages of new homes include:

- Modern bathrooms, a fully-fitted modern kitchen, central heating, modern facilities, low maintenance, good security and storage.
- No work to do and you can move in immediately.
- Fewer problems – new houses are generally maintenance-free and there are no costs or problems associated with renovation or modernisation.
- Lower running costs than old homes. Most new buildings use low maintenance materials and have good insulation and ventilation, providing lower heating bills and keeping homes cooler in summer.

- It's often cheaper to buy a new home than modernise or renovate an old property, as the price is fixed, unlike the cost of renovation which can soar way beyond estimates.
- Easier to obtain a mortgage.
- Comes with a builder's guarantee against defects (see below).
- It can usually be let immediately.
- Modern homes have good resale potential and are considered a good investment by most buyers.
- **You cannot be gazumped!**

The disadvantages of a new home include:

- Lacking the history, charm and character of an older building.
- Little individuality or exclusivity.
- Gardens lack mature plants and trees.
- Teething troubles.
- Slower capital growth than an old property (they lack 'rarity' value).
- Possible restrictive covenants.
- Unfinished development and communities without local shops and services.
- They're usually smaller than old properties with lower ceilings, smaller rooms (some are tiny!) and less sense of space.
- They may be impossible to expand.
- They rarely have a large garden or plot of land.
- You may need to buy off-plan and run the risk of the developer going bust or the property being worth less than you've paid when you take possession - although it's much more likely to be worth much more!

Quality Of Construction

The quality of new buildings in the UK is strictly regulated and they must conform to stringent building regulations and energy efficiency standards. However, the quality of new homes is extremely variable and some developments of apartments in major cities (where they sell off-plan) suffer from poor quality. Many developments in London and other cities are built for the investment (letting) market and aren't suitable for owner-occupiers. Your best insurance when buying a new house is the reputation of the builder and it pays to buy from a long-established builder with a reputation for quality. The price may be marginally higher than buying from a builder who uses 'cowboy' contractors and refuses to honour his warranty, but it will be well worthwhile in the long term. Before buying a new home you should check what other developments the builder or developer has completed recently and ask the owners what problems they've experienced.

Developers generally employ high standards of materials and workmanship and homes have higher specifications than old houses, including double or triple-glazing, cavity and under-floor insulation, and central heating. Luxury 'intelligent' homes have discreet systems that allow you to control the temperature, lighting, security, music and TVs via wall-mounted or remote controls. They may also have broadband (Internet) connections in all rooms. Some developers also offer specially-designed live-work homes for those who work from home.

New homes often contain a high level of 'luxury' features, depending on individual developments and (of course) the price. Executive homes with four or five bedrooms should have three or four en suite bathrooms with separate showers; built-in wardrobes in all bedrooms; four reception rooms; a double integral garage; solid oak doors; designer kitchens with top quality appliances; ceramic floors in kitchens, bathrooms and cloakrooms; a security system; conservatory; kitchen/breakfast room; utility room and possibly a cellar. You can also have a variety of 'custom' extras included at additional cost such as additional power points, upgraded kitchen appliances, special flooring and wall tiling, a conservatory, a hot tub or Jacuzzi, landscaping, special lighting and a wide variety of electronic gadgets. An added advantage is that the cost of extras can be included in your mortgage, although it's important to check that they offer good value for money (many developers overcharge on extras, which is a common cause of complaints).

Construction Methods

Most new homes are made of brick (some 10 per cent in England and Wales are of timber frame construction) and some employ steel-framed panels, a recent introduction to the UK, but used widely in Australia and the US. Frames are pre-fabricated with foam insulation board ready for bolting together, which increases fuel efficiency and sound insulation. Although rare, stone (usually from a local source) is again in vogue as a building material for new homes. Homes with thatched roofs have always been popular and specialist builders offer 'thatched' homes of almost any size.

Choice

A huge variety of new properties are available, including apartment and townhouse developments - some of which are conversions of old buildings, although for all intents and purposes these qualify as new homes - standard family homes built on new estates, and a wide range of individually designed detached houses (including vast mansions). Waterside homes are popular and many new harbour developments have been built in recent years. Although rare, golf properties are in demand and may include a year's free membership of a golf club. In some areas, new homes must be styled to blend in with existing homes and many builders offer a number of 'mock' period styles, possibly using recycled materials (e.g. bricks, tiles, oak timber beams, fireplaces, doors, etc.) from old properties, thus offering the best of both worlds for those who cannot decide between a period home and a maintenance-free new home. Some developers event create new houses in the style of barn conversions to keep up with demand.

Purpose-Built Developments

Many new homes are part of purpose-built developments, which offer a range of sports facilities such as a golf course, swimming pool, tennis and squash courts, a gymnasium or fitness club, and even a bar and restaurant. Some properties built on private estates have a resident's association or management committee to manage the upkeep of roads, landscaping, trees, plants, lighting, and so on, for which owners pay an annual fee. There are usually also a number of restrictive covenants that owners must adhere to (see page 66). The cost of land is usually included when buying a detached house on its own plot, unless you agree a separate contract for the land and the house. Most new homes are sold directly by property developers or builders, although they may also be marketed by estate agents (generally there's no difference in price, although the developer will have more leeway). New developments have a sales office and usually a show house or apartment. Homes built within private estates or grounds often have excellent security, including electronic gates, security lights and alarms linked to a central monitoring station (and are a good choice for those seeking maximum privacy).

Warranty

Most new properties are covered by the National House Building Council's (NHBC, ☎ 0845-845 6422, 💻 www.nhbc.co.uk), Buildmark 10-year warranty or the Zurich Municipal Building Guarantee (☎ 01252-

522000). Most lenders will refuse to lend against a new house without a warranty. The NHBC warranty covers the owner for claims of up to £10,000 against the builder's failure to complete the house, for the loss of a deposit (up to 10 per cent of the agreed price) or any expenses incurred in completing building work.

Buying new isn't all roses and it isn't unusual for new homes to have hundreds of (mostly minor) faults.

During the first two years the builder should make good any defects – termed 'snagging' – arising from his failure to meet NHBC requirements. During the first two years in a new home you should list all the things that require fixing which are the responsibility of the builder.

The NHBC warranty (which is half funded by developers) has been accused of being toothless when it comes to getting 'minor' faults rectified and the NHBC is slow to act and soft on builders (the building trade enjoys the luxury of self-regulation).

During the next eight years you're insured only against major structural damage caused by defects in the structure, subsidence or heave. If you find or suspect any building defects within the first two years, you should inform the NHBC in writing and have a survey done to ensure that your property is sound. The Zurich Municipal Building Guarantee provides a similar 10-year warranty, including protection against a builder going bust before a property is completed.

Buying Off-Plan

When buying a new property in a development, you're usually obliged to buy it off-plan, i.e. before it's built.

If a development is finished and largely unsold, particularly in a popular area, you should beware as it usually means that there's something wrong with it that the locals know about!

In recent years people have queued overnight to buy properties in many new developments. In a rising market it's possible to make a good profit buying off-plan, between the period when you pay the deposit and when the property is completed a year or two later.

The contract will contain the timetable for the property's completion; payment dates; the completion date and penalties for non-completion; guarantees for building work; and a copy of the plans and drawings. Payments are spread over the period of construction, with payments made in stages as building work progresses. If you're buying a property off-plan, you may be able to choose your bathroom suite(s), kitchen cupboards, wallpaper and paint, wall and floor tiles, and carpets, which may be included in the price. You may also be able to alter the interior room layout, although this will usually increase the price.

SURVIVAL TIP
It's advisable to make any changes or additions to a property during the design stage, as it will cost much more later.

Some analysts advise buyers against buying off-plan, which can be risky, particularly in a falling market. It may be better to wait until a property is almost complete before buying, otherwise you could end up paying more than a property is worth or the developer could even go bust. You must put down at least 10 per cent of the price as a deposit and pay over £500 in legal fees to exchange contracts, which legally obliges you to go through with the purchase. If the developer goes bust, you may have to wait years for a property to be completed and there's no guarantee that it will be finished to the original specifications. Added to which you could lose your loan if bad publicity has an adverse effect on the market value of the property. In 2003, many buyers pulled out of off-plan purchases (and lost their deposits), particularly in London, amid fears that the property wouldn't be worth what they had agreed to pay and that the rent wouldn't cover their mortgage payments. When buying off-plan, choose a large developer or one who's selling different types of property in different areas, as he's better placed to weather a storm.

Price

Whether you can haggle over the price of a new home will depend on demand and how fast they're selling. In a rising market a development may sell within a few days of being released for sale, with the majority of properties being snapped up by investors. If a development isn't selling well, the developer may be willing to negotiate over the price or include 'extras' free of charge. Some developers will also pay your deposit, stamp duty and legal fees to clinch a sale. Whatever the state of the market it's always worth trying to reduce the price. In 2003, shrewd buyers were getting discounts of 5 to 10 per cent on selected apartments in London and developers were slashing the price of their most expensive homes by as much as 25 per cent in a bid to attract buyers.

Part-Exchange

Some developers offer a part exchange deal on your existing home, although you should be wary of such schemes (see page 252). Part-exchange is a lucrative business for developers and relieves vendors of the hassle of selling their home and paying agents' and other fees. Many developers offer a part-exchange deal when you're buying a more expensive new home – usually the property you're buying must be worth 30 per cent more than the one you're offering in part exchange.

Resale 'New' Homes

Buying new doesn't necessarily mean buying a brand new home where you're the first occupant. There are many advantages in buying a modern resale home, which may include the following:

- Better value for money;
- An established development with a range of local shops, services and facilities in place;
- The eradication of teething troubles;
- Furniture and other extras included in the price;
- A mature garden and trees;
- A range of improvements made by the owner;
- The ability to assess the overall quality of a development, the neighbourhood and check on your neighbours.

With a resale property you can see exactly what you will get for your money, most problems will have been resolved, and the previous owners may have made improvements such as an extension, which may not be fully reflected in the asking price.

The disadvantages of buying a resale home depend on its age and how well it has been maintained, and may include:

- A poor state of repair and the need for refurbishment;
- Lacking the benefits of a brand new home unless it has been modernised;

- The need for redecorating and new carpets;
- Poorer build quality and inferior design;
- No warranty;
- Termite or other infestations;
- The possibility of incurring high assessments for repairs in leasehold properties.

Home and property magazines (see **Appendix A**) contain a wealth of information about new homes, including a list of new developments throughout the country, and numerous advertisements from builders and developers. Daily newspapers are a good source of information, particularly the quality Saturday and Sunday newspapers such as *The Times* and *The Telegraph* (Saturday editions) and *The Sunday Times* and *The Sunday Telegraph*. Many home and property exhibitions are held throughout the UK, including the 'Daily Mail Ideal Home Show', staged in March at the Earls Court Exhibition Centre (London), the biggest and best of all, the 'House & Garden Fair' (held in June at the Olympia Exhibition Centre, London) and the Evening Standard Homebuyer Show (💻 www.homebuyer.co.uk). You can also search for a new home on the Internet with Your New Home (💻 www.yournewhome.co.uk), new-homes.co.uk (💻 www.new-homes.co.uk) and Smart New Homes (💻 www.smartnewhomes.co.uk). See also **Appendix C**.

BUYING AN OLD HOUSE

In the UK, the term 'old house' usually refers to a building that's pre-1940, while homes built before 1914 are often referred to as period homes, for example Georgian, Victorian or Edwardian. If you want a property with charm and character; a building for renovation or conversion; outbuildings or a large plot of land; then you must usually buy an old property. The UK has a wealth of beautiful historic buildings encompassing village houses to castles, farmhouses to mansions (particularly 17th to 19th century townhouses and country mansions). When buying an old building you aren't just buying a home, but a piece of history, part of cultural heritage, and a unique building that represents the architects' and artisans' skills of a bygone age.

The advantages of an old house may include the following:

- History, charm and character in abundance;
- Individuality and exclusivity;

- Interesting architectural features such as inglenook fireplaces, exposed beams, wood or slate floors, and beautiful plasterwork (look behind boarded up chimney breasts, wall and bath panelling, painted doors and floor coverings and you may unearth some period treasures just waiting to be discovered);
- A mature garden with fully-grown trees and an abundance of plants;
- An absence of teething troubles;
- A mature community with abundant shops and services;
- More space than new properties with higher ceilings and larger rooms;
- Outbuildings that can be converted into a self-contained studio or apartment, study, office or workshop;
- The possibility to expand or convert it for a different use;
- A large garden or plot of land;
- Good capital growth (rising in value faster than a new home);
- Easier to sell than a new home ('rarity' value).

The disadvantages of old homes may include:

- Out-of-date bathrooms and kitchen, bulky storage heaters (or no central heating at all), poor security, poor insulation (high heating bills), lack of storage space, etc.
- Restoration, renovation or decoration may be necessary before you can move in;
- Large repair and maintenance bills, particularly if they haven't been lovingly cared for, and high running costs;
- Difficulty in obtaining a mortgage if the property needs major structural work;
- Hidden defects (you will have no guarantee unlike with a new home) such as dry rot, rising damp, subsidence or landslide, woodworm or other infestations – always have a survey done;
- Restrictive covenants or rights of way and if it's a listed building (see below) you will be severely restricted in what you can do regarding 'improvements';
- Not being able to let it immediately if it needs updating;
- The possibility of being gazumped at any time before contracts are exchanged.

Thatched Houses

Homes with thatched roofs are attractive and very popular. However, they're prone to fires (fire protection and an alarm system are essential), attract high insurance premiums and are expensive to re-thatch. Before buying a home with a thatched roof you should check that it's in good condition, as the skills are disappearing and roofs are expensive to replace. They last anything from 20 to 90 years depending on whether they use reeds or wheat straw (the long-staple straw required can be difficult to source). Don't be tempted to use plastic straws, which look awful and clatter in a high wind.

Conversions

Conversions of old buildings are popular and highly individual homes have been created from old schools, churches, railway stations, signal boxes, factories, coach houses, windmills, towers, mills and barns – you name it and it has been converted to a comfortable home somewhere in the UK. Barn conversions are extremely popular (and very expensive), but rare due to the lack of barns. (You can also have a 'barn' home built from new, which may be a lot cheaper than a conversion.) Expect to pay around £300,000 for a barn for conversion (usually with planning permission) and at least 50 per cent more turning it into a comfortable home. You can even buy a barn abroad (e.g. in France) and have it dismantled and reassembled in the UK. An economical way to live in an historic building (often within private grounds) is to buy an apartment or townhouse in a building that has been converted, which include former stately homes, hospitals, warehouses and factories.

Listed Buildings

Listed buildings (see also page 202) are buildings of special architectural or historic interest, which are protected throughout the UK. Buildings can be listed because of their age, rarity, architectural merit or method of construction. Occasionally buildings are selected because the building has played a part in the life of a famous person or were the scene for an important event. An interesting group of buildings, such as a model village or a square, may also be listed.

There are conservation areas in many historic towns and cities, where there are strict rules governing what can and cannot be done to the houses within them.

The older a building is, the more likely it is to be listed. There are over half a million listed buildings in the UK – around 350,000 grade I and II listed buildings in England and Wales, plus a further 175,000 in Scotland and Northern Ireland – most of which were built before 1840. They include all buildings built before 1700 that survive in anything like their original condition and most built between 1700 and 1840. After that date, the criteria become tighter with time, so that post-1945 buildings have to be exceptionally important to be listed.

In England and Wales, buildings are graded to show their relative architectural or historic interest as follows:

- **Grade I** – buildings of exceptional interest (only some 2 per cent of listed buildings are in this grade).
- **Grade II*** – particularly important buildings of more than special interest (some 4 per cent of listed buildings).
- **Grade II** – buildings of special interest warranting every effort to preserve them (over 90 per cent of listed buildings).

In Scotland and Northern Ireland Grades I, II* and II are replaced by the grades A, B and C.

The task of identifying and protecting buildings in the UK is under the control of the following organisations:

- **England** – English Heritage, 23 Saville Row, London W1S 2ET (☎ 020-7973 3000, 💻 www.english-heritage.org.uk).
- **Wales** – Cadw (Welsh Heritage – Cadw means 'keep' in Welsh), Cathays Park, Cardiff CF10 3NQ (☎ 029-2050 0200, 💻 www.cadw.gov.uk).
- **Scotland** – Historic Scotland, Longmore House, Salisbury Place, Edinburgh EH9 1SH (☎ 0131-668 8600, 💻 www.historic-scotland.gov.uk).
- **N. Ireland** – Ulster Architectural Heritage Society, 66 Donegall Pass, Belfast BT7 1BU (☎ 028-9055 0213, 💻 www.uahs.co.uk).

Renovation & Restoration

Inexpensive old houses are available in some areas, but most have been snapped up and modernised years ago, and those that are left are generally no longer the bargains they once were. In rural areas it's still possible to buy old properties requiring total renovation or even total restoration, although they're rarer nowadays and are by no means cheap. There is a passion for rescuing old tumbledown houses and restoring them to their former glory, and 'ruins' sold at auction often far exceed their reserve price.

It's very expensive to restore an old property and can cost much more than building a new house, particularly if you do it properly using reclaimed materials.

Many people are lulled into a false sense of security and believe they're getting a wonderful bargain, without fully investigating the renovation costs, which are invariably higher than you imagined or planned! Some properties even lack basic services such as electricity, a reliable water supply and sanitation.

SURVIVAL TIP
If you're planning to buy a property that needs renovation, have a full structural survey (see page 103) and obtain an accurate estimate of the costs before buying it!

While you may get more for your money when buying an old home, the downside is that they require much more maintenance and upkeep than new homes, and heating costs can be high unless a property has good insulation.

Good Value

Old properties can provide better value than new homes, although you must check their quality and condition carefully. As with most things in life, you generally get what you pay for, so you shouldn't expect a fully renovated property for a knock-down price. For those who can afford them, at the top end of the scale there's a wealth of beautiful mansions, castles and stately homes available with extensive grounds (some country homes even come with their own golf course!). Substantial period homes certainly don't come cheap, although this segment of the market has suffered in recent years and larger homes costing in excess of £750,000 are generally excellent value for money.

If you aspire to live the life of the landed gentry in your own stately home, bear in mind that the cost of their upkeep is usually astronomical. As a consequence many mansions have been converted into luxury apartments and townhouses in recent years.

If you're looking for something unusual try Pavilions of Splendour (22 Mount View Road, London N4 4HX, ☎ 020-8348 1234, 💻 www.heritage.co.uk) or SAVE Britain's Heritage (70 Cowcross Street, London EC1M 6EJ, ☎ 020-7253 3500, 💻 www.savebritainsheritage.org), a conservation charity that maintains a list of properties in need of restoration. See also **Chapter 6 – Home Improvements**.

BUYING AN APARTMENT

In the last few decades, apartments have become increasingly popular, particularly among the young and city dwellers. There's often little alternative if you wish to live in a city centre, where young professionals prefer to live in apartments rather than houses. The advantages include the following:

- Increased security (provided it isn't a basement or ground floor apartment);
- Lower property taxes than detached homes;
- A range of sports and leisure facilities;
- Community living with lots of social contacts and the companionship of close neighbours;
- No garden, lawn or pool maintenance;
- Fewer responsibilities than with a house;
- Ease and low-cost of maintenance;
- Lower cost than a house;
- The ability to live in a location where owning a house would be prohibitively expensive, e.g. a city centre.

The disadvantages of apartments may include:

- Excessively high service charges (owners may have no control over increases);
- Restrictive covenants and regulations;
- A confining living and social environment and possible lack of privacy;
- Noisy neighbours;
- Limited living and storage space;
- Obtaining the freeholder's permission to make structural changes;

- No private garden;
- Expensive covered or secure parking (or no secure parking).

Most property in the UK is owned freehold, where the owner acquires complete legal ownership of the property and land and his rights over the property, which can be modified only by the law or specific conditions in the contract of sale. Most houses, whether detached, semi-detached, terraced or townhouses, are sold freehold. Most apartments in England and Wales (rare in Scotland) are sold leasehold, which includes some 3 million homes (mostly in cities and on the south coast), where you buy the property, but not the ground on which it stands. The freeholder owns the site and charges the leaseholder an annual ground rent; the leaseholder must also pay an annual service charge to the freeholder to cover the maintenance and repairs of the building and its common parts.

Length Of Leasehold

The leasehold property is owned for a specified number of years, after which ownership reverts to the freeholder. Ownership is limited to the life of the lease, for example, 80 to 100 years for an old building and up to 999 years for a new building. (Unlike in most other countries, where apartments or condominiums are owned outright under a system of co-ownership.) Leasehold law means that you can pay a fortune for a home and technically still not be able to call it your own. At best, leaseholders pay only ground rent on their homes, but there can be restrictive rules whereby they can be forbidden to change their curtains, wallpaper or even keep pets. Abuses by landlords such as charging high 'administration' costs, presenting leaseholders with bogus bills and harassment are also commonplace.

A property can change hands several times during the life of a lease and when the lease expires the property reverts to the original owner (the freeholder). When buying a leasehold apartment, the most important consideration is the length of the lease, particularly if it has less than around 50 years to run, in which case you will have difficulty obtaining a mortgage. Most experts consider 75 years to be the minimum lease you should consider. Leases often contain special terms and conditions, which should also be taken into account. For advice or information about leases, contact the Leasehold Advisory Service (☎ 020-7490 9580, 💻 www.lease-advice.org), who can also provide an application form for a Leasehold Valuation Tribunal.

Buying The Freehold

Since 1993 when the Leasehold Reform, Housing and Urban Development Act became law, leaseholders have had the right to buy the freehold between them, called a joint freehold, and many apartments are now sold not with a lease, but with a share of the freehold. However, there are strict rules regarding residence and the procedure can be long and the cost uncertain, therefore it's essential to obtain advice from a experienced solicitor. Owners of a joint freehold can choose to manage the building themselves or employ a managing agent, although it's generally better to have a managing agent as it avoids the disagreements that inevitably arise when owners manage a building themselves.

The 1993 act also made it possible for some leaseholders to extend their lease by 90 years and if the freeholder decides to sell the freehold he must give the present tenants right of first refusal to buy it. New legislation should extend leaseholders rights and alter the balance of power between freeholder and leaseholder. Under a new type of ownership for apartments called commonhold, leaseholders have the right to buy the freehold and establish a commonhold association to manage the common parts of a property.

For information contact the Leasehold Enfranchisement Advisory Service (6-8 Maddox Street, London W1R 9PN, ☎ 020-7493 3116), which provides free advice and maintains lists of valuers and solicitors who specialise in leasehold properties. If you sell a lease that was drawn up before 1996, you must ensure that your solicitor includes am indemnity in the contract that allows you to pass liability for any debts on to the new leaseholder, otherwise you could be held liable. This anomaly was abolished in the Landlord and Tenants (Covenants) Act of 1995.

Types Of Apartments

Apartments are common in London and other cities, but rare elsewhere, particularly in small towns, where they're unpopular and tend to be budget accommodation. In the last few decades a wealth of old industrial sites and buildings have been transformed into chic urban apartments and loft penthouses with stainless-steel kitchens and designer bathrooms. In recent years, stately homes, hospitals, schools, warehouses, mills, offices and factories have all been redeveloped as apartments. So called 'mega-apartments', i.e. huge open plan apartments, and loft apartments with double or triple height 'cathedral' ceilings are popular in London and other cities, as are penthouses, some of which sell for £5 million (£1,000 per square foot!) or more in London.

They're often an emotive purchase, where you pay dearly for the panoramic views.

You can also buy a shell apartment – which is literally a shell with no internal walls or fixtures and fittings – which needs to be fitted out. With this type of apartment you can usually obtain a maximum 75 per cent mortgage and need to take out another loan to fit it out. This will cost around £25,000 to £50,000 for a 1,000ft^2 (92.9m^2) apartment.

Modern Apartments

New apartments (particularly in London) are invariably lavishly appointed, which is essential nowadays if they're to sell well. The best apartments are beautifully designed and fitted, with developers vying with each other to design the most alluring interiors. These include designer kitchens complete with top quality appliances; however, although kitchens full of gleaming stainless steel and gadgets may look great, they aren't always practical, well-designed or good for cooking. Other features include en suite bathrooms with separate showers and designer fittings; built-in wardrobes; telephone and TV points (including cable) in all rooms; fitted carpets and ceramic floors in kitchens and bathrooms.

Luxury apartments may come with a menu of high-tech options, including discrete, multi-room audio systems, home cinemas, ducted air-conditioning/heating, state-of-the-art security and broadband connections in all rooms. Luxury apartments may also have air-conditioning or what may be termed comfort cooling, air-cooling or a climate-controlled, refrigerated-air system. Security is a key feature of most developments, which may have a 24-hour caretaker/concierge, CCTV surveillance and a security entry system with entry phones – some even have a video entry system that takes a picture of callers who press your apartment button when you aren't at home!

Communal Facilities

Modern developments – so-called 'lifestyle' apartments – often have a leisure complex with swimming pool and gymnasium, sauna, Jacuzzi, tennis courts, plus secure parking and landscaped gardens. Sports facilities are often the clincher in an inner-city development. Some developments also have an in-house medical centre, business centre, private meeting rooms for residents' exclusive use, a restaurant and a bar.

Size

The size of apartments varies considerably, although new apartments are getting smaller, particularly in London. It isn't uncommon to find purpose-built student studios (or micro-apartments) of less the 250ft^2 (23m^2) and one-bedroom apartments of 425ft^2 (40m^2). When comparing the price of apartments, always take into account their size (in square feet or square meters) which is a huge factor. Most experts recommend that you avoid studios, which are invariably tiny, cramped and difficult to sell – for a bit more money you can buy a one-bedroom apartment (most people want a separate bedroom). However, studios and small one-bedroom apartments are becoming popular among commuters who stay in town during the week and return to their country homes at the weekend. They're more comfortable and cheaper than staying in a hotel and you also save money and time on travelling. Your apartment will also be a good capital investment.

Research

Before buying an apartment it's advisable to ask the current owners about the development. For example, do they like living there, what are the charges and restrictions, how noisy are other residents, are the recreational facilities easy to access, would they buy there again (if not, why not), and, most importantly, is the development well managed? You may also wish to check on your prospective neighbours. An apartment that has others above and below it's generally more noisy than a ground or top floor apartment. If you're planning to buy an apartment above the ground floor, ensure that the building has a lift. Ground or garden level apartments (along with penthouses) are more prone to thefts and an insurance company may insist on extra security before they will insure a property.

Note that upper floor apartments are both colder in winter and warmer in summer, although temperature-control problems will be offset by the panoramic views.

Cost

Prices of apartments vary considerably from as little as £30,000 for a studio or one-bedroom apartment in a small country town to over £300,000 for a new two-bedroom, two-bathroom apartment in London.

Prices in London, where many apartments are purchased by investors, have risen considerably in recent years and in 2003 were £600 to £700 per ft^2 (£6,500 to £7,500 per m^2) in prime areas. The price may include a year's free membership of a health club. Bear in mind that amenities such as a health club or gymnasium don't come cheap and there are often high service charges, e.g. £4,000 a year, which may include hot water and heating. Cheaper apartments are available in London's Docklands and south of the River Thames, where loft conversions can be purchased from around £250 per ft^2 (£2,700 per m^2). Apartments in cities are generally a good investment and have excellent letting potential, always assuming that the rental market doesn't become saturated. The best-selling apartments are spacious with at least two bedrooms and good views.

Note that in popular developments, you must usually buy off-plan long before a development is completed.

In an older development, you should check whether access to private grounds and a parking space are included in the cost. In new developments you usually need to pay extra for a garage or a space in an underground car park. If you're buying a resale property, check the price paid for similar properties in the same area or development in recent months, but bear in mind that the price you pay may have more to do with the seller's circumstances than the price fetched by other properties. Find out how many properties are for sale in a development; if there are many on offer you should investigate why, as there could be management or structural problems. If you're still keen to buy you can use any negative aspects to drive a hard bargain.

Service Charges

Apartment owners pay service charges for the upkeep of communal areas and for shared services, with charges calculated according to each owner's share of the development. A proportion of the common elements is usually assigned to each apartment owner depending on the number and size of apartments in a development. Service charges include such things as the items mentioned below:

- Garden maintenance;
- Cleaning (including roads and pathways), decoration and maintenance of communal areas and buildings;

- Caretakers, concierges or porters;
- Lift maintenance, entry phone and security;
- Lighting in communal areas and grounds;
- Water supply (e.g. for gardens);
- Pest control;
- Buildings insurance;
- Administration;
- General maintenance;
- Membership and upkeep of communal facilities such as a health club, gymnasium or swimming pool;
- Sink fund for major repairs.

Service charges may also include heating and hot water. Buildings insurance is provided by the freeholder, but you're usually required to have third party insurance for damage you may cause to other apartments (e.g. through flood or fire).

Always check the level of service charges and any special charges before buying a community property. Fees are usually billed monthly or bi-annually and adjusted at the end of the year (which can be a nasty shock) when the actual expenditure is known and the annual accounts have finalised. If you're buying an apartment from a previous owner, ask to see a copy of the service charges for previous years, as owners may be 'economical with the truth' when stating service charges, particularly if they're high. Fees vary considerably and can run to thousands of pounds (£5,000 a year isn't unusual) for luxury developments with a high level of amenities such as a health club and swimming pool. They may also increase annually.

An apartment block with a resident caretaker will have higher community fees than one without, although it's preferable to buy in a block with a caretaker. If a management company is employed to manage and maintain an apartment block, the service fees are likely to be higher, but the building is also likely to be maintained better. High fees aren't necessarily a negative point (assuming you can afford them), provided that you receive value for money and the development is well managed and maintained. The value of an apartment depends to a large extent on how well it's maintained and managed.

Disputes over service charges can be acrimonious and disagreements between owners and landlords should be heard by a Leasehold Valuation Tribunal (LVT) with a panel comprising a solicitor, a valuer and a third experienced person, and not by county courts. In the past, landlords have used threats of expensive court action to intimidate apartment owners into paying higher fees. Many landlords have increased their service charges significantly in recent years, which may bear little or no relationship to actual costs, and many people have been hit by high charges for major repairs (see below). It's essential when buying a leasehold property to take legal advice and have the lease checked by a solicitor.

Maintenance & Repairs

If necessary, owners can be assessed an additional service charge to make up for any shortfall of funds for maintenance or repairs. You should check the condition of the common areas (including all amenities) in an old development and whether any major maintenance or capital expense is planned for which you could be assessed. Beware of bargain apartments in buildings requiring a lot of maintenance work or refurbishment. Most developments have a sink or reserve fund to pay for one-off major repairs, which is funded from general service charges.

Ground Rent

Ground rent is a nominal rent for the land on which an apartment block is built and is usually around £100 to £200 per year. The lease should indicate whether the ground rent is fixed or whether it can be reviewed after a certain period.

Covenants & Restrictions

Covenants are legally binding obligations of the freeholder and leaseholder to do or refrain from doing certain things. Restrictions are regulations governing how leaseholders are required to behave. Restrictions usually include such things as noise levels; the keeping of pets; renting; exterior decoration and plants (e.g. the placement of shrubs); waste disposal; the use of gymnasiums and other recreational facilities; parking; business or professional use and the hanging of laundry. Check the regulations and discuss any restrictions you're unsure about with residents. Permanent residents should avoid buying in a development with a high proportion of rental apartments, i.e. apartments that aren't owner-occupied, although you may have little choice in London.

Private Gardens

Many London squares and developments have private communal gardens for the exclusive use of residents, which can add considerably to the cost of a property. London's shared gardens date back to the 19th century when the landed gentry came up to town for the season. Gardens often have strict rules and regulations such as no animals (although you may be able to exercise your dog), ball games, barbecues, large parties and unsupervised children - their peace and tranquillity adds to their charm. Residents pay an annual fee and receive a key.

BUYING A MOBILE HOME

Mobile homes (owners prefer to call them park homes) have increased in popularity in recent years and there are now around 1,250 sites in the UK with over 200,000 permanent residents. Park homes designed for residential use come in a wide range of styles, shapes and sizes and are built to a high standard, with luxury park homes almost indistinguishable from permanent homes. Homes have timber frames with weatherproof exteriors and double-glazed windows, and many have a higher insulation rating than a conventional brick and mortar home. Homes are plumbed with all mod cons and are cemented to the ground, although they aren't as structurally sound as brick-built homes and are more vulnerable to fires and high winds.

Despite the 'mobile' tag, modern park homes aren't very mobile, particularly as many have added rooms and carports permanently attached to the ground.

Homes cost from £25,000 to over £150,000 depending on the size and luxury, with two-bedroom homes costing around £80,000, or around half to two-thirds of the price of a similar size brick-built home. Resale homes are often sold furnished. When comparing prices, check the standard features and exactly what the price includes. Park homes offer good safety and security and are popular with retirees (many parks are exclusively for the retired). Some parks ban children as permanent residents and may also prohibit dogs and activities such as cycling. Parks are often like self-sufficient villages with their own village shop, pub, restaurant, meeting hall and amenities (such as a bowling green).

SURVIVAL TIP
Before choosing a mobile home park, you should talk with other owners and ask them about a park's ground rent (annual fees), facilities and management. Also read a contract carefully, so that you know exactly what's included and excluded from the rent.

Ground rents are typically £75 to £125 per month (£1,200 to £1,500 a year), depending on the park and its amenities. It's important to take the same precautions when buying a park home as when buying a traditional home and to have a sales contract checked by your solicitor. You should also ensure that a park is a member of the BHHPA (see below) or a similar organisation. The Mobile Homes Act 1983 provided park homeowners with security of tenure and gave them the right to sell their homes or leave them to close members of their family. Each time a home changes hands the landlord (park owner) usually receives 10 per cent of the purchase price. Note that equity-release schemes don't usually apply to park homes.

For information about parks, contact the National Park Homes Council (Catherine House, Victoria Road, Aldershot, Hants. GU11 1SS, ☎ 01252-336092, 💻 www.theparkhome.net) or the British Holiday and Homes Parks Association (BHHPA, Chichester House, 6 Pullman Court, Great Western Road, Gloucester GL1 3ND, ☎ 01452-526911, 💻 www.parkhome.co.uk).

BUYING A RETIREMENT HOME

For those who are retired or nearing retirement age, purpose-designed retirement or sheltered housing has grown in popularity in recent years (around 5 per cent of the over 65 population lives in retirement housing) and there are now retirement developments in most regions. Homes are usually situated in a town with easy access to public transport or in a country location with beautiful gardens, where owners live in their own apartments, townhouses or cottages, with a garage or off-road parking.

Most sheltered housing is restricted to those aged over 55 (the average age of buyers is actually over 70) and shouldn't be confused with residential or nursing homes, as owners generally need to be mobile and able to look after themselves. However, help may be provided ranging from shopping and cleaning (home help) to full domestic services (usually for an additional service fee). Thanks to the extra assistance provided, around 70 per cent of owners remain in retirement housing until they die, rather than go into nursing homes.

Communal areas usually include an owner's lounge, kitchen (possibly a restaurant), library, gardens and guest suites for visitors. Some of the larger developments are modelled on those in the US with private amenities such as a theatre, restaurant, bar, launderette, shop, putting and golf course, swimming pool, tennis and a bowling green. There are usually special features for the elderly and those with restricted mobility, including wide doors for wheelchairs, low level switches (electricity sockets, switches and panic buttons are located at waist height), manageable taps, easy-access storage, walk-in showers and wheelchair accessibility. One of the main advantages of purpose-built retirement housing is its high security (including security cameras), and it has a much lower incidence of burglary than all other types of housing. Help is usually on hand 24-hours a day, either from a live-in warden or caretaker, or via an alarm system linked to a control centre.

Properties are usually sold leasehold with leases from 125 to 999 years. Retirement homes can be **very** expensive and often cost much more (e.g. 15 per cent) than similar properties that aren't in a retirement housing development, therefore it's important to check that you're getting good value for money. There are relatively few mainstream developers in the retirement sector and demand far outstrips supply, which means that developers can and do charge what they like (which has led to charges of profiteering). At the bottom end of the market, one-bedroom retirement homes start at around £60,000, although most are luxury homes costing from £200,000 to over £400,000. Despite the relatively high prices, homes sell quickly and you usually need to buy off-plan in the most popular developments. Look at a wide range of existing schemes and consider putting your name down for both new-build and resales, where you've the advantage of joining an established community.

All developments levy annual service charges, which are usually between £1,500 and £4,000 a year (£30 to £80 per week) depending on the size of a property and the services and amenities provided. When you leave you can sell your property on the open market or may be able to take advantage of a guaranteed buy-back scheme, where the market value is determined by the price of the most recent comparable sale.

There are a number of specialist development companies, including the English Courtyard Association (☎ 0800-220858, 💻 www.englishcourtyard.co.uk), Beechcroft (☎ 01491-834975, 💻 www.beechcroft.co.uk), Pegasus (☎ 0870-120 8844, 💻 www.pegasus-homes.co.uk) and Retirement Homesearch (☎ 0870-600 5560, 💻 www.retirementhomesearch.co.uk), who will search the whole market for you. Other useful contacts include Age Concern England (☎ 020-8679 8000, 💻 www.ageconcern.org.uk), Age Concern Scotland (☎ 0131-220 3345, 💻 www.ageconcernscotland.org.uk), the Elderly Accommodation Counsel (☎ 020-7820 1343, 💻 www.housingcare.org) and Help The Aged (☎ 020-7278 1114, 💻 www.helptheaged.org.uk).

BUYING FOR INVESTMENT

Property has been an excellent investment in recent years, particularly in London and the south-east of the country, where many buyers buy new homes off-plan without even seeing them. In the last few years property has far out-performed the stock market and all forms of savings, and provides both capital growth and income (if you let a property). As a rough rule of thumb, house values in the UK double every seven years, although in recent years properties in many areas have doubled in as little as three or four years, even without the owners making any improvements (see **House Prices** on page 27). Prices in many areas have been fuelled by investors, with some two-thirds of all new homes in London purchased for investment! In mid-2003, the property market was flat or falling in many areas, despite which most large investors were still buying property. However, most market analysts have warned that price growth will slow in the next few years and that you shouldn't rely on double-digit growth.

> **SURVIVAL TIP**
> **Whatever the state of the property market, the best way to make money when selling property is to not pay too much in the first place!**

A property investment should usually be considered over the medium to long term, say a minimum of five and preferably 10 to 15 years. Bear in mind that property isn't always 'as safe as houses' and property investments can be risky over the short to medium term – unless you get an absolute bargain or add value. You also need to take into account income tax if a property is let (see **Taxation Of Property Income** on page 228) and capital gains tax (see page 253) when you sell a second home or an investment property. See also **Chapter 7 – Letting**.

There are various kinds of property investment. Your permanent family home is an investment (and should be regarded as a **business** investment) in that it provides you with rent-free accommodation and hopefully will make a profit when you sell.

SURVIVAL TIP
For most people who plan to live in a property for a long time it's best to buy a home, not simply a good investment! Nevertheless, it pays to have one eye on the investment potential of a home, as you never know when you may need to sell!

Think about how easy it will be to sell when buying – if it will be easy to sell it will also be a good investment. Bear in mind that although you may make a hefty profit on your home, it may be difficult to realise unless you trade down or move to another area (or country) where property is less expensive.

Of course, if you buy property other than for your own regular use (i.e. a property that isn't your principal home), you will be in a position to benefit from a more tangible return on your investment. There are essentially four main categories of investment property:

- **A holiday home**, which can provide a return in a number of ways. It can provide your family and friends with rent-free accommodation and you may also be able to let it to generate income. It may also produce a capital gain if property values rise faster than inflation (as they have done in recent years).
- **A second home** for when you're in town (it could be in London or any city that you visit regularly), which can be for business, pleasure or both. It can be a studio, a one-bedroom apartment or something grander – somewhere to crash while working, shopping or having a night out on the town, a place to stay from Tuesday to Thursday when working in town, or even a bachelor pad for guys (or girls) who are no longer bachelors (when a few friends can buy a place together).
- **A property purchased purely for investment**, which could be a capital investment, provide a regular income from letting or both. In recent years many people have invested in property to provide an income in their retirement. Many people also buy properties off-plan and sell on completion to make a quick profit. Usually the earlier you buy off-plan the better the deal, as developers are keen to get in some money and start the ball rolling.
- **A home for a student child**, which may also realise a capital gain. In recent years an increasing number of parents have purchased homes for their offspring while they're attending university, which they

generally share with their fellow students (who pay rent which can go towards the mortgage).

- **A commercial property**, which can be anything from bed and breakfast accommodation or a hotel to a shop or office. This is a more specialised market sector and not generally something for the novice investor.

Good investments generally include the following:

- A property that's under-priced;
- A property (at the right price) that needs refurbishing, modernisation or renovation;
- A property with a large garden, part of which can be sold off as a separate building plot;
- A property with the potential to add value such as a loft conversion, annexe or extension;
- A property in an up-and-coming area;
- A property with good transport links (road/rail) or planned links;
- A property with good amenities (shops, leisure facilities, parks, etc.);
- Homes with wide appeal;
- Properties with well-proportioned rooms (that will take 'proper' furniture);
- Period properties;
- Four and five-bedroom houses;
- A large property that can be converted into apartments or split into two semi-detached homes or terraced homes;
- Reasonably-priced apartments and maisonettes in the centre of cities;
- Large loft apartments and penthouses;
- A property with off-road parking or a garage (particularly in cities);
- Waterside properties, particularly in popular seaside resorts;
- Homes near good state schools and international schools;
- Property in a historic or university town.

Poor or indifferent investments generally include the following:

- A property that's over-priced;
- Small studio and one-bedroom apartments;

- Property in rundown areas or areas with high unemployment;
- Unusual or non-traditional houses without universal appeal;
- Poorly designed or quirky homes;
- Apartments attached to commercial premises (e.g. above shops);
- Houses near to any source of noise such as a busy motorway;
- Homes prone to regular flooding;
- Property in towns without private parking and no nearby on-road parking;
- Nondescript 'modern' homes built in the '60s, '70s and '80s (which can be difficult to sell).

Where To Buy

A desirable address (postcode) can upgrade a property from an ordinary house to a desirable residence – just one street (or even the opposite side of a street) can make all the difference in value.

SURVIVAL TIP
Property within a mile or two of a fashionable area may be much better value for money, simply due to a different postcode, and it will often have better potential for price increases.

If you're planning to buy in London, it may be more profitable to look for an up-and-coming area for maximum profit – for example Hackney is popular among creative people and the Elephant & Castle is undergoing a huge redevelopment – rather than an area that's already well-established with fashionable restaurants, pubs and shops. Trying to determine the next hotspot is a national sport among property investors.

The key to spotting an up-and-coming area is improved transport links, e.g. a new motorway, railway station or tram/metro link. It also pays to buy in a area where there are lots of jobs and insufficient homes, such as the Thames Valley, rather than a region where property is cheaper but in less demand as employment is falling. You can use websites such Up My Street (💻 www.upmystreet.com), Provisor (💻 www.proviser.com) or UK Online.gov.uk (💻 www.ukonline.gov.uk) to check the facilities and property prices in a town or suburb.

In autumn 2003, the top ten property hotspots (where property prices had risen fastest in the previous year) were all outside the south of

England, i.e. in the north of England, Wales or Scotland. Areas being touted as hotspots (or warm spots) in late 2003 include South Wales (e.g. Abertillery), Oldham (Lancs.), Hucknall (Notts.) and towns in Northumberland within commuting distance of Newcastle.

Any area where property is much lower than the surrounding areas is likely to be a good long-term investment, provided it isn't in terminal decline due to crime and urban blight.

Buying To Let

When buying to let (see page 206) you must ensure that the rental income will cover the mortgage, out-goings and vacant (void) periods. Bear in mind that in some areas rents are falling and there are doubts over whether the rental market can sustain the ever-growing number of buy to let properties. Average gross rental yields (the annual rent as a percentage of a property's value) have fallen from round 10 per cent to 5 per cent in London in the last year, with net yields a few per cent lower. Yields vary considerably depending on the region or city and the type of property, and have traditionally been highest on apartments in London, although they can be just as high or higher in cities such as Leeds and Manchester, where property costs much less.

Holiday Homes

Holiday or second homes have always been popular in the UK and in recent years this sector has grown tremendously as investors have looked for a safe haven for their spare cash. Before buying a holiday home you need to decide whether you want it to be solely for your family's and friend's use or whether you want to let it. If you want to let it - or could do so in future - you will need to buy with this in mind. You can cover your costs by letting for a few months each year and may even cover your entire mortgage repayments.

Renovation

The secret to making money on property is buying what nobody else wants to take on (at a knockdown price) and turning it around. When looking for a property that needs refurbishing or modernisation or one where you can add value with a loft conversion, annexe or extension, it's important not to pay too much for it. One of the most common mistakes that people make is to pay too much for a restoration property and to underestimate the cost of the work required. If you buy a ruin for restoration, you must be prepared to spend a lot of money and probably a lot more than you bargained for, as a major restoration almost never comes in on budget! It will also take you much longer than planned.

It isn't always easy to get a loan on a property requiring complete restoration, which is usually paid in stages as when building a new home (see page 78).

If you're planning to buy a property that needs restoration or renovation, you should arrange for a builder to inspect it and provide a quotation (add another 25 per cent for unforeseen problems). You need to know **exactly** what you plan to do before starting work and to have architect's drawings for all structural changes. You also need to know how much each job will add to the value of a property - so that you don't waste money doing non-essential work that adds little or no value - and obtain an accurate valuation of what the restored property will be worth. Spending too much money on renovation is a common mistake. A property must be well renovated, but there's little point in spending a fortune on a designer kitchen, fancy bathrooms and power showers if it's out of character with the property or the sort of buyer you can expect to attract won't be interested in paying for such things.

Somewhere between the estimated value after restoration and the cost of renovation is what you should pay for a property. For example, if the restored value is estimated at £300,000 and the cost of restoration will be £100,000, you should pay no more than £200,000 and probably much less.

You need to allow for budget over-runs, the fees associated with buying and selling and your profit margin if you plan to sell as soon as the restoration is completed. You also need to bear in mind that the property market could fall by the time that you're ready to sell.

Student Homes

If you've a spare 'few thousand' you may wish to buy a home for a child studying at college or university. Not only do they get to live in a better property and save on rent, but it's also an excellent investment as good rental property in university towns is always in demand. When your child finishes university you can sell at a profit or continue to let it. An ideal property must generally have good transport links and lots of bedrooms, but doesn't need to be in tip-top decorative condition.

> **SURVIVAL TIP**
> **It's better to place the letting of the other rooms (if applicable) with an agent, rather than put your offspring in an awkward position when a flatmate doesn't pay the rent.**

The sharing of bills must also be carefully considered and controlled. Theft can be a problem during holiday periods, when properties must be secure and valuables removed.

New property investors may wish to attend the Property Investor Show (💻 www.propertyinvestor.co.uk), held in September at the ExCel Centre in London. See also **Chapter 4 – Mortgages, Chapter 6 – Home Improvements, Chapter 7 – Letting and Chapter 8 – Selling Your Home.**

BUYING LAND

You must take the same care when buying land as you would when buying a home. The most important point when buying land is to ensure that it has been approved for building and that the plot is large enough and suitable for the house you plan to build. When a plot of land has planning permission, the maximum size of building that can be built is usually stated. If you buy land from an agent, it will usually already have planning permission, but if it doesn't it must be made a condition of purchase.

Some plots are unsuitable for building as they're too steep or require prohibitively expensive foundations. Also check that there aren't any restrictions such as high-tension electricity lines, water pipes or rights of way that may restrict building. Note that the cost of providing services to a property in a remote rural area may be prohibitively expensive and it must have a reliable water supply. Always obtain confirmation in writing from the local town hall that land can be built on and has been approved for road access. It's also worth checking whether a plot is in an area where there are high levels of radon gas (see page 103) or other problems such as subsidence – see Home Check (💻 www.homecheck.co.uk) or Enviro Search (💻 www.envirosearch.com).

Most builders offer package deals that include the plot and the cost of building a home. However, it isn't always advisable to buy the building plot from the builder who's going to build your home, and you should shop around and compare separate land and building costs.

SURVIVAL TIP

If you decide to buy a package deal, you must insist on separate contracts for the land and the building, and obtain the title deed for the land before signing a building contract. Obtain a receipt showing the plot is correctly presented in the land register and check for yourself that the correct planning permission has been obtained (don't leave it to the builder). If planning permission is flawed you may need to pay extra to alter the building or it may even have to be demolished!

Cost Of Land

The cost of land in England varies considerably depending on the area, e.g. from around £250,000 to £500,000 for a half-acre plot. Prices have escalated sharply in recent years in many areas, fuelled by the demand for new homes. As a rough guide, you should allow 25 per cent of your total budget for the cost of a plot and 75 per cent for construction. This means that if you budget is £250,000 you will need to buy a plot for around £62,500, which is difficult or impossible in many areas. However, you can save money on the construction by building a timber-framed home (see page 49) and doing some of the work yourself. Land can represent up to half the cost of building a home, although it's still possible in many areas to buy a plot of land and build a bigger and better home for much less than the cost of a property built by a developer or a resale property.

Prime sites are at a premium in many areas and many old homes on a large plot are purchased by developers who knock them down and build a development of apartments, townhouses or detached homes. One way for self-builders to save money is to buy a plot of land with a derelict building on it and divide the land into two (or more) smaller plots and sell one to recoup some of the cost. Alternatively you can buy a house with a large garden and use half or more of the garden to create a new building plot and sell the house with a smaller garden. This way you can even get your plot for free if you add value to the house before selling it, but you must ensure that the garden isn't too small or will be overlooked by your new house. You must also ensure that your plot has planning permission, separate road access and parking, and that your planned house doesn't overlook nearby homes.

Plotfinder (☎ 01527-834435, 💻 www.plotfinder.net), a service of *Homebuilding & Renovating* magazine (☎ 01527-083 4400, 💻 www.home building.co.uk), *Build It* magazine (☎ 020-7772 8300, 💻 www.buildit-online.co.uk) and Buildstore (🖳 www.buildstore.co.uk/findingland) are good sources of plots for sale. Homelands of England (☎ 01572-822111) sell building plots ready for building with planning permission, telephone lines, electricity, water, mains gas and drainage (called serviced land).

BUILDING YOUR OWN HOME

Self-building is increasingly popular in the UK, where over 30,000 people build their own homes each year. Building your own home allows you not only to choose where to build a home and to design it yourself, but to ensure that the quality of materials and workmanship is first class. If you want to be far from the madding crowd, you can buy a plot of land and have an individual, architect-designed house built to your own design and specifications, or to a standard design provided by a builder. You can even literally build it yourself, as many people do, although you will need professional help with some jobs and work must be approved by building inspectors. If you've got a choice, avoid building a house during the winter – start in the late spring and with a bit of luck you will have finished or be doing the interior when winter comes around.

Building permission can be difficult to obtain in some regions (depending on what you want to build) and building a home isn't recommended for the timid.

It's advisable to employ contractors and manage the project yourself if you're up to it, otherwise you will need to engage an architect or builder to do it for you. Some self-build schemes involve a group of families building their homes together under the guidance of a self-build project management company, such as Wadsworth Landmark (☎ 0117-940 9800).

Never forget that it will take longer, cost more and be much more work than you ever thought!

The good news is that on completion, self-build homes are typically valued at around 30 to 40 per cent more than the total building cost (land, labour and materials).

Planning Permission

If a plot doesn't have planning permission (see also page 186), you will need to decide whether to apply for outline planning consent or full planning permission. Outline planning consent is a sort of agreement in principle and a way of 'testing the water' if you're unsure whether full planning permission will be granted. The costs involved are less, but you cannot start building until full planning permission has been granted. When outline planning consent has been given, you can submit detailed plans for approval. Alternatively, you can make an application for full planning permission from the start. This will save you time, but if it's refused you will have wasted money on producing plans and drawings (although you can minimise the risks involved by taking expert advice). If you employ an architect, he will apply for planning permission on your behalf, although it can take weeks or even months for a decision. Application forms are available from your local council's planning department. The Department of the Environment publishes a booklet, *Planning Permission: A Guide for Householders*, available from planning offices, and the Royal Town Planning Institute (☎ 020-7929 9494, 💻 www.rtpi.org.uk) publish a leaflet entitled *Where to Find Planning Advice*.

Building Costs

When building your own home, land and building costs are usually separate, with the cost of the plot (see above) usually comprising around 25 per cent of the total budget. Building costs vary depending on the region, the quality and upon which of the following options you choose:

- Do most of the work yourself (DIY) with the help of sub-contractors (cheapest);
- Use all sub-contractors;
- Use sub-contractors and a main contractor;
- Employ a main contractor (most expensive).

The cost per square metre varies from around £46 per ft^2 (£500 per m^2) for a standard quality home in northern England using the DIY method, to around £130 per ft^2 (£1,400 per m^2) in Greater London for a job using top quality materials using only a main contractor. The average cost of a good quality, spacious, three to four-bedroom family home of around 1,600 ft^2 (150m^2) is around £75 per ft^2 (£800 per m^2) or £120,000. See

Homebuilding & Renovating magazine for information on how to estimate your building costs.

SURVIVAL TIP
If you're buying materials yourself, you must pay VAT on materials but it can be reclaimed on completion of the project by applying to your local Customs & Excise office.

Many companies sell pre-fabricated or kit homes for self-builders, which can be built in 12 weeks or less. The cheapest homes are kit, timber-frame houses, where you buy the frame and supply the bricks and other materials separately. American and Scandinavian-style timber homes are becoming increasingly popular and are offered by many companies, including Advanced Timber Technology (💻 www.adtimtec.com), Fleming Homes (💻 www.fleminghomes.co.uk), Frame UK (💻 www.frameuk.com) and Robertson Timberkit (💻 www.timberkit.co.uk). One of the advantages of timber homes is that they're energy-efficient and have exceptionally low heating costs. It's also possible to build a striking Japanese-style home, which can be built for around half the cost of a traditional architect-designed house, although you may have difficulty obtaining planning permission (which applies to anything out of the ordinary). However, you've a good chance if your plot is in a secluded position and doesn't over-look (or isn't over-looked) by other properties.

Mortgages

Special self-build mortgages are available for those who wish to sell a property at a profit after building it (see *Build It* or *Homebuilding & Renovating* magazine for a list of lenders). The average mortgage for self-builders is usually 75 to 80 per cent of the cost of the land and building combined (see page 148), with payments made in stages as building progresses.

Architect-Designed Homes

You should expect to pay at least 10 per cent more for an individually-designed house than for a standard builder's offering. An individual architect-designed house may also command a much higher selling price, as there are always buyers who will pay a premium for individuality.

SURVIVAL TIP
You must ensure that the architect will be available to supervise a project and you should also personally check periodically that nothing is going drastically wrong.

When looking for an architect and builder, it's advisable to obtain recommendations from local people you can trust or alternatively you can contact the Association of Self-Build Architects (☎ 0800-387310, 💻 www.asba-architects.org).

An architect should be able to recommend a number of reliable builders or contractors, but you should also do your own research, as the most important consideration when building a home is the reputation of the builder. You should be wary of an architect with his 'own' builder (or a builder with his own architect), as it's the architect's job to ensure that the builder does his work according to the plans and specifications (so you don't want their relationship to be too cosy). Inspect other homes a builder has built and check with the owners what problems they've had and whether they're satisfied.

⚠ **Planning permission and building plans must be obtained in advance and if you build without planning permission, in the wrong place or deviate from the plans, you could be forced to demolish the property! The local authorities in the UK never turn a blind eye to planning infringements.**

If you employ a builder you should ensure that his work is covered by the NHBC Buildmark 10-year warranty or the Zurich Municipal Building Guarantee scheme (see page 50).

Contracts

You should obtain written quotations from a number of builders before signing a contract, which must include the following items:

- A detailed building description and a list of the materials to be used (with references to the architect's plans);
- The exact location of the building on the plot;
- The building and payment schedule, which should be made in stages according to building progress;

- All costs, including the architect's fees (unless contracted separately), landscaping (if applicable), all permits and licences, and the connection of utilities (water, electricity, gas, telephone) to the house, not just to the building site;
- A penalty clause for late completion;
- The retention of a percentage (e.g. 5 to 10 per cent) of the building costs as a guarantee against defects;
- How disputes will be settled.

Before accepting a quotation, it's advisable to have it checked by an independent building consultant or engineer to confirm that it's a fair deal. You should check whether the quotation is an estimate or a fixed price, as sometimes the cost can escalate wildly due to contract clauses and changes made during building work. It's important to have a contract checked by your solicitor, as building contracts are often heavily biased in the builder's favour and give clients few rights. You will also need insurance for yourself, your architect and contractors.

Information about building a home is available from many sources, including:

- *Homebuilding & Renovating* magazine (☎ 01527-083 4400, 💻 www.homebuilding.co.uk).
- *Build It* magazine (☎ 020-7772 8300, 💻 www.buildit-online.co.uk).
- **The Association of SelfBuilders** (☎ 0704-154 4126, 💻 www.self-builder.org.uk).
- **Federation of Master Builders (FMB)**, Gordon Fisher House, 14/15 Great James Street, London WC1N 3DP (☎ 020-7242 7583, 💻 www.fmb.org.uk).
- **House Builders Federation**, 56-64 Leonard Street, London EC2A 4JX (☎ 020-7608 5000, 💻 www.hbf.co.uk).
- **Timber and Brick Homes Information Council**, Gable House, 40 High Street, Rickmansworth, Herts. WD1 3ES (☎ 01923-778136).

A National Self-Build Homes Show (☎ 020-7865 9042/020-8466 4066) is held at Alexandra Palace (London) in September and *Homebuilding & Renovating* magazine organises a number of shows for self-builders throughout the UK (💻 www.homebuildingshow.co.uk). A wealth of books are published for self-builders (see 💻 www.buildstore.co.uk/whyselfbuild/books), including *The Housebuilder's Bible* by

Mark Brinkley (Rodelia Books – ☎ 01487-824704). See also the list of trade associations in **Appendix A**.

GARAGES & PARKING

A garage or off-road private parking space isn't usually included in the price when you buy an apartment or townhouse, although private parking may be available at an additional cost, possibly in an underground garage. Modern semi-detached and detached homes always have a garage or car port. Smaller homes usually have a single garage, while larger 'executive' homes often have integral double garages or even garaging for up to four cars.

Urban period homes (such as Georgian townhouses) rarely have a garage or parking area. However, parking isn't usually a problem when buying an old home in a rural area, although there may not be a purpose-built garage.

When buying an apartment or townhouse in a new development, a garage or parking space may be available at extra cost. You should think carefully before deciding not to buy a garage or parking space (even if you haven't got a car!), as it will be worth its weight in gold when you sell and could clinch a sale. In suburban and rural areas, a garage is essential and a double garage is even better. The cost of parking is an important consideration when buying in a town or city, where on-road parking (even with a resident's parking permit) can be difficult to find. It may be possible to rent a garage or parking space, although this is difficult and can be prohibitively expensive in cities. Bear in mind that in a large development, the nearest resident parking area may be some distance from your home. This may be an important factor, particularly if you aren't up to carrying heavy shopping hundreds of metres to your home and possibly up several flights of stairs.

Without a private garage or parking space, parking can be a nightmare, particularly in cities or during the summer in busy holiday resorts. Bear in mind that the customers of nearby hotels, B&Bs and other businesses could monopolise on-street parking. In London and other cities, tradesmen often refuse work when there's nowhere to park! You can usually get the council to suspend a parking bay for a period, but it costs around £20 per day and you need to apply around a week in advance (not much good in an emergency!). Free on-street parking can be difficult or impossible to find in cities and large towns, and in any case may be inadvisable for anything but a wreck. A lock-up garage is important in areas with a high incidence of car theft (e.g. most cities) and is also useful to protect your car from climatic extremes such as ice, snow and extreme heat.

Garages and parking spaces are at a premium in cities such as London (where a single garage can sell for as much as £100,000!) and are in huge demand. A garage can add tens of thousands of pounds to properties in city centres and as much as 15 per cent in London.

SURVIVAL TIP

When buying an apartment or townhouse where a garage or parking space is optional, you should *always* buy one (or two if possible) if you can afford to, even if you've no car and don't plan to buy one. It will be appreciated by your visitors and guests and will make a home much easier to sell.

Z
Z
Z
Z
Z
HOME
SWEET
HOME
WIPE
YOUR
FEET

Jim Watson

3.

THE BUYING PROCESS

From a legal point of view, the UK is one of the safest countries in the world in which to buy a home and buyers have a high degree of protection under the law, although you must take the usual precautions regarding contracts, deposits and obtaining proper title. Nevertheless, many people have had their fingers burnt by rushing into property deals without proper care and consideration, and it's all too easy to fall in love with a home and sign a contract without giving it sufficient thought. If you're uncertain, don't allow yourself to be rushed into making a hasty decision, e.g. by fears of an imminent price rise or because someone else is interested in a property. It's vital to do your homework thoroughly and avoid the 'dream sellers' who will happily tell you anything to sell you a property.

SURVIVAL TIP
You should never pay any money or sign anything without first taking legal advice. You will find the relatively small cost of legal advice (compared to the cost of a home) to be excellent value for money, if only for the peace of mind it affords.

Trying to cut corners to save a few pounds on legal costs is foolhardy in the extreme when a large sum of money is at stake. It's wise to check the credentials of all professionals you employ and not to rely solely on advice proffered by those with a financial interest in selling you a property, such as a developer or estate agent (see page 39), although their advice may be excellent and totally unbiased.

The sequence of events when buying a home in the UK (except for Scotland – see page 126) is as follows:

- Arrange a mortgage in principal;
- View a number of properties;
- Make an offer on a property;
- Offer is accepted;
- Give your solicitor's (or conveyancer's) details to the selling agent or owner;
- Obtain a valuation and obtain a written mortgage offer;
- Arrange a survey;
- Complete the conveyancing work;
- Agree a completion date, which is included in the contract;

- Exchange contracts, pay the deposit and take out buildings insurance on the property;
- Check the property's condition and whether anything is missing a few days before the completion;
- Completion;
- Move in;
- Start organising the house-warming party!

Bear in mind that the whole procedure from agreeing a sale to moving usually takes from one to three months (but can be longer), so don't be in too much of a hurry!

This chapter includes the following topics:

- Avoiding problems;
- Viewing;
- Inspecting a property;
- Valuations & surveys;
- Making an offer;
- Conveyancing;
- Purchase contracts;
- Completion;
- Fees;
- Buying at auction;
- Buying in Scotland.

AVOIDING PROBLEMS

The most common problems experienced by buyers include the following:

- Buying in the wrong area (rent first!);
- Paying to much for a property;
- Losing a property due to being in a chain;
- Gazumping and 'gazundering' (see below);

- Buying a property that needs renovation and underestimating the costs and the resale value;
- Not being able to obtain planning permission for alterations;
- Not having a survey done on an old property;
- Not taking proper legal advice or including additional clauses in a contract;
- Taking on too large a mortgage.

Wrong Area

Buying in the wrong area is usually the result of not doing your homework and researching the market properly (see **Chapter 1 – Choosing the Location**). This may mean buying in an area that's unsuitable for your family (poor schools, lack of public transport, etc.), buying in a run-down area where values are falling or simply buying in the wrong street. If it's feasible, it's advisable to rent a property for a period (in the area where you're planning to buy) before buying in an unfamiliar area.

Paying Too Much

Again, this is the result of lack of research and being in too much of a hurry. If you're unsure what a property is worth, have it valued by a professional valuer.

Chains

The dreaded chain is the curse of the UK housing market, as buyers and sellers in England and Wales are free to pull out of a deal at any time before the exchange of contracts without penalty (in Scotland once a bid has been accepted it's legally binding).

If you're a first-time buyer there will be nobody 'above' you, but the vendor may be part of a chain below you.

You can try to avoid chains by doing the following:

- Pay in cash (i.e. don't take out a mortgage);
- Sell your home and rent before buying another;
- Buy a new home from a developer;

- Buy at auction;
- Buy a property with vacant possession (where the owner has already moved out).

Most house sales are part of a chain of sellers and buyers – around seven or eight isn't uncommon – and only one link needs to fail (which is commonplace) to jeopardise a whole series of sales.

If someone drops out of a chain, it's likely to delay the sale of your property or the purchase of a new one. If your purchase looks as if it's in jeopardy, you could just hang on and hope that the vendor doesn't find another buyer who can complete sooner. However, if this happens you should be prepared to lose the new home and start the process all over again. You may be able to obtain a bridging loan which will allow you to go through with the purchase, although this is risky and expensive. If you've sold your home, but lost the home you planned to buy due to a break in the chain, you may wish to consider renting accommodation until you find a new home rather than lose your buyer.

Gazumping

In a sellers' market, gazumping – where a seller agrees to an offer from one prospective buyer and then sells to another for a higher amount – is rampant and **isn't illegal**. When buying a resale home (you cannot be gazumped when buying a new home after you've paid a deposit) in England, Wales or Northern Ireland, prospective buyers make an offer which is subject to survey and contract. (There's virtually no gazumping in Scotland, as neither side can pull out of a deal without penalty once an offer has been made and accepted.) Either party can amend or withdraw from a sale at any time before the exchange of contracts – when a sale is legally binding – which is usually around 12 weeks after the acceptance of an offer. In a sellers' market your chances of being gazumped are very high and it has been blamed for wrecking as many as one in seven deals.

SURVIVAL TIP

Gazumping is so prevalent that you can take out insurance against being gazumped after having paid for a survey and legal fees!

Sellers and estate agents may not take a property off the market when an offer has been accepted because the buyer may change his mind or take too long to complete the deal. However, agents should agree not to show a property to other prospective buyers and you should make this a condition of an offer being accepted. However, agents are legally obliged to tell vendors about any other offers on a property, even when an offer has been accepted and it has been taken off the market. For example, if someone who previously viewed a property makes an offer, the agent must tell the vendor. Don't take it personally if the vendor receives a better offer after accepting yours and asks you to match or better it – if you really want the property it may be better to swallow your pride. Note that around 30 per cent of offers that are accepted fail to reach completion for one reason or another.

You can reduce the chances of being gazumped by exchanging contracts as soon as possible and encouraging a vendor to sign a lock-out agreement where you've the exclusive right to buy for a number of weeks. Because of the fears of gazumping, some buyers agree to buy two or more homes, which inevitably leads to them pulling out of a sale at the last minute. Sellers also frequently cancel sales before contracts are exchanged and may take a property off the market altogether if they think they can get a better price later. To try to prevent gazumping, some agents insist that vendors sign a binding agreement that states that any further offers they receive after they've accepted one must be refused.

To avoid gazumping, the American system which allows contracts to be exchanged the same day a sale is agreed has been introduced by some solicitors. Most people agree that the present system is immoral, with both buyers and sellers reneging on deals with impunity, often just days before they're due to exchange contracts (and after a prospective buyer has paid hundreds and possibly thousands of pounds in legal fees and a survey).

From 2004, sellers will need to provide a 'home information pack' (see page 251) at a cost of around £500 before putting their home on the market. This will include commissioning a survey, collecting the title deeds, conducting local council searches and providing details of warranties, planning permission (etc.). It's hoped that this will reduce the risk of gazumping, although without a financial penalty (such as the forfeiture of a deposit as in other countries) it's very unlikely that gazumping will be eradicated, particularly when some buyers are willing to pay much more than the asking price in a hot market and may even pay in cash!

Gazundering

This is the term used when a prospective buyer threatens to pull out at the last minute unless the seller reduces the price. Often the vendor has already arranged to buy a new home and is forced to go through with the deal. Although rare, gazundering is more common in a flat housing market where prices are static or falling and buyers are thin on the ground. To get their own back on 'gazunderers', some vendors strip houses bare, removing carpets and anything that wasn't specifically included in a sale - one vendor even went so far as to dig up the tennis court!

Renovation

If you're planning to buy a property that requires renovation or you plan to carry out major structural changes, ensure that you've an accurate estimate of the costs (see **Chapter 6 - Home Improvements**).

Planning Permission

If you plan to make structural changes to a property, particularly a large extension, you must ensure that you will be able to obtain planning permission (see page 186).

Surveys

A survey is vital, particularly if you're buying an old property or a property with a large plot of land (see page 76).

Legal Advice

Your solicitor or conveyancer (see page 110) will carry out the necessary searches regarding such matters as ownership, debts, rights of way, use of land before building (landfill, mines or industrial sites) and planned developments (motorways or railway lines, radio or mobile phone masts, industrial sites, etc.). Enquiries must be made to ensure that the vendor has a registered title and that there are no debts against a property. Your solicitor must make sure that the person selling a property is the sole owner or has the right to sell. It isn't unknown for a husband or wife to sell a home without telling his or her spouse, forge the spouse's signature and disappear with the proceeds, in which case you can end up owning only half a house. It's also important to check that a property has the relevant building licences, conforms to local planning conditions and that any changes (alterations, additions or renovations) have been approved by the local council.

Contracts & Clauses

If a sale or purchase is dependent on something beyond your control, such as the sale of a property, or you're buying additional items (such as carpets, curtains or furniture) with a property, they must be included in the contract.

Mortgages

It's important not to take on too large a mortgage because if interest rates rise you could be in negative equity (where your loan is more than a property is worth – see page 150) or unable to pay your mortgage and have your home repossessed.

VIEWING

You should view a property (see also **Inspecting A Property's Condition** below) a number of times before agreeing to buy it – and you shouldn't allow yourself to be rushed. Bear in mind that properties take on a different character at different times of the day and in different weather (view on bright and dull days), therefore you should view them on different days and on both weekdays and at weekends. It's advisable to take someone with you when viewing a property and obtain their opinion – in any case, a woman should always be accompanied by an agent or friend (for security). Don't view anything that doesn't meet your requirements or is much too expensive and don't waste time viewing a property that you take an immediate dislike to.

Ask lots of questions, make copious notes and take lots of photographs. Obtain a large-scale map of the area where you're looking, which may even show individual buildings, thus allowing you to mark the places that you've seen. You could do this using a grading system to denote your impressions. If you use an estate agent, he will usually drive you around and you can return later to those that you like most at your leisure (provided you've marked them on your map!). However, bear in mind that you won't be able to view a property (i.e. the interior or garden) without making an appointment with the agent or owner.

When viewing a property, note your immediate impressions:

- Do you like the street and general area?
- Do you get a good feeling about it?
- Is it light and spacious (or can the light and size be increased)?
- Is it ready to move into or can it be renovated for a reasonable investment?
- Does it have good potential to add value?

Potential

Although you should present a property in its best light when selling, many people don't bother. If you can see through their clutter and dirt and have a vision of what a property could be with a bit of 'tlc', you could snap up a bargain that most people wouldn't touch with a barge pole. Most buyers are unable to visualise how a property could be transformed with a bit of money and elbow grease, and want somewhere they can move into tomorrow without lifting a finger. To help spot the hidden potential you should try to do the following:

- Ignore the vendor's clutter, ghastly décor and tatty furnishings;
- Use you imagination to see how it could look after renovation – you can always install a period fireplace, cornicing, new windows and doors, and even a new staircase;
- Look for interesting period architectural features (such as fireplaces, staircases, cornicing and ceiling roses, tiled or woodblock floors, stained glass, etc.) that can be exploited;
- Assess the space and light and how it can be enhanced;
- Look for potential areas that can be improved such as knocking two small rooms into one, adding an extension, conservatory or loft conversion;
- Calculate the property's value when it has been done up.

Good Vibrations

How does the house feel? Does it feel right and comfortable or do you feel uneasy and get bad vibes? Trust your instincts – if it doesn't feel right, don't buy it. The Chinese and an increasing number of westerners put their faith in Feng Shui – the Chinese art of placement of buildings, doors, windows and furniture in order to create good health, harmony and wealth. You can move the furniture around, but you cannot do much about a house that has been built with bad Feng Shui. Houses tend to give off good and bad vibes, which is why you may feel immediately at home in one house, yet feel strangely uncomfortable in another. Houses can also be affected by ley (energy) lines and underground streams.

Size & Light

Many tricks are employed to make a property look larger and lighter, including mirrors, artful lighting, removing curtains to increase light, small (toy) furniture and beds, pale colours, removing doors and attractive accessories. This is particularly common in show homes when you're buying off-plan.

While these are good tips when selling, you should be aware of them when buying!

Always check the room sizes (given in feet and inches) and measure them if you aren't sure. This is particularly important if you need space for large items of furniture or the rooms are relatively small. Are rooms an unusual shape for furniture? Is there room to expand? Is there lots of natural light? Are bedrooms facing east to catch the morning sun and does the living area face west to get the evening sun?

Area & Surroundings

What is the road and surrounding area like? Is it on a busy street with public transport? – if it's on a bus route this can be a bonus, although a red route in London can reduce property values. What are the neighbouring buildings like? What are the neighbours like? It's particularly important to check your prospective neighbours when buying an apartment. For example, are they noisy (you can check by viewing in the evening), sociable or absent for long periods? Do you think you will get on with them? If the vendor has had a dispute with a neighbour, particularly an acrimonious one that has resulted in litigation, he must declare it when selling.

Parking & Access

Is there a garage or off-road parking? Is the house on a steep slope and if so, is there a flat area for parking? Can you park on the street? Is there a residents' parking scheme? How far is the nearest parking area from the property? If you need to park a long way away, how do you feel about carrying heavy shopping hundreds of yards to your home and possibly up several flights of stairs? You may also wish to check whether a property allows wheelchair access and whether it has been designed with the elderly or disabled in mind.

Garden

Does it have a garden, patio or balcony? How large is the garden and is it south facing? Are outbuildings such as sheds and greenhouses included in the price? Is the garden secluded or overlooked? Does it have mature trees and plants? Check for any surrounding trees on a neighbour's property or possible extensions and walls that could block your light (**you've no legal right to light**). If a house overlooks a village green (or green field land), don't assume that it will always be so as some greens have been sold off by councils to developers. Check that trees aren't too close to a property and could cause subsidence (see page 98).

General

Does the property has sufficient storage space, power points and light fittings? Is it in good condition, e.g. good windows, roof and floorboards? If not, is it reflected in the price? If you're planning to buy an apartment you may wish to check whether pets are permitted and there may also be other restrictions (see **Buying An Apartment** on page 59).

Value For Money

Does the property seem to be good value, taking into account any work that needs to be done? Is anything included in the price such as appliances, furniture, carpets/curtains, garden ornaments (etc.).

If you still like a property after taking into consideration all its negative points, you should consider making an offer subject to a survey (see below). See also **Chapter 1 – Choosing The Location**.

Inspecting A Property's Condition

When you've found a property that you like, you should make a close inspection of its condition – not to be confused with a professional survey (see below). Obviously this will depend on whether it's an old home in need of renovation or a modern home. Some simple checks you can do yourself include testing the electrical system, plumbing, mains water, water pressure, hot water boiler and central heating. Don't take someone's word that these are functional, but check them yourself. Although building standards in the UK are generally high, you shouldn't assume that a building is sound, as even relatively new buildings can have serious faults (although rare). Before commissioning a survey there are a number of obvious signs of damage or decay that you can spot without being an expert. Checks you can make or questions to ask include the following:

- Look for signs of subsidence such as cracked walls and doors that don't hang correctly or stick. External signs may include a bent chimney stack, an uneven floor line, walls that aren't vertical, or bulging or cracked walls. Check whether there are any nearby trees with roots that could undermine a property's foundations – some trees are notorious for drying out the soil, which can lead to subsidence. Cracks in walls may indicate signs of subsidence, although a few small cracks don't necessarily indicate a problem, as many small cracks happen naturally in houses due to routine changes in humidity or temperature. Bear in mind that houses built before 1960 are more likely to be prone to subsidence, because foundations tended to be shallower. Note that a house covered in ivy may look nice, but it can seriously damage walls (Virginia Creeper is okay).
- Does the property have a damp-proof course? Check for signs of damp or damp smells. Check internal and external walls for tidemarks or discoloured plaster, particularly on the ground floor or in the basement. Feel walls for moisture, which can be caused by condensation, and check windows for condensation. Damp is one of the most difficult and expensive problems to eradicate (if any damp proofing or other repair work has been carried out, check whether it's guaranteed). If you find signs of damp, always have it checked by a surveyor or damp expert.
- If possible, check an old property after a heavy rainfall, when any leaks (in guttering, roof tiles, tiling, etc.) should come to light.
- Check the state of the brickwork and rendering, and if it's a stone house check the pointing – if it's crumbling the house will be (or become) damp. If there are air-bricks they must not be blocked by earth or plants.
- Check the roof (with binoculars if necessary) for signs of missing or dislodged tiles and leaks in the roof space, damaged chimneys and blocked or damaged guttering. Also check flat roofs thoroughly as

they're vulnerable to the elements and a constant source of trouble (most need to be re-surfaced every 10 to 15 years).

- Check that windows are double-glazed and in good condition. Are they uPVC or inappropriate for the house? Examine wooden window frames for signs of rot or patching.
- Check the state of the floorboards. If a floor is springy it could be a sign of rotting joists.
- How old is the piping – lead piping will need replacing – and are the pipes and boiler insulated or lagged?
- Is their wall cavity insulation? Check whether the loft is well insulated – with the light off you shouldn't see any daylight. Check the roof timbers for signs of damp, woodworm or other boring insects.
- How old is the central heating system? Is it gas, oil or electric powered? Ask to see heating bills.
- Examine the state of the interior and exterior decoration. If it's poor it may indicate that more important repairs have been neglected or fixed temporarily. Be wary of new paint or wallpaper, which may conceal cracks or damp patches.
- Have a good look at old plasterwork and if it looks unsound tap it – a hollow sound means that it has blown and will need replacing.
- Check the quality of any building work or 'improvements' that have been carried out and whether it's guaranteed (when it should be backed by an industry-recognised warranty).
- Check the state of the garden and whether it will need professional work (landscaping is expensive).

If you're happy with the condition of a property after inspecting it you should have a valuation or survey done, depending on the age and type of property. In Scotland (see page 126) a valuation or survey must be carried out before making a formal offer, while in the rest of the UK offers are made subject to contract and a satisfactory survey.

VALUATIONS & SURVEYS

Before making an offer on a property in Scotland or before exchanging contracts in the rest of the UK, it's important to have a survey, although over half of all buyers rely on a basic valuation. This can be extremely risky, particularly when you consider that around one in five properties are found by surveyors to have major faults, such as damp, dry rot or insect infestations. Serious defects are more likely in old buildings, although they sometimes found in properties less than ten years old.

It's false economy and a huge gamble to buy an old property without having a survey.

If a survey reveals any problems they can usually be used as a bargaining tool to justify a lower price. A property vendor doesn't need to inform prospective buyers of any defects that might exist, although there are plans to include a survey as part a new 'home information pack' (see page 251) designed to speed up the buying process and reduce gazumping.

There are three levels of property inspections carried out by surveyors: a valuation, a homebuyer report and a full structural survey (described in detail below). Which one you choose usually depends on the age and type of property you're buying. If you're buying a relatively new home of standard construction, a valuation will probably suffice, particularly if it's still covered by the builder's warranty (see page 51). However, if you're in doubt about the condition you should have a more thorough survey carried out, particularly if it's over 50 years old, when you should have a full structural survey. An old home can have a variety of problems such as dry rot, rising damp, woodworm or other infestations, a leaking roof, rotten window frames, frost damage to stone and brickwork, subsidence or land-slip, rusty pipes and gutters, poor electrical and plumbing installations, and poor insulation. If new windows (e.g. double-glazing), central heating, re-wiring or re-plumbing are required it will be expensive and should be reflected in (or deducted from) the asking price.

Surveys should be carried out only by a qualified surveyor, who should be a member of the Royal Institute of Chartered Surveyors (RICS), which now incorporates the Institute of Surveyors and Valuers (ISVA), or the Royal Institute of Chartered Surveyors in Scotland (RICSS). (See **Appendix A** for addresses and contact numbers.) Members of these organisations have professional indemnity insurance, which means that you can happily sue them if they do a bad job! Most good surveyors will also have an ISO 9002 certification, which is an independent verification of the quality of their services.

SURVIVAL TIP

In Scotland you should have a valuation or survey before making an offer, which will help you determine how much to bid (see Buying In Scotland on page 126).

Put instructions in writing and include anything you particularly want inspected, plus details of any major work that you're planning to have done. Check what you will receive for your money and obtain a written estimate which includes VAT and all expenses. It's important to find a surveyor you can trust to do a good job, as a bad survey can be just as expensive as none at all (as some buyers have found out to their cost). A home inspection can be restricted to a few items or even a single system only, such as the wiring or plumbing in an old house. If you want an inspection on an unusual property, such as a thatched cottage or period home, you should choose a surveyor with experience of these.

Valuation

Lenders insist on a valuation before approving a loan, although this usually consists of a perfunctory check to confirm that a property is worth the purchase price. The valuation takes into account a property's age, condition, area and the price of similar properties locally. Although it's carried out by a qualified surveyor, it's merely a cautious assessment of the value of the property and not a survey. If you're obtaining a loan to purchase a property, your lender must be satisfied that the property provides sufficient security for the loan, and he will therefore carry out an independent valuation, which you must usually pay for (whether or not you go through with the purchase). The cost (which may be refunded when the mortgage is finalised) varies depending on the lender and the value of the property, and is approximately as shown below:

Value	**Fee**
£100,000	£175
£150,000	£225
£250,000	£275
£350,000	£325
£450,000	£375
Over £450,000	Negotiable

It's a gamble to rely on a valuation report as it's no guarantee that a property is structurally sound. You may be able to combine a homebuyer report or full structural survey with your lender's valuation, which should save you money, although you may prefer to use a surveyor who has been personally recommended to you or whom you've used before.

If your lender's valuation is less than the asking price, you may have to pull out of the deal if you cannot get the seller to reduce the price or raise more cash.

Homebuyer Report

A homebuyer report (or homebuyer survey and valuation report/ HSVR) is a concise report on the condition of a property, together with a valuation. In addition to a mortgage valuation, it includes the current open market value and an opinion of how saleable the property will be in future. Any major defects in the property will be listed, along with recommendations about further investigations required.

The property will be inspected only where it's reasonably accessible or visible and no test is made of the plumbing, heating, electrical or drainage systems (etc.).

It's recommended for conventional houses and apartments that appear to be in a reasonable condition. A homebuyer report isn't usually considered adequate for large houses over say 2,000ft^2 (around 200m^2), old properties (say pre-1940), and converted or purpose-built apartments.

Bear in mind that a homebuyer report isn't much cheaper than a full structural survey and therefore, unless you've a good reason not to, you should consider having a full structural survey.

If you combine a homebuyer report with a lender's valuation, which is refunded by your lender, you only pay the difference between the cost of the valuation and the homebuyer report. The cost of a homebuyer report varies depending on the value, age and condition of a property, and is roughly as follows:

Value	Fee
£100,000	£250
£150,000	£350
£250,000	£450
£350,000	£550
£450,000	£650
Over £450,000	Negotiable

Full Structural (Or Building) Survey

Around one in four property buyers has a full structural survey, which is usually tailored to individual requirements and is particularly suited to larger, older (e.g. over 50 years old), more complex properties, which may be outside the scope of a homebuyer report. This includes property over three stories in height, buildings of unusual construction (thatched, timber, etc.) and when you're planning to carry out major alterations such as extending or converting a property. Some people delay having a full structural survey done until both parties are ready to exchange contracts, as it's expensive having a report done for every house that you're interested in. The surveyor will examine everything that's reasonably visible, in addition to reporting on the construction and condition of a property. A structural survey includes the structural condition of all buildings, particularly the foundations, roofs, walls and woodwork; plumbing, electricity and heating systems; and anything else you want inspected.

Extent Of Survey

Discuss with the surveyor exactly what will be included in a survey, and most importantly, what will be excluded. You may need to pay extra to include certain checks and tests, such as an environmental survey and an energy efficiency rating. The surveyor will also advise on any repair costs and the suitability of proposed improvements or extensions you plan to make. Although the scope of a full structural survey is greater than a valuation or homebuyer report, there will still be some inaccessible parts of the structure and limitations. If you want a detailed survey, make sure that the vendor will allow your surveyor free access to the property, e.g. to the roof space (loft), and allow him to pull up carpets to examine floorboards. You will receive a written report on the structural condition of a property, including anything that could become a problem in the future. Some surveyors will allow you to accompany them and may produce a video of their findings in addition to a written report.

It's important to find out what the land a house is built on (and any land that comes with it) was previously used for, as some homes have been built on unsafe sites such as rubbish tips or chemical factories. You should also check what's in the ground (e.g. radon gas) and what's under it (e.g. an old mineshaft). Many houses in the UK are built on clay, which is prone to shrinking in prolonged hot weather, resulting in houses literally cracking up (usually due to inadequate foundations). If this isn't visible to the eye as cracked walls, ceilings or floors, a structural survey should reveal whether there's a problem. You should also have a house checked for termites and other pests, which are common in some areas. Your surveyor should also note any trees near to a house which may have caused (or could cause) structural problems, either due to damage caused by their roots or drying the soil which can lead to subsidence.

The cost of a full structural report depends on the value, size, age and condition of a property, and can vary considerably. You should shop around and obtain a few quotes (you may be able to negotiate a lower price). The table below is a rough guide to what you can expect to pay:

Value Of Property	Survey Fee
£100,000	£350
£150,000	£450
£250,000	£550
£350,000	£650
£450,000	£750
Over £450,000	Negotiable

Condition

Sometimes the valuation or surveyor's report shows that a property is in poor condition or that there are structural faults or other problems such as dry rot, woodworm or rising damp. If the poor condition isn't already reflected in the asking price, you should negotiate a reduction to cover the cost of repairs or renovation. If a property needs work doing on it, you should obtain a quotation in writing from a local builder or specialist.

A lender may refuse a mortgage on a property in poor condition or may insist that certain work is carried out before a mortgage is approved.

Don't be put off too much by problems brought to light by a survey, but check what they would cost to rectify. You may find that other prospective buyers are scared off by problems and that you can negotiate a good reduction for the necessary work. If a property needs renovating, arrange for a builder to inspect the property and give you a quotation (**add another 25 per cent to the total for safety**). If you're buying as an investment and plan to sell a house after doing it up, you need to know how much each job will add to the value of the property in order not to waste money doing non-essential work that adds little or no value.

Buying Land

When buying a rural property you may be able to negotiate the amount of land to be included in the purchase. If you're buying a property with a large plot of land or a property that's part of a larger plot of land owned by the vendor, the boundaries should be redrawn – you should engage a surveyor to measure the land and draw up a new plan, which must be registered with the Land Registry. You should also check with the Land Registry to find out what the land can be used for and whether there are any existing rights of way.

Complaints

Bear in mind that many surveyors miss problems or include non-existent problems and recommend unnecessary specialists. Many surveys are hedged with get-out clauses that try to limit the surveyor's liability.

> **SURVIVAL TIP**
> **If your new home turns out to have damp or dry rot or to be infested with death-watch beetles, which your surveyor has failed to discover, you can usually successfully sue him for damages – especially if you've given him written instructions in respect to these and other possible problem areas (always advisable).**

Complaints should be made in the first instance to your surveyor or his professional body (see **Appendix A**). Members of the RICS (see page 100) have an in-house complaints' procedure and also have compulsory arbitration schemes in the event of a dispute.

MAKING AN OFFER

When buying a property it pays to haggle over the price, even if you think it's a bargain. Don't be put off by a high or unrealistic asking price, as most sellers are willing to negotiate. Many properties sell for much less than their original asking prices – the average is around 5 per cent less – particularly properties priced at over £500,000. Sellers generally presume buyers will haggle and rarely expect to receive the asking price, although some people ask an unrealistic price and won't budge a penny. If you're in doubt about a property's value, it may be worthwhile obtaining an independent valuation (appraisal) – if it's less than a vendor is asking it may encourage him to lower his price.

Haggling

Buying property is one of the few times when you're expected to haggle over the price (like buying a used car!), although if a property has been realistically priced you shouldn't expect to get more than a 5 to 10 per cent reduction. However, in a buyer's market, such as London in late 2003, you should haggle like mad over the price. This applies equally to new and old properties. In 2003, asking prices in London and southern England were around 10 per cent higher than the selling price and buyers could negotiate as much as 20 per cent off the asking price of £1 million plus houses (although many vendors are reluctant to reduce their asking price or accept offers). In London, many developers offer inducements to buyers of new apartments such as paying stamp duty and legal fees, although you may be able to negotiate a 10 per cent discount (or more) if a development is selling slowly (some developers will throw in a free garage with luxury penthouses valued at up to £75,000). Cash buyers may be able to negotiate a considerable reduction for a quick sale, depending on the state of the property market and how urgent the sale. Your bargaining position may also be strengthened if you aren't part of a chain.

Initial Offer

When making an offer, don't be panicked into over-bidding. If you make an offer that's too low you can always raise it, but it's impossible to lower an offer once it has been accepted. If your first offer is accepted without haggling, you will never know how low you could have gone, although it's rare to have a first offer accepted if it's below the guide price. Calculate what's a reasonable price based on other properties in the same area (location is the prime factor in determining value), the state of the property market (whether properties are selling fast or slowly) and the amount of work that needs to be done. Don't show your hand by indicating that you will go higher, but try to give the impression that your offer is a high as you can stretch to.

You may need to pitch your offer close to the asking price in a booming market when a property is particularly desirable. If an offer is rejected it may be worth waiting a week or two before making a higher offer, depending on the market and how keen you are to buy. Agents sometimes invent rival buyers and bids – if an agent says he has a higher bid it may be worthwhile confronting him face to face and asking for written evidence (you could also ask the vendor). However, if you fall in love with a property, don't procrastinate but **make an offer immediately** and increase it until it's accepted. If it's fairly priced and you really want it, you should make an offer at the asking price if there has been a lot of interest.

Bear in mind, however, that you can still be gazumped after an offer has been accepted (except in Scotland).

Negotiating

If you make a low offer, it's advisable to indicate to the owner a few negative points (without being too critical) that merit a reduction in price. You may be able to negotiate a substantial reduction if there's a lot of work to be done – in any case you will have to renegotiate if major problems are discovered during a survey (presuming you still want to buy it). Bear in mind, however, that if you make a very low offer an owner may feel insulted and refuse to sell to you! An offer should be made in writing (supported with information about funding and legal arrangements), which is likely to be taken more seriously than a verbal offer. Before agreeing a price, make sure that both the vendor and agent are aware of the terms of your offer, which should include the following:

- A list of fixtures and fittings (and anything else you've agreed with the seller) that are included in the sale.
- Any work that's to be done on the property before completion.
- The offer being subject to a survey and contract – if the survey brings to light any work that needs doing you may need to renegotiate the price.
- The vendor taking the property off the market in order to lessen the risk of being gazumped.

Getting The Best Deal

If you simply want to buy a property at the best possible price as an investment, shopping around and buying a 'distress sale' from an owner who simply must sell is likely to result in the best deal. Obviously you will be in a better position if you're a cash buyer and able to complete quickly. However, if you're seeking an investment property it's advisable to buy in an area that's in high demand, preferably with both buyers and renters.

> **SURVIVAL TIP**
> **Always be prepared to walk away from a deal rather than pay too high a price.**

Research

You should find out as much as possible about a property before making an offer, such as the following:

- When it was built;
- How long the owners have lived there;
- Whether it's a principal or second home;
- Why the owner is selling (although getting a straight answer can be difficult);
- How urgent a sale is;
- How long it has been on the market (and why it hasn't sold);
- Whether the asking price has been dropped;
- The state of the property market;
- The condition of the property;
- The neighbours and neighbourhood;
- Whether the asking price is realistic.

Timing

Timing is of the essence in the bargaining process and it's essential to find out how long a property has been on the market (generally the longer it has been for sale, the more likely a lower offer will be accepted) and how desperate the vendor is to sell. A good clue is when a property has been reduced in price, which may be indicated in an advertisement or an agent's data sheet. Some people will tell you outright that they must sell by a certain date and that they will accept any reasonable offer. You may be able to find out from neighbours why someone is selling, which may help you decide whether an offer would be accepted. If a property has been on the market for a long time, e.g. longer than six months in a popular area, it may be overpriced (unless it has obvious faults). If there are many apparently desirable properties for sale in a particular area or development that have been on the market a long time, you should find out why. Buying when the market is flat or during the winter when there are few buyers around may also net you a bargain.

> **SURVIVAL TIP**
> **For your part, you must ensure that you keep any sensitive information from a seller and give the impression that you've all the time in the world (even if you're desperate to buy immediately).**

All this 'cloak and dagger' stuff may seem unethical, but you can rest assured that if you were selling and a prospective buyer knew you were desperate and would accept a low/lower offer, he certainly wouldn't be in a hurry to pay you any more!

Bargains

In an overheated property market there are few real bargains around, and if you think you've found one it will probably need lots of work doing – once you've renovated it, it won't seem like such a bargain! Most bargains are snapped up by developers and buyers who have ready cash and are able to complete fast (buying at auction – see page 123 – can also net you a bargain).

> **SURVIVAL TIP**
> **If a property is offered for a seemingly bargain price, try to find out why before viewing it, as there's usually a good reason.**

Taking A Property Off The Market

An offer should be conditional on the vendor taking the property off the market, even if only for a number of weeks – say three or four – while you obtain a mortgage, have a survey and your conveyancer conducts searches. You may be able to get the vendor to agree to sign a lock-out agreement, whereby he takes the property off the market for a period during which contracts are exchanged.

Sealed Bids

A vendor in England or Wales may invite sealed bids (as is standard practice in Scotland), although this is rare. There are two kinds of bids; a formal or an informal tender. With a formal tender, once the bids are opened and a bid is accepted, the sale is complete and binding on both parties. With an informal tender, a sealed bid is subject to a survey and contract and until contracts are exchanged either party can withdraw.

CONVEYANCING

Conveyancing (or more correctly 'conveyance') is the legal term for the process by which ownership of property is transferred from one person to another. A conveyance is a deed (legal document) that conveys a house from the vendor (seller) to the buyer, thereby transferring ownership. Most people employ a solicitor or licensed conveyancer to do the conveyancing, although you can do it yourself. There are two main stages when your conveyancer will become involved. The first stage takes you up to the exchange of contracts (see page 115) and the second leads to the completion of the sale (see page 116), when you become the new owner.

Finding A Conveyancer

Property conveyancing is usually done by a solicitor, a solicitor's agent (Scotland) or a licensed conveyancer. (You can do it yourself - see below - but for most people it's highly inadvisable.) Ask your friends, neighbours and colleagues if they can recommend a solicitor or licensed conveyancer, as personal recommendations are always best. It's advisable to use a local professional who knows the area and is familiar with local planning restrictions. Estate agents and local lenders may give you the name of a solicitor if you ask, but they're usually reluctant to give recommendations. Some large estate agents offer an in-house conveyancing service, although you may be better off with an independent solicitor or conveyancer, as an agent's services could lead to a conflict of interest.

Failing a recommendation, you can also find a solicitor via the Law Society (☎ 020-0870-606 6575, 💻 www.solicitors-online.com) or the National Solicitors' Network (☎ 020-7244 6422, 💻 www.tnsn.com) and a licensed conveyancer through the Council for Licensed Conveyancers (☎ 01245-349599, 💻 www.theclc.gov.uk).

SURVIVAL TIP
If possible you should engage a solicitor who has been personally recommended, as frauds committed by solicitors aren't unknown and have risen in recent years.

Online Conveyancers

In recent years, dozens of online conveyancing services have sprung up, including the following:

- www.conveyancing24-7.com
- www.easier2move.co.uk
- www.e-zeemoves.com
- www.goodmigrations.co.uk
- www.movingahead.co.uk
- www.onlineconveyancing.co.uk
- www.perfectlylegal.co.uk
- www.titleabsolute.co.uk

What Conveyancing Involves

- Ensuring that a 'good' title is obtained and verifying ownership.
- Checking whether the land has been registered and the existence of any restrictive covenants or rights of way.
- Checking that any structural alterations (extensions, loft conversions, etc.) have the necessary planning permission and building licences, and whether they have a warranty.
- Carrying out local authority searches.
- Ensuring there are no debts against a property or that they're cleared before completion.
- Checking the lease and its clauses (leasehold apartments only).
- Drawing up a contract of sale.
- Arranging registration of the title in the new owner's name after the sale of the property.

Other Checks

Things that you may wish to specifically ask your conveyancer to check could include:

- Checking who owns adjacent vacant land or fields and what degree of development, if any, would be allowed. Beware if it has been 'zoned' for commercial activities.
- Checking what the land under and surrounding a house was originally used for, particularly if it's a relatively modern house. This could include mining, industrial sites (pollution), landfill, waste sites, a burial ground for dead animals (e.g. foot and mouth disease, etc.) and military use (unexploded ordnance), all of which should be avoided.
- Checking whether a property is prone to flooding and whether it has been flooded in recent years.
- Checking whether there are any planned developments in the vicinity that could affect the value of the property such as a railway line, motorway or industrial plant, radio or mobile phone mast, electricity sub-station or plant, sewage works, landfill site, etc.
- Ensuring that the person selling a property is the sole owner or has the right to sell. It isn't unknown for a husband or wife to sell a home without telling his or her spouse, forge the spouse's signature and disappear with the proceeds, in which case you can end up owning only half a house.

Land Registry

HM Land Registry guarantees the title to (and records the ownership of) interests in registered land in England and Wales. Anyone has the right to inspect the Land Registry's records and check who owns land or property registered in England and Wales, whether or not there's a mortgage attached to it and any restrictions of use or unusual rights of way (in Scotland it's also possible to inspect the Registry's copies of registered mortgages). A free leaflet entitled *The Open Register – A Guide To Information Held By The Land Registry* is available from HM Land Registry, Lincoln's Inn Fields, London WC2A 3PH (☎ 020-7917 8888, 💻 www.landreg.gov.uk) and regional offices. Land registry is handled by Registers of Scotland (💻 www.ros.gov.uk) in Scotland and by Land Registers of Northern Ireland (💻 www.lrni.gov.uk) in Northern Ireland.

Duration

Conveyancing can theoretically be completed in a few days but usually takes weeks, with the whole process from agreeing a sale to the exchange of contracts taking two to three months (amongst the slowest in the world and on average around twice as long as in many other countries). Completion can theoretically be done the same day as contracts are exchanged, but in practice it's usually a number of weeks later and can be several months later. Certain aspects of conveyancing can be speeded up, for example you can opt for a personal search which will speed up the local authority searches from weeks or months to just a few days. There is an extra cost for this service of around £50.

A new service in recent years has been introduced by the National Land Information Service (NLIS, 💻 www.nlis.org.uk), which provides online conveyancing searches via the Internet to solicitors and licensed conveyancers. When it's in widespread use this is expected to vastly reduce the time required for searches, with information available within hours rather than days. Using this system a typical sale should take just ten days instead of the current four weeks. Prices are competitive, but the major selling point isn't price but speed. Many online conveyancers charge a basic fee of around £300 plus disbursements and VAT, and they may offer a no completion, no fee guarantee – so it's in their interest to ensure that your sale or purchase goes through.

Costs

Prior to 1988, the cost of conveyancing was kept artificially high in England and Wales by the monopoly maintained by solicitors. Since 1988 buyers have been able to employ a licensed conveyancer, which has brought costs down to the current average of 0.5 to 1 per cent of the purchase price (still a nice earner for a bit of paperwork that's often relegated to a solicitor's clerk). Expect to pay between £750 and £1,000 for a home costing £150,000, although many lenders offer an inexpensive fixed-fee service. Most solicitors and conveyancers will tell you over the telephone what they charge and you can also obtain quotes via websites. Obtain a quotation in writing before any work starts and check what's included and whether it's 'full and binding' or just an estimate. A low basic rate maybe supplemented by more expensive 'extras'. Disbursements, which include fees such as stamp duty, Land Registry fees and search fees, are payable separately on completion (see page 116) and VAT is added to the total.

Conveyancers' Requirements

Your conveyancer will need to know the name of the selling agent (if applicable), the property details, a list of any special points such as items included in the sale (carpets, light fittings, appliances, furniture, garden ornaments, etc.), and anything agreed regarding the condition of a house. If the vendor is taking anything that can reasonably be considered to be fixtures and fittings, such as plants or shrubs, this should be agreed with the buyer and included in the contract. If applicable, your converyancer will need details of your sources of finance (bank, building society, etc.) and the contact name and telephone number of your lender. He will also need to know when you'd like to take possession.

If you're selling, your solicitor will need details of where the deeds are, your mortgage account number (if applicable), the name of your lender, and the branch office and telephone number. He will require copies of planning consents for any work you've had done on the house and details of any warranties still in force. If the sale is linked to another purchase, he will need all the details listed above for buyers, plus the date by which you'd like the transactions completed. If you're buying with someone other than your spouse, ask your solicitor to draw up a formal agreement setting out your rights and responsibilities (see **Chapter 2 - What To Buy**), as this is important when you decide to sell. When you're buying and selling, you must pay conveyancing fees on both properties.

Complaints

If you've got a complaint about your solicitor, in the first instance you should try to resolve it personally with him personally. If you've a legitimate complaint a threat to report the matter to the Office for the Supervision of Solicitors (OSS) can often yield quick results. If you need to take it further you can contact them at: OSS, Victoria Court, 8 Dormer Place, Leamington Spa, Warks. CV32 5AE (☎ 01926-820082, 💻 www. lawsociety.org.uk).

DIY Conveyancing

It's possible and perfectly legal to do your own conveyancing and there are a number of good DIY books available. You will need to do at least ten hours work and require a good grasp of details, plus a measure of patience. However, it isn't recommended for most people as it's complex, time-consuming and can be risky. If you miss a mistake in the contract, you could be left with a property you cannot sell and unable to find a new property – if a solicitor or licensed conveyancer is at fault, you can at least sue them. Many people do, however, successfully perform their own conveyancing. If you're short of cash and fancy giving it a try, obtain a copy of the Consumers' Association (see **Appendix A**) action pack, *Do Your Own Conveyancing*, or a good DIY conveyancing book.

SURVIVAL TIP
If you do your own conveyancing it's advisable to have the paperwork checked by a solicitor or conveyancer, which may cost only £100 or so.

PURCHASE CONTRACTS

When buying or selling property in England, Wales or Northern Ireland, prospective buyers make an offer subject to survey and contract. The procedure is different in Scotland and is covered separately (see **Buying In Scotland** on page 126). Either side can amend or withdraw from a sale at any time before the exchange of contracts – at which time a sale is legally binding – or a seller can accept a higher offer from another buyer (called gazumping – see page 91). There are no preliminary contracts in England, Wales and Northern Ireland, where a purchase becomes legal only after the exchange of contracts when a 10 per cent deposit (negotiable) is payable.

Exchange Of Contracts

The exchange of contracts is literally that – a contract with the buyer's signature is sent to the vendor's solicitor, while at the same time a contract bearing the signature of the vendor is sent to the buyer's solicitor. Completion (see below) usually takes place around four weeks after the exchange of contracts, although it can be shorter or longer, as agreed between the parties.

SURVIVAL TIP
Note that once you've exchanged contracts (or had an offer accepted in Scotland) you should take out buildings insurance on a property, which is mandatory if you have a mortgage.

Contract Names

A property can be owned by a number of joint-owners. Co-buyers don't need to have equal shares and they can be proportionate to the deposit paid and the repayments made. The percentage owned by each co-buyer must be registered on the title deeds and all co-buyers registered as 'tenants in common' rather than 'joint tenants'. You will also need a 'declaration of trust' so that if one person wants to sell, the others have the option of buying them out – if not the property would need to be sold.

Conditions

If there are any conditions to a sale, these must usually be fulfilled before completion. If a condition of purchase is that certain work must be done or repairs carried out, a 'specification of works' must be drawn up by your solicitor detailing the work to be done before completion. If it's agreed that planning permission must be granted or certain work done between the exchange of contracts and completion, there's usually an agreement to deposit a portion of the purchase price in a bonded (escrow) account. This money is held post-completion until the agreed work has been satisfactorily completed or planning permission obtained.

COMPLETION

Completion (or closing) is the name for the final act of buying a property when the balance of the price is paid and the title deeds are handed over. The date of completion is specified at the exchange of contracts and is usually around four weeks (28 days) after the exchange, although it can be shorter or longer as agreed between the parties (if it's longer it may be referred to as 'delayed completion'). You should try to arrange the completion for early in the week in case there are any problems, which can usually be sorted out the next day (if you plan to complete on a Friday – the most popular day – you may need to wait until Monday).

Note that completion delays are common and should be allowed for. Unlike other countries, it isn't usual for the vendor or buyer to attend the completion unless they're doing their own conveyancing. Your solicitor will give you a bill for stamp duty and Land Registry fees before completion, which must be paid by completion day.

Final Checks

Property is sold subject to the condition that it's accepted in the state it's in at the time of completion, therefore you should be aware of anything that may have occurred between the exchange of contracts and completion, e.g. storm damage. If you're buying through an estate agent he should accompany you on this visit. You should also do a final inventory immediately before completion (the previous owner should have already vacated the property) to ensure that the vendor hasn't absconded with anything that was included in the price.

Inventory

You should have an inventory of the fixtures and fittings and anything that was included in the contract or purchased separately, e.g. carpets, light fittings, curtains or kitchen appliances, and check that they're present and in good working order. This is particularly important if furniture and furnishings (and major appliances) were included in the price. You should also ensure that expensive items (such as kitchen apparatus) haven't been substituted for inferior (possibly second-hand) items, and that all period features (such as fireplaces) are still intact and haven't been ripped out or replaced when buying a period property.

Any fixtures and fittings (and garden plants and shrubs) present in a property when you viewed it should still be there when you take possession, unless otherwise stated in the contract.

SURVIVAL TIP

If you find anything is missing, damaged or isn't in working order, you should make a note and insist on immediate restitution such as an appropriate reduction in the amount to be paid. You should refuse to go through with the completion if you aren't completely satisfied, as it will be difficult or impossible to obtain redress later.

If it isn't possible to complete the sale, you should consult your solicitor about your rights and the return of your deposit.

Payment

The balance of the price (after the deposit and any mortgages are subtracted) must be paid by banker's draft on the day of completion or transferred to your solicitor's bank account before completion day (make sure that you allow sufficient time for the transfer to be made).

> **SURVIVAL TIP**
> **Note that paying by banker's draft allows you to withhold payment if there's a last minute problem (see Final Checks above) that cannot be resolved.**

If you've got a mortgage, the money will be paid to your solicitor by your lender before completion, and will be sent by him to the vendor's solicitor by bank telegraphic transfer on completion day. When the final payment has been made, the deeds to the property are handed over to the buyer's solicitor, including the conveyance or transfer of ownership. Your solicitor will also receive the keys.

After Completion

After completion your solicitor will do all the things mentioned below:

- Have the conveyance stamped and pay the stamp duty on the property purchase to the Inland Revenue.
- Register the transfer of ownership with the Land Registry or register the land if it was previously unregistered (this can take several months).
- Notify your lender that the sale has been completed and inform the life insurance company (as applicable).
- Send the title deeds to your mortgage lender who holds them as security until the loan is paid off or the property is sold.
- Notify the leaseholder of the sale if the property is a leasehold apartment.
- Send you a completion statement listing all the transactions that have taken place, along with his final bill.

FEES

The total fees (also called closing or completion costs) payable when buying a house in the UK are among the lowest in the world and total between 3 and 5 per cent for a property costing below £250,000. The average fees for a first-time buyer are around £6,000, which includes conveyancing and other solicitor's fees, survey fee, stamp duty and removals. Most fees are calculated as a percentage of the cost of a property, therefore the more expensive the property, the higher the fees. Even removal costs will be higher if you've got a large house (unless you've a lot of empty rooms). If you're buying and selling, you must consider the cost of both transactions.

Note that a number of fees are associated with a mortgage and if you're a cash buyer your fees will be lower. The fees for buying or selling a home aren't tax deductible.

Fees vary considerably depending on the price, whether you've a mortgage, whether you're buying via an agent or privately, and whether you've employed a solicitor or other professional such as a surveyor. There's no such thing as the declared value in the UK and fees are always paid on the actual price paid. Theoretically it would be possible to under-declare the price (so that a buyer can save on stamp duty and a vendor on capital gains tax) and for a vendor to receive part of the price 'under-the-table', although this practice is virtually unknown (but see **Stamp Duty** below). If you're buying a property without selling one, you will be faced with the following fees:

Stamp Duty

If you're buying a property costing over £60,000 you must pay a property tax, called stamp duty. Stamp duty isn't payable on 'fixtures and fittings' (legally called chattels) such as carpets, curtains, light fittings, kitchen appliances and garden ornaments (basically anything moveable), which may be included in the purchase price. You can legally pay for fixtures and fittings separately, which you should do if it will bring the price below the £250,000 or £500,000 threshold (saving around £5,000 in each case). However, the Inland Revenue is investigating sales just below the £250,000 and £500,000 thresholds when it's suspected that the buyer has fraudulently over-valued fixtures and fittings in order dip below a stamp duty threshold. From 1st December 2003, buyers have had to complete an eight-page, self-assessment form and take personal responsibility for paying stamp duty. Stamp duty rates are shown below:

Property Price	Stamp Duty*
Below £60,000	Zero
£60,000 – £250,000*	1%
£250,000 – £500,000	3%
Over £500,000	4%

* In 2001, an exemption from stamp duty on property transactions up to £150,000 was introduced in the most disadvantaged areas (indicated by postcode). See the Inland Revenue website (💻 www.ir.gov.uk/so/disadvantaged.htm) for a list of exempt areas.

Solicitor's Or Licensed Conveyancer's Fees

There's no fixed charge, but you should allow for 0.5 to 1 per cent of the purchase price (plus VAT). Some conveyancers charge a fixed fee. Fees usually include searches (see page 93), although these may be charged separately as disbursements (which generally includes Land Registry fees).

Valuation

You must pay for the valuation of a property before a lender will offer you a loan, even if you decide not to go ahead with the purchase. Check the cost in advance, which varies depending on the lender and the value of the property. The valuation for a £100,000 property costs from around £175 (plus VAT), although many lenders now waive this fee.

Survey

You should consider having a 'homebuyer report' or a 'full structural survey' carried out, particularly on an old property. The homebuyer report is an assessment of the general condition of the property, together with a valuation, and costs from around £250 (plus VAT) for a £100,000 property. A full structural survey is much more detailed and usually costs from around £350 for a £100,000 property, depending on the surveyor, the property and what's included in the report. When combined with the lender's valuation, a homebuyer report or structural survey should be cheaper.

Land Registry Fees

These are payable each time a property is sold and are to record the change of owner in the Land Register. The fee varies depending on whether the land is already registered (most property in England and Wales is registered - see 💻 www.landreg.gov.uk). Land in Scotland is registered in the General Register of Sasines or the Registers of Scotland and in Northern Ireland in Land Registers of Northern Ireland. There's a sliding scale of charges depending on the value of the property, as shown in the table below:

England & Wales

Value of Property	Land Registry Fee
Up to £50,000	£40
£50,001-£80,000	£60
£80,001-£100,000	£100
£100,001-£200,000	£150
£200,001-£500,000	£250
£500,001-£1,000,000	£450
Over £1,000,000	£750

Northern Ireland

Value of Property	Land Registry Fee
Up to £20,000	£50
£20,000 – £30,000	£100
£30,000 – £40,000	£150
£40,000 – £50,000	£200
£50,000 – £60,000	£250
£60,000 – £70,000	£300
Over £70,000	£350

Scotland

In Scotland, Land Registry fees are divided into smaller bands. Sample fees are shown below:

Value of Property	Land Registry Fee
£50,000	£110
£100,000	£220
£150,000	£330
£200,000	£440
£300,000	£500
£400,000	£550
£500,000	£600

Mortgage Indemnity Guarantee (MIG)

If you borrow more than a certain loan-to-value (LTV), which varies depending on the lender, you must usually take out a mortgage indemnity guarantee (also called a high lending fee or mortgage risk fee). This is to protect the lender in the event that you're unable to repay the loan and the lender is forced to repossess and sell the property. Many lenders insist on a MIG if you borrow over 70 or 80 per cent of the value of a property, although some have dropped MIG on loans of up to 90 per cent of the value of a property.

Arrangement Or Acceptance Fee

The Arrangement or Acceptance Fee is usually from £150 to £400 and is paid when you apply for a mortgage or when you accept one.

Lender's Legal Fees

Your lender's legal fees are usually around £300 (plus VAT) on a £100,000 property, although some lenders waive this fee.

Buildings Insurance

It's a condition of your lender that a property is fully insured against structural damage (etc.) from the time contracts are exchanged (see page 115).

Removal Costs

Although it isn't a fee as such, the cost of moving house must be taken into account when buying a property and should include insurance against breakages or loss (see page 156). You should expect to pay around £500 for moving the contents of a typical three to four-bedroom house.

Running Costs

In addition to the fees associated with buying a property, you must also take into account the running costs, which may include the ones mentioned below:

- Council tax;
- Buildings insurance;

- Contents insurance;
- Mortgage protection insurance;
- Standing charges for utilities (electricity, gas, telephone, water);
- Ground rent and service charges for a leasehold apartment (see page 59);
- Garden and pool maintenance;
- General maintenance, including any essential work that need doing immediately;
- Management fees if you let a property.

Annual running costs usually average around 2 to 3 per cent of the cost of a property.

You must register with your local council when you take up residence in a new area and you may be liable to pay council tax from your first day of residence.

BUYING AT AUCTION

Buying at auction is increasingly popular and the number and variety of properties (from terraced houses to country mansions) sold at auction is over 30,000 a year. Apparently December, is one of the best times to buy at auction, as most people are busy spending their money and time on Christmas. Auctions really came into their own in the early '90s when lenders used them to dispose of thousands of repossessed properties, although these now comprise only a small percentage of properties sold at auction. One of the main reasons for buying a property at auction is to obtain a bargain, but you should bear in mind that many properties sold at auction are those that are difficult to sell and/or need serious renovation – the price you pay must reflect the condition and the cost of any necessary work. Others are hugely desirable mansions that sell for well above the guide price.

When buying at auction you usually need to move fast, as they're often advertised only three to six weeks in advance and payment must be made in full within four weeks (20 working days) of a successful bid. In addition to being a quick way to buy a home (no chains), you can also save money and there's no possibility of being gazumped! The disadvantages include survey and legal costs, which will be wasted if you're out-bid. You must know what you're doing and what a property is worth, otherwise you can end up paying well over the odds.

Bear in mind that when buying a property for modernisation or renovation the costs can be astronomical (see Chapter 6 – Home Improvements).

It's advisable to attend a few auctions before bidding in order to familiarise yourself with the procedure. Before bidding at an auction, you must have the purchase contract and title (properties with title problems are often auctioned!) checked by your solicitor; obtain a valuation or survey, which may be provided by the auctioneer; and arrange a mortgage (if necessary). Vendors are usually required to provide a legal pack containing the title deeds, leases, planning permission, searches, special conditions of sale and other information.

Note that the same rules apply to surveys as when buying the conventional way.

SURVIVAL TIP
If you plan to bid on a large (over three stories), old (e.g. over 50 years of age) or unusual (thatched, timber, etc.) property, or you plan to carry out major alterations such as extending or converting a property, you should have a full structural survey.

Properties aren't always sold with vacant possession and some are tenanted or part vacant, so ensure that you understand how a property is being offered.

When you've had a bid accepted at auction, the property is legally yours and you must pay a deposit of around 10 per cent (in cash or by banker's draft) and have just four weeks in which to pay the balance. You must also prove your identity (so take some form of ID with you) and your solicitor's details. Bear in mind that when bidding at auction you bid unconditionally and if you're successful your deposit is at risk if you cannot complete the purchase for any reason (you cannot back out as with a private purchase in England, Wales and N. Ireland). You should arrange buildings insurance immediately after the sale is completed.

Guide prices tend to be deliberately conservative in order to attract as many prospective buyers as possible and the actual selling price is often much higher than the guide price (over double isn't unusual).

The guide price isn't the same as the reserve price, which is the lowest price the seller is willing to accept. If no-one bids above the reserve price, a property will remain unsold. When bids pass the reserve price the auctioneer announces that a property is 'on the market' and will be sold.

If you're among the last bidders for a property that fails to reach the reserve price, you should tell the auctioneer afterwards if you're willing to improve your bid, as the seller may accept an offer. An auctioneer may also bid up a property (in increments of £5,000 or £1,000) to the reserve price himself, which isn't illegal and is a common practice when bidding is slow.

You should take care not to go above the amount that you've decided a property is worth or what you're willing to pay (if you go above a mortgage valuation you must fund the extra yourself) – it's easy to get carried away when bidding! However, bear in mind that many unsuccessful bidders wish they had chanced another bid, so don't lose a property for the sake one more bid.

It isn't necessary to attend an auction in person and you can engage a solicitor to bid on your behalf (when you must provide written instructions), bid over the phone or by proxy in writing, by fax or via the Internet – but you must complete a registration form and provide a cheque to cover the deposit beforehand. It may also be possible to buy a property before an auction – when prior offers are invited the publicity may contain the words 'unless previously sold' – in which case a purchase contract must be signed before the auction for a property to be withdrawn. If you plan to bid for a property you should register your interest before the auction so that you can be informed if it's sold beforehand. The auctioneer's fee is usually the same as when buying from an estate agent (e.g. 2.5 per cent), but may vary depending on the value of the property and in some cases may be subject to negotiation.

Information about auctions is available from the Royal Institute of Chartered Surveyors (☎ 020-7235 2282, 🖳 www.rics.org/property_auctions) and many websites, including Property Auctions.com (🖳 www.propertyauctions.com), , UK Auction List (🖳 www.ukauctionlist.com), UK Property Auctions Guide (🖳 www.uk-property-auctions-guide.co.uk), Auction Property for Sale (🖳 www.auctionpropertyfor-sale.co.uk) and the Essential Information Group (🖳 www.eigroup.co.uk). Number One 4 Property (☎ 01772-621909, 🖳 www.numberone4property.co.uk/Auctions/auction_home.htm) provides a subscription Investment Property Database Service (IPDS) for a period of one or three months or one year. You can also visit auctioneers' websites such as Allsop & Co. (☎ 020-7494 3686, 🖳 www.allsop.co.uk), the UK's largest property auctioneer, which provide online catalogues and details of individual homes for sale. Auctioneers also publish catalogues that are sent to prospective buyers. A good book for anyone planning to buy property at auction is *Buying Bargains at Property Auctions* by Howard R. Gooddie (Law Pack Publishing).

BUYING IN SCOTLAND

The process for buying property in Scotland is quite different from the rest of the UK. Almost all property (including apartments) is owned on feudal tenure and there's no such thing as freehold or leasehold property. Instead of being owned outright, property is held from another person – similar to a lease that a tenant holds from a landlord. In feudal terminology, the person holding the land is termed the vassel and the person from whom the land is held is called the superior. In practice vassels regard themselves as the true owners of the land, although the original landowner or developer (the superior) may have laid down conditions regarding its use or which prevent alterations, which may be in force in perpetuity unless waived or modified.

The feudal tenure was abolished by the Scottish Parliament in 2000, but the rights of superiors had not been removed at the time of writing.

When buying an apartment you should examine the whole building for defects and ensure that any repairs to the common elements or structure are shared equally among the owners.

Purchase Procedure

The sequence of events in Scotland is different from the rest of the UK (see page 88), the procedure is detailed below:

- Apply for a mortgage;
- Engage a solicitor or conveyancer (mandatory in Scotland);
- Find a property you wish to buy;
- Ask your solicitor to 'note interest';
- Complete a mortgage application;
- Get a valuation or survey;
- Have the mortgage application agreed;

- Make an offer on the property;
- Complete the mortgage application;
- Offer is accepted;
- Fix a settlement date;
- Arrange buildings insurance;
- Solicitors complete missives (contracts);
- Settlement (completion);
- Move in!

Solicitors

When buying property in Scotland you need to engage a solicitor to act on your behalf. The Law Society of Scotland (☎ 0132-226 7411, 💻 www.lawscot.org.uk) provides a Directory of General Services listing Scottish solicitors. You should obtain quotations from a number of solicitors, as there are no set fees. When you've found a property you wish to buy your solicitor will contact the seller's solicitor and register your interest (the correspondence between solicitors is termed 'missives'). Once the seller's solicitor has had sufficient interest, he will usually fix a closing date by which time all offers must be submitted in writing.

Surveys

Before making an offer it's vital that you have a valuation or survey done (and have the necessary finance), as once your offer in writing is accepted it's legally binding. The main problem with the Scottish system is that each prospective buyer must have his own survey done before making an offer. This has prompted a proposed change in the law where the seller is responsible for having a survey carried out before selling a property – an excellent idea provided that the surveyor is legally responsible to both the vendor and buyer for any errors he makes.

Making An Offer

Most property is advertised as 'offers above a certain price', e.g. offers above £150,000, which is called the 'upset' price. Asking prices may be set artificially low to attract interest and they're often exceeded by up to 30 per cent or more in popular areas and by around 5 to 10 per cent in less popular areas. It can be difficult to know where to pitch an offer as you don't want to lose a property for the sake of a few hundred or thousand pounds, but you also don't want to grossly overbid. You should discuss an offer with your solicitor and pitch it slightly above a round figure, e.g. £155,150 rather than £155,000.

Occasionally properties are advertised at a fixed price, when you must be quick off the mark as the first reasonable offer is accepted (this is also the normal procedure when buying a new home from a builder or developer). If the seller gives a closing date for offers, all interested parties must make sealed bids, which are opened on that date. The seller normally accepts the highest bid, although he isn't legally bound to do so and can reject all offers, although this rarely happens. If the vendor wants a quick sale and you can complete almost immediately – the entry date is included in the offer – your lower offer could be accepted.

It's virtually impossible to be gazumped in Scotland, as once an offer in writing has been accepted it's legally binding and you cannot pull out. Therefore it's vital that you have a valuation or survey done (and have the necessary finance) before making an offer. If your offer is unsuccessful, you will have wasted time and money (on a survey) and you may have to do this a number of times before you're successful!

Note that you must not make an offer without your lender's approval, otherwise you could find yourself legally committed to buying a property without the necessary finance!

After your offer is accepted a formal moving in date is set which makes it easier to co-ordinate a sale and purchase, and removes some of the problems of being in a chain. Once an offer has been accepted and the missives (contracts) concluded, you're responsible for insuring the property.

Conveyancing & Completion

In Scotland, conveyancing (see page 110) is carried out after an offer has been accepted, when your solicitor or conveyancer examines the deeds and initiates proceedings towards settlement (completion), which is usually four to five weeks after acceptance of an offer. On completion day, settlement takes place whereby the solicitors acting for the two parties meet and exchange a cheque for the keys. After completion, you pay your solicitor's fees, stamp duty and registration fees for the disposition (the legal document that transfers ownership), which is registered with the General Register of Sasines or the Land Register of Scotland (depending on the area).

4.

MORTGAGES

Mortgages are available from an huge number of lenders, including building societies, high street and foreign banks (including offshore banks), direct lenders, finance houses and credit companies, insurance companies, developers, local authorities and even employers. The UK has a fiercely competitive mortgage business with around 150 lenders offering over 3,000 different mortgage products vying for your business. There are over 11 million mortgages in the UK worth a staggering £750 billion in 2003 – equal to the annual take home pay of the entire country! The average loan of a first-time buyer is over £90,000 and for someone moving up the property ladder is over £100,000.

However, in 2003 mortgage rates were the lowest for 50 years and you could easily knock 2 per cent off the standard interest rate for several years, pay off some of your loan without charge or switch to another lender for a better deal. In fact, there had never been a better time to change your mortgage! A survey by Clear Cut Mortgages in autumn 2003 showed that homeowners were losing out on potential savings of £7.5 billion a year by failing to switch to more competitive home loans.

SURVIVAL TIP

Note also that overpaying on your mortgage in order to pay it off early will save you tens of thousands of pounds in interest and is advisable when the interest paid on savings is low.

In England, Wales and Northern Ireland you can apply for a mortgage after an offer on a property is accepted. However, in Scotland (see page 126) you must apply for a mortgage and have it approved before making an offer on a property. If the offer is successful it's legally binding and you're contractually obliged to complete the purchase, which isn't the case in the rest of the UK.

BRIDGING LOANS

If possible, it's best to complete on a new property before selling your current home. You can do this by obtaining a bridging loan after you've exchanged contracts on the sale of your current home and are fairly certain that the sale with go through (few people pull out after having paid a deposit). There are two types of bridging loan; a closed loan where you've exchanged contracts and both sides are committed to a deal, and an open loan where you aren't yet committed to adeal and there's no final date for completion. Financial experts advise that you only take out an open loan – which is more difficult to obtain – when you've very good reason to assume that you home will be sold quickly and you can afford to maintain the loan for six months or longer.

ADVICE & INFORMATION

Whatever kind of mortgage you want, you should shop around and take the time to investigate all the options available. Most high street banks and building societies offer similar products and you may get a better deal from a small regional building society, although they may not offer fixed rate mortgages.

Mortgage advice offered by lenders is often misleading and biased and not always to be trusted (the mis-selling of mortgages was widespread in the '90s).

One way to find the best deal is to contact an independent mortgage broker, who can save you considerable money. In addition to finding the lowest rates (the best deals from some high street banks are only available through brokers), they may be able to offer free valuations and generous cashbacks. However, bear in mind that lenders offer inducements to encourage brokers to push their products, so you may not always receive independent advice, and you may have to pay a fee of around £300.

The best independent advice is found in surveys carried out by publications such as *Which?* magazine (see **Appendix A**), which accept no advertisements, and daily newspapers. The best variable, fixed-rate and discount mortgage rates are shown on TV teletext services, published in daily and Sunday newspapers such as *The Sunday Times*, *The Sunday Telegraph*, *The Observer* and *The Independent on Sunday*, and in listed in monthly mortgage magazines such as *What Mortgage* (💻 www.whatmortgageonline.co.uk), *Mortgage Magazine* and *Home Buyer & Mortgage Advisor* (💻 www.homebuyermag.co.uk). You can also make comparisons of mortgage products via numerous websites (see **Appendix C**).

A voluntary Mortgage Code for lenders was introduced in the '90s which sets standards of good mortgage advisory practice and provides safeguards for clients. Details are contained in a booklet (published in large print, audio and Braille formats) available from lenders or from the Council of Mortgage Lenders, 3 Saville Row, London W1S 3PB (☎ 020-7440 2255 – recorded information, 💻 www.cml.org.uk). **However, the code has been criticised as too vague and is broken by many lenders.**

INCOME

Three factors determine whether you can obtain a mortgage and its size: income, credit history and the property itself (**lenders won't lend on a ruin**). If you're an employee in steady employment, you should have no problem obtaining a mortgage, although whether it will be enough to buy a home is another matter entirely.

You can usually borrow up to 3.5 times your gross (pre-tax) salary or 2.75 times the joint income of a couple. For example if you earn £30,000 a year and your wife £25,000, you'd qualify for a £151,250 mortgage (2.75 x £55,000). However, with average prices in 2003 for first time buyers around £105,000, a single person would need to earn £28,000 rising to over £53,000 in London where the average property price is around £200,000!

SURVIVAL TIP
Note that lenders are flexible and some will lend 3.25 times your salary plus the salary of a partner, while others will lend much more to those with good career prospects (e.g. graduates). Some lenders will even lend professionals up to five times their annual salary.

The amount you can borrow also depends on how large a deposit you can put down. Up to four people can legally share the ownership of a property (although most lenders allow a maximum of three co-owners), when the incomes of all co-owners are taken into account (see **First-Time Buyers** on page 44).

Most lenders will give you a 'conditional' decision over the phone and will provide a written 'mortgage promise' that you can show sellers to prove that you're a serious buyer. If you're refused a mortgage, you can ask the Council of Mortgage Lenders (see above) for advice.

GUARANTOR MORTGAGES

If you don't qualify for a mortgage because your income is too low, you may be able to get someone to act as a guarantor, such as your parents. However, it's more difficult to obtain a mortgage, which usually requires a deposit of at least 25 per cent, although there are lenders that don't require such a high mortgage (try Northern Rock or Scottish Widows). Scottish Widows only require parents to guarantee the part of the mortgage that isn't covered by their child's income. Parents must usually have at least 30 per cent equity in their own home to act as guarantors and can be released from the arrangement when the mortgage holder is earning sufficient income to take on the loan.

> **SURVIVAL TIP**
> **There are also family offset mortgages (see page 147), where parents can link a savings account to the offset mortgage of a family member.**

The balance of the account is offset against the value of the loan and the borrower only pays interest on the difference. However, no interest is paid on savings.

GRADUATE MORTGAGES

Some lenders provide special graduate and professional mortgages for young people (with good income prospects) and will lend up to five times annual salary. Lenders may also waive MIG (see page 136) on graduate mortgages of up to 95 per cent to value. There are also special deals for first-time buyers and 100 per cent mortgages - some lender even offer up to 125 per cent mortgages!

MORTGAGE PROTECTION INSURANCE

You may find it worthwhile taking out mortgage payment protection insurance, which covers your mortgage payments if you cannot work due to illness or unemployment, although it can be prohibitively expensive.

LOAN-TO-VALUE

The loan-to-value (LTV) is the size of the mortgage as a percentage of the price or value of a property. A £180,000 mortgage on a house worth £200,000 is equal to a LTV of 90 per cent. Most borrowers can obtain 90 to 95 per cent mortgages and some lenders offer 100 per cent mortgages (some lenders even offer up to 125 per cent mortgages!).

> **SURVIVAL TIP**
> **Note that the larger the deposit you can pay (as a percentage of the value), the larger the mortgage you can obtain and the wider the choice of mortgages and deals available.**

In certain cases a lender will reduce the LTV, for example if you're buying a shell apartment (which needs to be fitted out), you usually receive a maximum 75 per cent mortgage and will have to take out another loan to fit it out.

MORTGAGE INDEMNITY GUARANTEE (MIG)

If you borrow more than a certain loan-to-value, which varies depending on the lender, you must usually have a mortgage indemnity guarantee (also called a high lending fee, mortgage risk fee or maximum advance premium). This is to protect the lender in the event that you're unable to repay the loan and the lender is forced to repossess a property (see page 149). Many lenders insist on a MIG if you borrow over 90 per cent (can be lower) of the value of a property. However, a number of lenders don't levy MIG, including HSBC, the Nationwide Building Society, the Co-perative Bank and Northern Rock, although they may charge a higher interest rate when the loan-to-value is over 90 per cent.

Where applicable, the difference between the LTV and the MIG threshold is the amount on which you must pay MIG, which typically costs around £2,000 on a £100,000 loan. The interest rate charged for MIG varies and it can be paid up front or added to the mortgage (some lenders allow you to pay it over a few years without interest).

Note that if you add it to the mortgage the MIG premium is likely to cost you three times as much over 25 years and if you pay off the mortgage early you don't receive a refund of a portion of the MIG!

HIGH-RISK BORROWERS

Many high street lenders won't lend to so-called 'high-risk' borrowers or when they do they levy a higher interest rate. High-risk borrowers generally include (as far as lenders are concerned!) the newly self-employed (without three years' accounts), contract workers (who are often treated as self-employed), those who have had a lot of jobs in a short period of time, single mothers and divorced women. High-risk borrowers also include those seeking a mortgage for a risky property, e.g. an apartment attached to commercial premises such as a shop or an apartment with a short lease (e.g. under 65 years). Other high-risk borrowers include those with a poor credit rating, someone who has had mortgage payment arrears (or been repossessed) and those with county court judgements (CCJs). Around three in ten people are turned down for a mortgage by high street lenders. Lenders usually insist that a self-employed person has two or three years' audited accounts to qualify for a standard mortgage or special deals.

However, all is not lost. There are a number of lenders who specialise in lending to high-risk borrowers, although you will be charged a higher rate of interest and won't usually be eligible for special deals or discounts. Many people use specialist lenders as a stopgap to rebuild their credit rating or until they can find a better deal, although you need to be wary of redemption penalties and avoid the sharks. Some lenders specialise in lending to the self-employed, such as the Bank of Scotland (☎ 0800-810810) and UCB (☎ 0645-501500 – a subsidiary of the Nationwide Building Society). Lenders who specialise in lending to 'high-risk' borrowers include Future Mortgages (☎ 0118-951 4940), the Kensington Mortgage Company (☎ 020-7376 0110), the Money Store (☎ 0800-783 4448) and Paragon Mortgages (☎ 0121-712 2345). Alternatively you can use a mortgage broker, who will charge a fee of around £300 to find you a mortgage.

SELF-CERTIFICATION MORTGAGES

Self-certification mortgages are targeted at the self-employed (a huge market which includes some 3 million people) and allow borrowers to estimate their earnings rather than provide proof of income. Borrowers can usually obtain a mortgage of between 75 and 85 per cent of the value of a property. The rates offered to high-risk borrowers are typically around 2 per cent above the standard rates for new customers. Some brokers encourage buyers to fraudulently obtain self-certification mortgages that are up to ten times their gross income (six or seven times income is common)!

If you're tempted to lie you should bear in mind that it's not only fraud (there are custodial sentences for offenders), but you could easily get into payment difficulties and lose your home!

INTEREST RATES

With a repayment mortgage, payments include part interest and part capital repayments. You can generally choose between fixed and variable rate mortgages. An important aspect of a mortgage is how interest is calculated, which may be daily, monthly or annually. Daily is the best method for borrowers, as when you make payments (or overpayments) they take effect immediately.

When interest is calculated annually the outstanding debt doesn't decrease daily or even monthly, but once a year. This results in you paying interest on money you've already repaid!

Fixed Rate

Fixed loans for up to 25 years are rare in the UK (unlike in Europe and the US) and aren't popular with borrowers or lenders. In recent years (with falling rates) they've been at a record low, although in 2003 many market analysts were recommending fixed-rate loans to avoid being caught out by future interest rate rises. Those on tight budgets who cannot afford an increase in their mortgage repayments are better off with a fixed-rate mortgage, where the interest rate is fixed for a number of years (e.g. one year to the whole mortgage term) no matter what happens to the base rate in the meantime. The longer the fixed-rate period, the lower the interest rate offered. If interest rates go down, you may find yourself paying more than the current rate, but at least you will know exactly what you must pay each month.

To judge whether a fixed-rate mortgage is worthwhile, you must estimate in which direction interest rates are heading - a difficult feat even the so-called experts cannot manage. The standard variable rate is usually around 1.5 per cent above the base rate. Building societies typically offer standard variable rate mortgages that are around half a per cent below high street banks. Note that if you've a fixed rate for a pre-set period there are high penalties for switching lenders during this period. The interest rate returns to the standard variable rate (SVR) after the fixed rate period.

Fixed-rate mortgages, where the rate is fixed for the whole term, often have crippling early repayment costs, e.g. £50,000 or more! This is because the lender 'purchased' the money for the loan at a fixed interest rate when the borrower took out the loan. Many people on fixed-rate loans are paying hundreds or even thousands of pounds a year more for fixed rate mortgages taken out in the years before interest rates started falling.

Variable Rate

Most property buyers choose a variable rate mortgage, where the interest rate goes up and down depending on the base rate.

Theoretically, when the base rate (set by the Bank of England) changes, the variable rate should rise or fall by the same percentage. However, when the base rate falls many lenders don't pass on cuts (or the whole amount) to borrowers, ostensibly to protect savers, because when mortgage rates are cut the interest paid to savers must also be reduced. In recent years the cost of a standard variable-rate mortgage has fallen considerably and in late 2003 the Bank of England base rate had fallen to 3.5 per cent (the lowest rate for over 50 years), with most lenders offering even lower short-term rates.

Tracker Mortgages

Tracker mortgages are a variation on variable rate mortgages, where the rate tracks the Bank of England's base rate, with interest rates lowered or raised automatically when the base rate changes. This protects you from lenders hiking their rates, as lenders must pass on a rate cut to borrowers with a tracker mortgage.

Note, however, that some tracker mortgages track the base rate for a number of years only, before reverting to the lender's standard variable rate.

Loans may be linked to hefty redemption penalties and you may need to take out life insurance to obtain the best rate (always read the small print). Although relatively new, tracker mortgages are becoming increasingly popular with borrowers, particularly as most lenders have failed to pass on cuts in the base rate in full to borrowers in recent years. Some lenders offer discounts on tracker mortgages for a number of months or years. Rates vary, e.g. from 0.7 to 1.45 per cent above the base rate, so you should shop around for the best rate.

Repayments

The gross monthly payments per £1,000 borrowed for repayment and interest-only mortgages over 25 years are shown below. To calculate your mortgage repayments simply find the payment that applies to your mortgage interest rate and multiply it by the amount of your mortgage. For example if you borrow £150,000 at 4.5 per cent your monthly repayments for a repayment mortgage would be £5.62 x 150 = £843. The interest-only figures apply only to the interest on your mortgage and the cost of the investment element (e.g. endowment, ISA or pension) that's intended to pay off the capital at the end of the loan period must be added.

Interest Rate (%)	Repayment Mortgage	Interest Only Mortgage
2.00	£4.27	£1.67
2.25	£4.39	£1.88
2.50	£4.52	£2.08
2.75	£4.65	£2.29
3.00	£4.79	£2.50
3.25	£4.92	£2.71
3.50	£5.06	£2.92
3.75	£5.19	£3.13
4.00	£5.33	£3.33
4.25	£5.48	£3.54
4.50	£5.62	£3.75
4.75	£5.77	£3.96
5.00	£5.91	£4.17
5.25	£6.06	£4.38
5.50	£6.21	£4.58
5.75	£6.36	£4.79
6.00	£6.52	£5.00

Many websites (such as 💻 www.yourmortgage.co.uk), including most banks' and building societies' websites, provide a mortgage calculator. You simply enter the mortgage required, the repayment period and the interest rate, and obtain an instant calculation of the monthly repayment (usually for both repayment and interest-only mortgages).

DISCOUNTS

In recent years lenders have offered a variety of discount mortgages, which usually extend from one to five years, after which the current variable interest rate applies. Although these deals look attractive there's usually a price to pay. Cheap loans usually come with heavy penalties and can be a costly choice if you want to change lenders or pay off your mortgage.

You can be locked into a fixed rate deal that costs much more than the current variable interest rate and there may also be other restrictions such as early repayment penalties and no capital repayments during the period of a limited fixed, discounted or capped rate of interest. The best deals are offered to new lenders and often have a maximum loan of £200,000 or £250,000, which excludes 'wealthy' buyers and existing borrowers. A lender cannot require you to buy expensive buildings and contents insurance through them, but will insist that you have buildings insurance and will require evidence.

When considering a discount mortgage it's advisable to check the following:

- The repayment method and time scale;
- The consequences of early repayment and lump sum payments;
- The type of interest rate;
- When interest is calculated (should be daily);
- What the future repayments will be after any fixed or discounted period;
- Whether you must take out any insurance through the lender;
- Fees such as start-up costs;
- Monthly administration charges;
- Whether the same terms apply if you move house.

Deposit-Free Loans

You should be wary of deposit-free loans as they may have hidden catches. For example, you may be required to pay interest on only a portion (e.g. 70 per cent) of a 100 per cent loan.

Your lender will take a share of any future rise in the property's value, which could cost you tens of thousands of pounds.

Discounted Rate

This provides a discount on the standard mortgage rate for a pre-set period, usually one to five years. Larger deposits and smaller loans attract bigger discounts. Bear in mind that your repayments will rise when the discounted rate ends, when the interest rate returns to the standard variable rate. Note, however, that some lenders offer a very low fixed rate for a number years (e.g. two), after which they raise the interest rate to around two per cent above the base rate for a further period (e.g. four years), with a hefty redemption penalty if you want to change lenders.

Cashback

A form of discount mortgage (usually variable rate) offering up to £20,000 cashback (which you can spend on furniture, decorating and improvements), which is calculated as a percentage of the loan.

Although this sounds great – you take out a mortgage and the lender gives you cash! – there's a hidden price, including high fees, interest rates and hefty penalties for early redemption or switching lenders (you may also have to pay the cash sum back).

They aren't the best deals around and without a cashback you can obtain a discount off the variable rate for up to five years.

Capped (& Collar) Rate

With a capped rate you pay the variable rate up to a pre-set ceiling for a pre-set period, which offers protection against interest rate rises. With a collar, there's a floor or collar, below which your rate cannot fall.

TERM

The usual repayment term is 25 years, although it can be up to 35 years or a much shorter period (particularly when re-mortgaging). The shorter the term, the less interest you pay, although your payments will be higher. Reducing the term, say from 25 to 20 years, will save you a lot of money. Most mortgages allow you to pay off lump sums at any time, which can also save you thousands of pounds in interest and reduce the term of your loan. There are usually minimum lump sum payments, e.g. £500 or £1,000, and lenders may credit lump sum payments immediately, monthly or annually. There are usually penalties with fixed rate loans, although it may still pay you to pay off your mortgage early.

MORTGAGE FEES

Various fees are associated with mortgages. All lenders charge an arrangement fee (also called a completion, booking or reservation fee) for arranging a loan, which is either a fixed amount or a percentage of the loan. This is usually from £150 to £400 and is paid when you apply for a loan or when you accept a mortgage. This has been branded a rip-off by mortgage brokers and others in the loan business, particularly as some 20 per cent of purchases fall through and lenders keep the fee. Some lenders charge an advance application fee and a completion fee when you accept the mortgage. Mortgage brokers may also levy a fee, e.g. 1 per cent of the value of the loan or a fee starting at around £300 to find you a deal, although many charge no fees to borrowers. Always check whether fees are refundable if a purchase falls through. There's usually a valuation fee of around £200 and the lender's legal fees, although many lenders now waive these.

STANDARD MORTGAGES

Once you've calculated how much you want to pay for a home, you must decide what kind of mortgage you want. Although there are many different mortgages on the market, all fall into two main categories: repayment and interest-only. Most interest-only mortgages are linked to an endowment, investment (such as an ISA) or a pension plan. You can also have a part repayment or part interest-only mortgage.

Note mortgages with an investment element have performed badly in recent years and many have made huge losses – most plans are worth a third less than the sum saved!

Repayment Mortgages

Repayment mortgages account for some 80 per cent of all mortgages in the UK. They're so called because you repay the original loan and interest over the period of the mortgage, similar to most personal loans. Your monthly payment includes interest (mostly interest at the start) and capital (mostly capital towards the end of the term) payments. As interest rates rise and fall, your repayments go up or down, but assuming a constant interest rate your payments would remain the same for the period of the loan. One advantage is that the term of the loan can be extended if you've trouble meeting your monthly repayments.

One disadvantage of a repayment mortgage is that you don't have a life policy and you must therefore take out a 'mortgage protection' policy to ensure that your loan is paid off if you die.

This policy isn't expensive as it pays off the mortgage only if you die before the term of the loan is completed (and the term and amount owed decreases over time). For the majority of people, a repayment mortgage together with adequate life insurance is the best choice, as it's the only loan that guarantees to pay off your mortgage by the end of the term (provided you maintain the stipulated payments).

Interest-Only Mortgages

Interest-only mortgages account for around one in five of all mortgages – you take out a mortgage loan in the normal way and pay interest as usual. However, instead of agreeing to repay the loan at a fixed date in the future, the loan simply stays in existence until you (not the lender) decide to repay it, which could be anytime from six months to 60 years. Interest-only loans are good for single people with no dependants, heavily-mortgaged families, those whose earnings fluctuate, people who expect to receive an inheritance and those whose salary is likely to rise substantially in the future.

It isn't necessary to have an insurance policy to repay the loan should you die, but it's advisable if others are dependent on your income. Most lenders will only lend from 50 to 75 per cent of a property's value on an interest-only mortgage **without** a linked investment. For most people it's essential to make provision for repaying the capital sum at the end of the original mortgage term, which can be done with an investment (such as an ISA), endowment or pension mortgage (see below). An Individual Savings Account (ISA) can be invested in cash, stocks or life insurance, and the pay-out is tax-free. However, due to the high charges and poor performance of these products in recent years, particularly endowments, interest-only mortgages are no longer so popular. They're favoured by the majority of buy to let investors and are a good way to get on to the housing ladder as your repayments are lower, although you will inevitably have to pay more later.

Endowment Mortgages

With an endowment mortgage you pay interest over the length of the loan. You also take out an endowment life insurance policy, which will hopefully provide a large enough lump sum to pay off the mortgage at the end of the term, usually 25 years. Your monthly mortgage payments are made up of an interest payment and an insurance (endowment) payment. The policy also carries life insurance, which ensures that if you die the mortgage is paid off in full and any money left over is paid to your estate. The loan and endowment are separate and you can obtain them from different sources. You should obtain independent advice and try to find a lender with a low interest rate and an insurance company with a good track record.

Like all endowment policies, you could be left with a tax-free sum at the end of the term after your loan has been paid off, although there are no guarantees. Investments depend on the stock market, which has performed very badly in recent years. In 2003, over 75 per cent of endowment policies were facing a shortfall amounting to thousands of pounds, which means that some 7.5 million endowments could fail to repay mortgages. Some endowments are worth less than the holders have paid in, even after ten years!

In recent years mortgage advisers have advised most borrowers to avoid endowment mortgages like the plague!

More recently, policyholders with under-performing endowments have been officially notified via special letters:

- A **green letter** means that the policy needs to grow by more than 6 per cent a year to reach its target.
- An **amber letter** alerts policyholders that there's a problem if the fund doesn't grow by between 6 and 8 per cent.
- A **red letter** indicated that there's a high risk that the endowment won't pay out the target amount at the end of the term because the fund must grow at 8 per cent or more.

If your endowment is under-performing, you can switch part of your mortgage to a repayment mortgage, increase payments to reduce the shortfall or consider re-mortgaging. Don't, however, be tempted to cash in your endowment but make it 'paid up', which means that you don't make any further payments but continue to receive bonuses and a pay-out when it matures. If you surrender an endowment policy you stand to forfeit thousands of pounds as a penalty. Endowment mortgages aren't recommended for first-time buyers with limited financial resources and low salaries, who should consider a repayment mortgage, which is more flexible if you've trouble meeting your repayments. However, they remain the best choice for people who have faith in the stock market (a rare animal in 2003!).

Endowment mortgages used to account for some 80 per cent of all mortgages, largely because they were heavily promoted by sales people on high commissions. Not surprisingly, lenders didn't tell borrowers about the disadvantages, such as high commissions and fees, or the alternatives. Hundreds of thousands of people were mis-sold endowment mortgages in the '80s and '90s, most of whom have been paid or are entitled to compensation.

Investment-Linked Or ISA Mortgages

Investment-linked mortgages are generally linked to an Individual Savings Account (ISA), which is a tax-free savings scheme. With an ISA mortgage you set up the finance for a home in the usual way, but you repay only the interest (not the capital) on the debt each month. At the same time you take out an ISA where your tax-free monthly contributions should grow over the mortgage term to enable you to repay the capital debt (hopefully with a surplus), in the same way as an endowment mortgage.

The main advantage is that you don't need to pay income tax or capital gains tax on your ISA investment. ISA home loans are more flexible than endowment mortgages as they don't have high start-up fees, they have a fixed life and you can withdraw some of your investment to repay your loan early. You can also usually stop, start and vary contributions without penalty. You do, however, need to take some investment risk and near the end of the term it's important that your investment is switched to low-risk investments to guard against a stock market crash.

Note that ISAs are guaranteed to exist only for a limited period, although if they're withdrawn they're likely to be replaced with a similar tax-free savings scheme.

Some lenders insist that you also take out a life insurance policy, although it isn't usually compulsory. However, not having life cover generally only benefits a single person with no dependants, because if they die the property would be sold and the lender would recoup his money.

Pension-Linked Mortgages

These are broadly similar to endowment mortgages, where monthly interest is paid on the loan. However, with a pension mortgage you pay into a personal pension plan that pays off your mortgage on retirement and also pays you a pension. This can be a good choice for the self-employed and for employees who aren't members of a company pension scheme, as the pension premiums attract tax relief at your highest tax rate and you can pay in from 17.5 to 40 per cent of your annual earnings, depending on your age. They are, however, inflexible and you must stipulate a retirement date from the outset. When you retire, 25 per cent of your fund can be taken as a lump sum and used to pay off your mortgage, although there's no guarantee that the pension will produce enough to repay the mortgage.

SPECIAL MORTGAGES

There are a number of special mortgage products which are variations on the standard mortgages described above, i.e. you still need to choose between a repayment and interest-only mortgage.

Flexible Or Current Account Mortgages (CAM)

One of the best innovations for homebuyers in the last decade has been the flexible or current account mortgage (also called an 'All-In-One' or 'One' account), where you operate your mortgage as a current account within certain limits. With a CAM you must have your salary paid into your mortgage account, which automatically reduces your mortgage debt and saves you interest until you withdraw money (interest is calculated daily). You also earn the same interest rate on your savings as you pay on your mortgage and you can borrow additional funds at any time (up to the maximum agreed mortgage) at the same interest rate you pay for your mortgage.

A CAM is ideal for people with savings, the self-employed (who need to put aside money to pay their taxes) and those who receive periodic lump-sum payments. You can usually vary your monthly payments, make over-payments, underpay (if you've over-paid) and take payment holidays. Most analysts agree that CAM accounts are difficult to beat and if you make full use of the account you could save tens of thousands of pounds by paying off your loan years early. CAM mortgages were introduced in the mid-'90s (from Australia, where they're the standard mortgage) and now account for some 20 per cent of all mortgages.

Offset Mortgages

This is a variation on the current account mortgage (see above) where you nominally have separate current and savings accounts, and your savings are offset against the mortgage sum, although loan repayments are based on the original loan. This means that if you've a mortgage of £150,000 and savings of £10,000, you will pay interest on £140,000 and will repay your mortgage quicker. No interest is paid on your savings, but you will save thousands of pounds in mortgage interest.

Self-Build Mortgages

If you wish to build your own home (e.g. buy a plot of land, engage an architect and builder, etc.) you can obtain a self-build mortgage, where the money is released in stages (usually four) after building has begun until the loan is fully drawn.

> **SURVIVAL TIP**
> **Bear in mind that some lenders make funds available at the beginning of each stage and others after a stage has been completed, which will make a big difference to your budget.**

Most lenders will lend a maximum of 75 to 85 per cent for both the land and the building costs, although some go as high as 95 per cent. See the table of lenders in magazines such as *Build It* and *Homebuilding & Renovating*. The sum you can borrow is calculated on the valuation rather than the cost of a home, therefore you should easily be able to borrow enough to build a home. For further information see **Building Your Own Home** on page 78.

Buy To Let Mortgages

In recent years, special 'buy to let' mortgages have been introduced for those planning to buy an investment property and have proved extremely popular. Most lenders will lend a maximum of 75 or 80 per cent of the value of a property (and will also lend to first-time buyers), with interest rates typically around 1 per cent higher than standard residential loans. Some mortgages offer a discount for a number of years – **shop around for the best deal** (also do this periodically and switch to a better deal whenever possible).

Note that if you decide to take out a second mortgage, you must inform both lenders that you're paying two mortgages, otherwise you will be committing mortgage fraud.

If you happen to have any surplus rental income it can be used to make overpayments on your mortgage and you can also choose to have your rental payments paid directly into your mortgage 'account' if you've got a flexible mortgage (see above).

RE-MORTGAGING & REDEMPTION CHARGES

A decade or so ago homebuyers used to get a mortgage and stick with it for 25 years until it was paid off. Nowadays the wise homeowner is continually checking the market to see whether he can get a better deal from another lender, and if so has little hesitation in switching lenders (penalties permitting). If your mortgage is more than three years old, free of redemption charges and you've a good credit rating, the chances are you're paying too much for it. In today's cut-throat mortgage market, lenders are offering attractive deals which weren't available a few years ago, as well as a variety of new flexible and current account mortgages that make better use of your money. Mortgage equity withdrawal (MEW), where homeowners take out a new mortgage to cash in on the increase in their home's value, was at an all-time high in 2003 and accounted for around half of all loans in mid-2003.

Bear in mind, however, that most fixed, capped, discounted and cashback deals come with severe penalties if you repay your loan early or switch to another deal. Penalty clauses typically keep you tied in for up to seven years and if you redeem the loan early you must repay any benefits or pay up to around nine month' interest.

Nevertheless, as the base rate has fallen sharply in recent years, many people find that they can re-mortgage and still save money. Note that fixed-rate mortgages - where the rate is fixed for the whole term - often have crippling early repayment costs (see page 139).

Some websites, such as that of mortgage broker London & Country (www.lcplc.co.uk), have a redemption penalty calculator which calculates whether paying a penalty will save you money in the long term.

PAYMENT PROBLEMS

Don't over-stretch yourself financially and take on a larger mortgage than you can afford to pay, as you run the risk of losing your home.

Note that lenders are required by law to print the following warning in all advertisements and literature: 'Your home is at risk if you don't keep up repayments on a mortgage or loan secured on it.' It means exactly what it says!

If you run into payment problems you should discuss it with your lender as he may be able to help by reducing your payments (e.g. by extending the term or changing to another mortgage product) or offering a payment holiday if your financial problems are only temporary. Other options may include letting a room (or rooms) to help pay the mortgage or even letting your entire home and renting a cheaper place for yourself.

You should avoid at all costs borrowing from lenders who offer loans to homeowners (secured on your home) at extortionate interest rates, as you're only likely to dig yourself in deeper.

If you fall too far behind with your mortgage payments, for example six months or over one year, or stop paying altogether without notifying your lender, they will eventually take steps to repossess your home. Over 2 million people fell behind with their home loan payments in the '90s and around 50,000 people a year had their homes repossessed by their lenders. If your home is repossessed it will be sold at auction and if the amount recovered is less than that owed to your lender, you can be sued for the balance by your lender or the MIG company (see page 136). The good news is that in 2003 repossessions were at their lowest level for some 20 years.

Negative Equity

During the recession in the '90s there was an unprecedented collapse in property values, resulting in almost 2 million households with negative equity – where the amount owed on the mortgage exceeded a property's value. Negative equity was widespread in the south-east, where over 25 per cent of owners were affected in some areas, although there was virtually none in Scotland and Northern Ireland. Thanks to the booming property market in recent years, negative equity has been eradicated and it's unlikely to become a problem again unless there's another property crash, which most analysts think is unlikely.

MORTGAGES FOR SECOND HOMES

Taking out a second mortgage to fund the purchase of a holiday home isn't easy even if you plan to let it for part of the year (see **Chapter 7 – Letting**), as most lenders insist that you're able to afford the repayments without earning any rental income. Therefore your income will need to be sufficient to cover your existing mortgage and your holiday home (normal income multiples apply - see page 134). You also need a minimum deposit of around 25 per cent on a second home, although you can use any spare equity in your principal home as security. Buy to let mortgages (see page 148) don't apply (unless you plan to let a second home long-term) and most buy to let lenders won't lend on holiday homes. You can obtain a better deal if you claim that a second home is for personal use only, although if you buy a home to let and don't tell the lender, you're committing mortgage fraud. If you decide to let a second home, you must inform your lender.

However, some lenders will take half the expected rental income into account as well as earned income, while others will lend on the basis of rental income alone, although their terms can be restrictive (they may expect rental income to cover around 140 per cent of mortgage interest!). It's best to take out an interest-only mortgage on a second home, as interest can be offset against your income tax bill.

Note also that buildings and contents insurance are more expensive on holiday homes when letting and can be around three times as high as for a principal home. You must tell the insurance company when a property is a second home or is to for letting.

FOREIGN CURRENCY MORTGAGES

It's possible to obtain a foreign currency mortgage, e.g. in euros, Swiss francs, US dollars or Japanese yen, to buy property in the UK. However, you should be extremely cautious about taking out a foreign currency mortgage, as interest rate gains can be wiped out overnight by currency swings. Most lenders such as high street banks and building societies, advise against taking out foreign currency home loans unless you're paid in a foreign currency (such as euros). This offers lower interest rates than sterling, but usually requires a higher deposit (e.g. 30 to 40 per cent) and fees.

The lending conditions for foreign currency home loans are stricter than for sterling loans and are generally granted only to high-rollers (those earning a minimum of around £50,000 to £75,000 a year) and may be for a minimum of £100,000 and a maximum of 60 to 70 per cent of a property's value. If you take out a foreign currency loan with an offshore bank, switching between major currencies is usually permitted and may be done automatically. When choosing between a sterling loan and a foreign currency loan, be sure to take into account all charges, fees, interest rates and possible currency fluctuations.

5.

MOVING HOUSE

When moving house there are many things to be considered and a 'million' people to be informed. The information and checklists contained in this chapter are designed to make the task easier and hopefully help prevent a nervous breakdown – provided you don't leave everything to the last minute.

Note that only divorce or a bereavement can cause more stress than moving house!

Moving home is an ideal opportunity to be ruthless and throw out all your old furniture, clothes and other belongings that you haven't used in years. This is a good time to have a (car) boot or garage sale, as it not only gets rid of all the junk but may also bring in a surprising sum. It also allows you to assess your lifestyle, particularly when moving to a new region or city. You will need to give a multitude of government departments, organisations and companies your new address, which is an ideal opportunity to save money by looking around for better deals and cancelling anything you don't really want. This particularly applies to utilities and other service providers, telephone companies, insurance, banking and credit cards.

DIY OR REMOVAL COMPANY?

The first decision you will need to make regarding moving house is whether to use a removal company or do the move yourself. It's possible to rent a self-drive van or truck (a standard car driving licence covers you for vans with a laden weight of 7.5 tonnes) and rope in a few friends to help you. However, although you can save money, for most people it's inadvisable unless it's a simple job, e.g. a few items of furniture and personal effects only.

Moving house is a back-breaking job which involves wrapping and packing everything in boxes (taking care to protect fragile items from damage), loading it all into a van, driving to your new home, unloading it and possibly repeating this a few times until you're finished or have collapsed!

It's no fun heaving beds and wardrobes up stairs and squeezing them into impossible spaces. It may be better just to move selected fragile and valuable items yourself and leave everything else to the professionals.

Note that most insurance policies have limitations and may not cover items above a certain value or breakages unless they were packed by the removal company.

Cost is obviously the main factor when making the decision whether to do a move yourself or employ a removals company. This varies considerably, depending on the distance between homes, how accessible both properties are, when you want to move (the day or time of the year), the size of your home and the amount of possessions you have, and exactly what is being moved. To move personal possessions and a few pieces of furniture may cost only a few hundred pounds, while the contents of a large house can run to several thousand. If you're moving only a relatively short distance, don't have a lot of things to move, or are moving to or from an apartment with lifts rather than stairs, it may be a straightforward job which you can do yourself. However, you will need to calculate the cost of hiring the van (and possibly paying someone to drive it), petrol, insurance and the possible loss of a day's earnings. You will also need to take into account the time involved, which may be an important consideration when time is money.

FINDING A REMOVAL COMPANY

Most people choose to use a removal service when moving home, as it reduces the chaos of packing to one or two days. If you're moving a relatively long distance (say over 200mi/320km), you should look both in the area that you're moving from and where you moving to, which may reveal surprising differences in cost. Unless a small company is highly recommended, it's best to use a major removal company with a good reputation. You can ask for references from previous customers, although this isn't usually necessary if someone is a member of a trade association such as the British Association of Removers (BAR).

Members Of The BAR

Members (some 650) of the British Association of Removers (☎ 020-8861 3331, 💻 www.bar.co.uk) have fair contract conditions, an approved code of practice, approved insurance cover, use environmentally-friendly packing materials, and have access to the BAR conciliation and arbitration service. BAR members also have access to Careline, an insurance policy to help customers deal with emergencies (such as emergency accommodation, legal advice, breakdowns or accidents and even burst pipes) during the first three months in a new home. Membership of BAR doesn't guarantee that nothing will be broken, but at least it will ensure that you're dealing with professionals who won't disappear with your belongings!

Quotations

You should obtain at least three written quotations before choosing a company, as costs can vary considerably. Don't forget to include everything, such as the contents of your garage, garden, attic, loft, cellar, annexe and workshop, as quotations can increase dramatically if you include things later. Most major companies provide a variety of levels of service which may include a standard move (load and unload only), fragile packing, full packing service, and combination service (e.g. packing and unload but not unpack). They may also provide storage services. A company may give a rough quote over the phone or a website, which will give you a good idea of the final cost, but they should send a representative to provide a detailed quotation after assessing the volume of your home's contents.

Companies base quotes on the number of hours they expect is needed to complete the loading and unloading, the amount of fuel required, driving time and extras such as packing, carpet laying, navigation of difficult stairs, using winches to access upper floors, etc. If there are access or parking restrictions for a large truck (the ground must also be firm enough to support a heavy vehicle) at either end, you should warn the remover as this is likely to influence the quotation (otherwise the bill will need to be adjusted later). If furniture needs to be taken in through an upstairs window, you may need to pay extra.

Check whether a quote includes packing and packaging, as these are optional extras with some companies and part of the standard service with others. A company may provide different packing services such as packing only breakables or packing everything, while others won't pack anything, but will provide packing materials (sometimes they won't even do this). Check whether the quote includes insurance and VAT.

SURVIVAL TIP

Always try to negotiate on price, as you may be surprised at the reduction (or extras) you can get simply by asking.

Insurance

It's highly recommended that you insure your belongings when moving house. Most people take up the insurance offered by their mover, which is specially designed to cover the risks involved in moving house. However, it isn't usually advisable to insure with a removal company that carries its own insurance (some do), as they may fight every penny of a claim. Insurance premiums are usually 1 to 2 per cent of the declared value of your goods, depending on the type of cover chosen. Find out what is covered and ask them to provide a list of exclusions, which is easier than trying to wade through the small print. Make sure that they have insurance for injuries to their staff during the move, as you don't want to be sued when one of the removal men falls down the stairs (most companies have insurance for injuries to staff).

Most insurance policies cover for 'all-risks' on a replacement value basis, although you may be able to choose between replacement basis ('new for old') or indemnity basis ('like for like' with an allowance for age, wear and tear). Note that china, glass and other breakables are usually only included in an 'all-risks' policy when they're packed by the removal company. Insurers may pay for the loss or damage to goods packed by a customer only if there's the total loss of a consignment.

If there are any breakages or damaged items, they should be noted and listed before you sign the delivery bill, although it's obviously impractical to check everything on delivery. If you need to make a claim, be sure to read the small print, as some companies require clients to make a claim within a few days, although 7 or 14 is usual. Send a claim by registered post. Some insurance companies apply an 'excess' of around 1 per cent of the total shipment value when assessing claims. This means that if your shipment is valued at £50,000, claims must be over £500.

It's prudent to make a photographic or video record of valuables for insurance purposes. Alternatively, you may wish to keep your valuables out of harm's way by renting a safety deposit box for the duration of the move. You may also wish to photocopy your important documents and leave the originals in a safe deposit box. If you're taking valuable with you, you may wish to ensure that they're covered by your home contents insurance while in transit.

Packing

Most companies will pack your belongings and provide packing cases and special containers. It can, however, be very expensive, although it's worthwhile if have a lot of good glass or ceramics (and can afford it!). Ask a company how they pack fragile and valuable items, and whether the cost of packing cases, materials and insurance (see above) is included in a quotation. If you're doing your own packing (as most people do), most shipping companies will provide packing crates and boxes, but you may have to pay for them. You will also need a number of rolls of strong tape and possibly a trolley to move boxes after you've packed them. Some items such as books, which should only be packed in small boxes, can be very heavy.

If money is no object, the best advice is probably to leave it all to the professionals, particularly as anything you pack yourself won't be covered by insurance. However, most people choose to pack small items, leaving the removers to deal with (and protect as necessary) larger items of furniture. Take care to pack small, valuable items (such as jewellery) separately and carry them yourself, which in any case are usually excluded from liability in a contract and insurance policy. If you've any questions about how to handle pets, fish, plants, antiques, fine art, wine cellars or anything else of particular importance or value, discuss it with your removal company well in advance. See also **Doing Your Own Packing** on page 160.

Storage

If you're unable to ship your belongings directly to your new home, you may need to put them into storage for a period. It's advisable to use your removal company to store your goods, which will minimise the number of people handling them and also reduce the cost. Most removal companies have their own storage facilities and they may even allow a limited free storage period before shipment, e.g. 14 days. Storage costs are based on volume and there may also be handling fees. You may have no access to your belongings while they're in storage, so take care not to pack anything that you may need before you move into your new home.

When leaving items in storage for a long period, you should ensure that they're adequately protected against temperature changes, damp and humidity. Warehouses are rarely heated and in winter the temperature is much lower than in a centrally-heated home. Bear in mind that items can be damaged by mould or mildew if they're left in storage for a long time.

If you need to put your household effects into storage, it's imperative to have them fully insured as warehouses have been known to burn down!

Contracts

Although most people cannot be bothered, it's advisable to read the small print in removal and insurance contracts, for example some insurance policies require owners to declare the value of all goods that are fragile or breakable above a certain nominal amount, e.g. £50. However, if it can be proven that a contract isn't reasonable, you may have a case for compensation. Removers are responsible for loss or damage caused by their negligence, although what this actually includes is debatable. Without insurance, a removal company's contract will limit their liability to a paltry sum in the event of damage or loss and will exclude liability for jewellery and other valuables.

Bookings

The first thing you will need to do – on which everything else will hinge – is to decide your moving day and book a removal company (or hire a van if you're doing your own move). Book a removal company well in advance for the best price – at least one month's notice is advisable. If you book at short notice you may not be able to make a booking on the day that you want and may need to pay more, particularly as a company will be aware that your options are limited and may increase its rates. At the very least it may not be willing to negotiate a lower rate.

Avoiding peak times such as bank holidays (or the week in which bank holidays fall), school half-term holidays and Fridays is advisable if you want to save money. Friday is the busiest day of the week, although if you've any problems you may not be able to contact anyone over the weekend to fix them. You will need to book well in advance if you wish to plan a move during a peak period.

You should be prepared for your moving date to change at the last minute! Bear in mind when moving home that everything that can go wrong often does, therefore you should allow plenty of time and try not to arrange your move from your old home on the same day as the new owner is moving in. That's just asking for fate to intervene!

Instructions

Give the removal company an itinerary for moving day with approximate arrival times, and provide them with a map and instructions how to find your new home. You should also give them a key, even if you're sure that someone will be there to meet them. Give them a mobile phone contact number (or two in case your phone packs up at the last minute, you forget to recharge it or a pay-as-you-go phone runs out of money). This could be the number of a friend who you can get in touch with. You should attach a floor plan of your new house and the colour-coded guide for the carton labels (see page 162), so that they know where to put things.

If there are access or parking restrictions for a large truck (the ground must also be firm enough to support a heavy vehicle) at either house you should warn the remover, as the cost can increase significantly if access or parking is restricted. These may include double yellow lines, metered or resident parking or any other obstruction that's going to cause the job to take longer than would otherwise be expected. If necessary, arrange with the local council to suspend a parking bay (or two) or the police to cone off a parking area around a week in advance. If you don't have access for a large vehicle (some are the size of a double-decker bus), your removal company may be able to use a smaller vehicle and make a number of trips. If access to upper floors is restricted by narrow doorways or stairways, small (spiral?) staircases, lack of lifts, etc., you may need to arrange for furniture to be hoisted on a pulley or 'lift' and be taken in through an upstairs window or balcony.

DOING YOUR OWN PACKING

If you're using a removal company but doing your own packing, there may still be certain items that you cannot deal with or would prefer the experts to handle. If you've any questions about how to deal with pets, plants, tropical fish (ask at a pet shop), antiques, chandeliers, fine art, wine cellars or anything else of particular importance or value, discuss it with your removal company. Take care to pack small, valuable items (such as jewellery) separately and carry them yourself, as they're usually excluded from liability by insurance companies. Note also that anything you pack yourself won't be covered by the removal insurance policy. Check that your home contents insurance covers your belongings in transit and insure your possessions from the day of arrival in your new home.

SURVIVAL TIP

Take care not to pack anything that you will need on moving day (see Survival Rations on page 163).

Packing Materials

Most shipping companies will provide packing crates and boxes, but you may have to pay for them. Start collecting packing materials if your removals company isn't providing them. You can obtain free boxes from supermarkets and other stores, although it may be better to obtain stronger boxes from your removal company (there's usually a small fee). Note that you will need lots of small boxes for books and other heavy items. You will also need a few rolls of strong plastic tape (with a dispenser), coloured marker pens, coloured tie labels or tape, bubble wrap and tissue paper for delicate items, corrugated cardboard or thick foam sheeting (for packing mirrors and pictures), and a plentiful supply of plastic bags and newspapers. If you've access to a shredder you can use it to convert newspapers into packing material for fragile items. You may also need some old blankets or sheets to protect large delicate items such as mirrors and light fittings.

Start Early

Start packing early – for example at least two weeks before you're due to move. It's surprising how long it can take to pack, particularly if you've little free time in the evenings and at weekends. If two people are packing you will need to allow at least three full days (or two weekends) to pack the contents of an average 4-bedroom house. Get your children to help pack their own belongings, but check that they're doing it correctly. Two weeks before you move you should have finished sorting your cupboards, loft, garage, cellar, etc. and have discarded, sold or given away anything that you don't need to charity shops or a recycling dump.

Packing Boxes

Ensure that your boxes and other containers are strong enough (they will be if the removal company provided them) to permit stacking in the van without damaging the contents. Don't over-fill boxes (all boxes should be sealed and flat) and don't fill large boxes with heavy items such as books, as they will be too heavy to lift. You can pack the bottom half of large boxes with books and other heavy items and fill them with lighter items.

Fragile Items

Pack fragile items in tissue or bubble wrap with plenty of padding, and mark boxes 'FRAGILE' or 'GLASS' in large red letters. Pictures and mirrors should be securely wrapped in corrugated cardboard or foam sheeting (available from removal companies) and have their corners protected – you can also buy special cardboard corner protectors and special picture boxes. Special care must be taken with valuable paintings, which you should move yourself. Wrap the legs on chairs and tables to prevent damage. Remove bulbs from lamps and other items and wrap plugs to prevent them damaging lamp bases. Large pieces of silver should be wrapped in acid-free tissue paper, especially if they're going into storage, which prevents them getting tarnished. If you've any really fragile or valuable items, you should transport them yourself in your car.

Marking Boxes & Items

Make a floor plan of your new home and where you want your belongings to be stacked by the removers by 'colour-coding' each room. You can then mark boxes and items with a coloured pen, labels or tape, so movers can readily identify where to put them. (Don't forget to give your removers a copy of the floor plan and colour-coding along with a map and instructions how to find your home, plus spare keys.) Mark boxes on the top and the side(s), as the top of a box may be obscured when it's stacked. Tie coloured labels to items that aren't boxed or mark them with coloured tape or sticky labels. Pack things together that you will need in the same room when they're unpacked – don't be tempted to throw things at random into boxes that belong in different rooms!

Special Items

When it comes to packing, certain items may need special consideration or handling, these include:

- **Self-Assembled Furniture** – This usually needs to be dismantled before you can move it and you may need to arrange with the supplier or a specialist to do this (a removal company may also do it). If possible move small items in one piece, although this won't be possible with large items of furniture such as wardrobes and sideboards.
- **Kitchen Appliances** – Cookers, washing machines, refrigerators, freezers and dishwashers should all be disconnected before moving day. The drums of washing machines must be secured with the proper brackets (obtainable from the vendor or a local agent) to avoid damage. Refrigerators and freezers should be washed with detergent and dried thoroughly to avoid unpleasant odours, and if they're going into storage wedge the doors open to allow air to circulate and tape them in place.

- **Fixtures & Soft Furnishings** – Curtains, blinds and fixed items such as shelves and lamp fittings need to be taken down before moving day and cleaned – soft furnishings should be washed or dry-cleaned.
- **Clothing** – Clothing on hangers can be transported in special wardrobe cartons available from major removal companies. Clothing in chests of drawers may be able to be left in situ, although if in doubt pack them separately (the drawers may need to be removed to lighten the load).
- **Computers, Audio & Video Equipment** – This is best moved in its original packaging. Items should be secured for transit in accordance with the manufacturers' instructions.
- **Food Stuffs** – When moving food you should ensure that all bottles and jars are tightly sealed, and packages and cartons securely closed, if necessary by using tape. Wrap anything that may leak in a plastic bag and put loose food in plastic food boxes. Refrigerated food should be kept in a separate box, with different foodstuffs wrapped in separate plastic bags. Frozen food should have been eaten or defrosted a few days before your move. However, if you're moving the contents of a freezer, put items into large polythene bags (ideally inside cool boxes) so that they can quickly be transferred to the freezer on arrival. Only transport frozen food if the journey is short enough for it not to defrost (**don't re-freeze food that has defrosted as it can lead to food-poisoning**).
- **Flammable Items** – Note that you removal company won't be insured to transport any flammable substances, old tins of paint, creosote, paraffin, matches, gas bottles or similar items. Containers and bottles should be securely sealed with tape to prevent leakage.

SURVIVAL RATIONS

You should pack anything that you may need on moving day (or before unpacking your boxes) and take these with you on moving day. Take care not to pack these in boxes beforehand. These may include all or some of the following:

Essentials

- Keys for your new home;
- Directions to you new home and a local map;

- Removal contract (in case of queries);
- Mobile phone (and charger), address book (with numbers of estate agent, removal company, solicitor, vendor, your buyer, neighbours, utility companies, etc.);
- A fixed-line phone of the roamer variety (if the line is connected);
- Notepad, pen/pencil;
- Medication (headache pills!) and first-aid kit;
- Wallet/handbag with cash, credit/debit card, cheque book, etc;
- Driving licence, car registration and insurance papers;
- Briefcase with copies of important documents.

Tools & Equipment

- Vacuum cleaner;
- Broom, dustpan/brush and mop;
- Cleaning materials;
- Light-bulbs, plugs, adapters and fuses;
- Self-sealing plugs (for sinks and bath);
- Tool kit with an adjustable spanner, large and small (electrical) screwdrivers, hammer, picture hooks, tape measure and pen knife;
- Camera (you may wish to take pictures of your old or new home);

Basics

- Small TV (with remote!) and/or computer (to pacify children!);
- Radio/CD player and CDs;
- Portable computer;
- Camping stove, matches/lighter, candles, torch and oil lamp;
- Electric kettle, saucepan(s), frying pan, teaspoons, teapot, cups/mugs, tin opener, can and bottle opener, corkscrew and a sharp knife;
- Plastic or disposable cups, plates and cutlery;
- Washing-up liquid, dishcloth and rubber gloves;
- Toilet paper, tissues and wipes;

- Toiletries (soap, toothpaste, deodorant, etc.);
- Make-up bag;
- Change of clothes and slippers for all the family;
- Nappies and toys;.
- Bed linen, duvets and towels;
- Hot-water bottle!

Provisions

- Tea, coffee, milk (long-life or powder), sugar (sweeteners), biscuits, soft drinks, juice, bottled water and alcohol;
- Breakfast cereals, snack food (fruit, crisps, cheese, bread, etc.), prepared meals for lunch/dinner and tinned food;
- Pet food, bowls and litter;
- Baby food;
- Bottle of bubbly or wine for when the removal men have gone!

SURVIVAL TIP

Note that it may be easier to eat out somewhere in the evening than to cook a meal!

COUNTDOWN TO MOVING DAY

As soon as you know when you will be moving – ideally at least four weeks before your moving date – you should begin to plan your removal.

In general you should be wary of arranging things or giving anyone your new address before you've exchanged contracts, as some 30 per cent of sales fall through before the exchange of contracts.

On the other hand, you shouldn't leave things too late, particularly if you're planning to move house the same week as you exchange contracts, when you will just have to play things by ear. The key to a smooth move is to consider all aspects well in advance and make a timetable of when jobs need to be done – and stick to it!

You also need to allow for Murphy to throw a spanner in the works at the last moment!

The way to ensure a smooth move is to make a number of checklists of jobs to be done before moving day, split into periods of from four weeks before the move to the actual moving day itself. These checklists relate solely to the task of moving your family and belongings from one home to another. They don't include other activities involved in the buying or selling process, therefore you should bear in mind that there will be many other things going on that could affect your schedule. To help you plan a move, the jobs to be completed before moving day have been divided into the timeframes shown below.

- Four weeks before moving;
- Two weeks before moving;
- One week before moving;
- Three days before moving;
- The day before moving;
- Moving day;
- On arrival;
- After moving.

Note that the checklists below are only a guide and you may prefer to do some things earlier or later than indicated. To help you keep track of what you have and haven't done the checklists are repeated in **Appendix D** (page 284) with tick boxes.

Four Weeks Before Moving

There are a number of things you need to do well in advance of a move. Some jobs can be left until one or two weeks before your move, but you should at least be aware of them and make sure that they're on your 'jobs to do' list.

- Book a removal company or van or reconfirm the moving date with the removal company or van hire company.

- You need to start of the process of cancelling services or insurance at your old address and re-arranging them at the new address, possibly with a different company.
- Notify your landlord if you live in rented accommodation. Obviously this will need to done in accordance with your rental contract, so check your notice period well in advance.
- Let your employer know when you're moving and arrange to take time off work, if necessary. Some employers give employees a day of two off work to move house.
- If you will need a bridging loan (see page 132) until the sale of your current home goes through, discuss this with your bank manager well in advance.
- Arrange alternative accommodation if you're selling your home before buying a new one, or if you don't plan to stay in your old or new home amidst the chaos of moving. If you will need hotel or self-catering accommodation you should book well in advance, particularly if you're moving during the summer months.
- You may wish to arrange for a few friends to help you move, which you will need to organise well in advance, particularly if they need to get time off work.
- If you require a residents' parking permit or special permission from the council or police for the removals van to park outside your current or new house, you will need to make an application for a permit around a week in advance.
- Arrange for a friend or neighbour to look after your pets on moving day or book them into a kennel/cattery. If they will be travelling with you they may need to be sedated – contact your vet for advice.
- Find a babysitter or someone to look after your children for the day of the move.
- Contact your insurance companies, for example private health, car, buildings and home contents. You should insure your new home from the day you exchange contracts. Check whether you're entitled to a rebate on your car, buildings and home contents insurance, which will apply if you're moving to a cheaper home or to an area with a lower insurance rating for car and home contents insurance, e.g. when moving from a city to the country. However, if you're moving from a rural area to a city, you will usually have to pay more! Shop around for new insurance as moving home is a good opportunity to save money.

- Contact government agencies such as the Department of Social Security, Child Benefit Agency, Department of Pensions, etc. If you're self-employed you will need to contact your local DSS office and give them your name, date of birth and National Insurance number.
- Contact your local tax office quoting your tax number, shown on your P60 or a payslip.
- If you've a driving licence or car you will need to get both your licence and your car registration papers updated with your new address (failure to do so is against the law). Complete the appropriate section on your car registration document and send to DVLA, Swansea, SA99 1AR (☎ 0870-2400010, 💻 www.dvla.gov.uk). Complete section 1 of your paper Counterpart Driving Licence (D740) and send it with your photocard licence and the fee to DVLA, Swansea, SA99 1BN (☎ 0870-2400009). Note that the DVLA no longer issues paper licences and if you have one you must obtain a photocard application pack from a post office or the DVLA.
- If you've got a TV licence, contact TV licensing (☎ 0870-850 1202) and give them your licence number and new address. If you've cable or satellite TV (or special aerials), contact your provider with your new address or to cancel your agreement (you can compare the cost of digital TV from different providers at 💻 www.uswitch.com). If you've a satellite system you will need to arrange for the dish to be moved to you new house or for a new one to be installed if you aren't taking it with you. This also applies to your television aerial.
- Contact your Internet Service Provider (ISP). If you've a broadband connection in your old home, you may need to make arrangements to have this service in your new home.
- Inform your children's current schools of the leaving date if known or warn them that you will be moving **as far in advance as possible**. This also applies to colleges, universities and local educational institutions where any members of your family are studying or plan to study. Obtain a copy of any relevant school reports or records from schools and arrange to visit schools in the area where you're moving to if you haven't already done so.
- If you're taking your carpets, appliances (such as a cooker or dishwasher) or anything requiring specialist removal and installation, arrange for someone to remove or disconnect them and

reconnect/refit them in your new home. Some removal companies will do this or will arrange for someone to do it. If you need to buy new carpets or curtains for your new home, arrange a visit to take measurements and order them well in advance.

- Notify your stockbroker, share accounts, company registrars and other financial institutions.
- Make arrangements for the cleaning of your old home or for furniture disassembling and assembling if you won't be doing it yourself. You may also wish to arrange for your new home to be professionally cleaned after the seller has moved out (**few people leave a home spotless and the best time to spring clean is when it's empty**).
- Arrange for any work to be done on your new home that needs doing before you move in. This not only includes essential work – such as fixing a hole in the roof – but also such things as changing the locks, installing an alarm system, or special electrical or plumbing installations.
- Start running down food stocks, particularly frozen foods. If your fridge and freezer are going into storage, they will need to be thoroughly cleaned and dried in order to prevent mould developing (or store them with their doors ajar).
- Make a list of all the major items that you plan to leave behind in your old home and give it to your solicitor. It's important that this is accurate as it will be appended to the contract and every item must be left when you move.
- Start sorting through your belongings in cupboards, loft, garden shed, workshop, garage, annexe, etc. and discard, sell or give away anything you don't plan to take with you. Investigate local car boot sales (or Ebay?) and charity shops.
- Make a list of all the major items you're taking with you for insurance purposes, including the cost, and date and place of purchase.
- Go through all your papers and copy any important documents – store the originals in a safe or safety deposit box. These may include birth certificates; driving licences; marriage certificate, divorce papers or death certificate (if a widow or widower); educational diplomas and professional certificates; employment references and curricula vitae; school records and student ID cards; medical and dental records; bank account and credit card details; insurance policies (plus records of no-claims' allowances); and receipts for valuables.

Two Weeks Before Moving

By now you should have finished sorting your cupboards, loft, garage, cellar, etc. and have discarded, sold or given away anything you don't plan to take with you. You should also have accumulated packing materials ready to start packing items you won't need in the next few weeks. Other jobs to do in the next week include:

- Start packing anything you won't need until after your move.
- Cut the lawns short so that you won't have to do them again. Drain any fuel from garden equipment such as lawnmowers, clean your BBQ, and ensure that all outdoor equipment is clean enough to transport. Make a list of plants and shrubs that you're taking with you and ensure that you've proper pots and tubs to transport them. Make a note of any garden ornaments and other items (shed?) that you're taking with you and dismantle any children's play equipment such as swings or climbing frames (keep all the nuts and bolts together in a plastic bag).
- If you haven't already done so, start running down the contents of your freezer. This is necessary if you need to defrost it - either to clean and leave or to take with you.
- Sort through your kitchen cupboards and start packing any equipment, tinned food, crockery and cutlery that you won't need before you go. Dispose of anything you don't want.
- Make a backup copy of any important data on your computer to floppy disks, a zip drive or a CD-ROM. (After making a backup, check that you can read the backup files - there's nothing worse than a backup file you cannot read!)

Bear in mind that computer hardware doesn't always travel well and the last thing you want to find is that you've lost vital data due to a hard disk crash and you don't have a backup!

- Obtain written instructions from the vendors of your new home regarding: the operation of appliances and heating and air-conditioning systems; the maintenance of grounds, gardens and lawns (the name of their gardener); care of special surfaces such as slate, wooden or tiled floors; and the names of reliable local maintenance men who know the property and are familiar with its quirks.

- Arrange to do a final check or inventory of the new property a few weeks before you moving.
- Contact banks, building societies, post office, credit union, stores and other institutions where you have accounts. If you're staying with the same bank, arrange to transfer your account to the nearest branch to your new home or workplace. If you've a safety deposit box or documents in safe keeping at your bank, you will need to collect them and make alternative arrangements at your new bank. Arrange for any direct debits or standing orders for your old home to be cancelled at the appropriate time. If you change your bank account you will need to ensure that all your direct debits or standing orders are switched to the new account or cancelled.
- Contact credit, charge and store card companies and give them your new address and bank account details (if applicable). Also notify your card protection insurer if you've one.
- Contact insurance companies such as mortgage payment protection, permanent health insurance, pet insurance, travel insurance, income insurance, life insurance, private health or dental insurance, etc.
- Make arrangements with gas, electricity and water companies to read meters and transfer your account to your new address. Although most companies officially require only a few days notice, it's advisable to contact them one or two weeks in advance and confirm the meter reading appointment a few days before. You may wish to take the opportunity to save money by changing your electricity or gas supplier. You can compare rates via Uswitch (💻 www.uswitch.com) or the Energy Helpline (💻 www.energyhelpline.com).
- Contact your telephone companies, both fixed and mobile. If you're moving locally you may be able to retain your existing phone number. You can compare the rates of the main phone companies at 💻 www.uswitch.com.
- Contact your local post office if you've got a pension book, as they will need to arrange for you to collect your pension from a post office close to your new home.
- If you've got some premium bonds you will need to notify the Bonds and Stock office (the form is available at post offices).
- Give your new address to your private pension companies, accountant, solicitor, and professional or regulatory bodies.
- Contact hire purchase and loan companies, and local businesses where you have accounts.

- Give your family doctor, dentist, optician and other health practitioners your new address. If you have regular prescriptions, ensure that you've adequate medicines to last until you've registered with a new doctor. If you're moving to a new area you will need to register with a new (NHS) doctor and dentist and arrange to have your records transferred (if possible, take them yourself). If you're undergoing hospital out-treatment, notify a new doctor as soon as possible and arrange to continue treatment in the new area.
- Notify private clinics or health practitioners such as a chiropodist, chiropractor, optometrist, osteopath, physiotherapist, etc.
- Contact anyone necessary to tell them that you're moving. These may include your accountant, alarm company (home), babysitter, car breakdown service (AA, Green Flag, RAC), car washer, catalogue shopping companies, charities, cleaner, chiropodist, football pools coupon collector, gardener, gym or leisure centre, hairdresser, library, masseur, milkman, national savings/premium bonds, newsagent, nursery or playgroup, online shopping accounts (e.g. Amazon or Ebay), pension provider, religious organisations, store cards, trade unions, tutors, vet, website hosting companies and window cleaner. It's unnecessary to give everyone you new address, but it will save time to have a 'change of address' sheet printed to distribute to your family, friends and those listed above.

One Week Before Moving

One week before you should have completed most of your packing and should only have minor items to pack such as food and clothes.

- Check that you haven't forgotten anything that you didn't agree to leave such as bathroom cabinets, shelving, mirrors, pictures and light fittings. If you haven't already done so, now is a good time to dismantle any furniture that cannot be moved in one piece (keep all the nuts and bolts in a labelled bag).
- Have your post redirected at the local post office. Redirection costs £6 per month, £13 for three months, £20 for six months and £30 to transfer all post addressed to one surname for a year. The post office requires one week's notice. Alternatively you can have post held for you if you're moving locally or arrange for a friend or your buyer to forward post (not that some post may get through even if it's redirected by the post office).

- Contact the local authority and inform them of the day you're moving. You may be entitled to a refund of part of your council tax.
- Arrange to drop off your keys with your estate agent and collect the keys to your new home at the earliest opportunity.
- Give the kitchen a thorough spring clean.
- Start finalising your 'survival rations' (see page 163).
- Make lots of copies of the map and instructions (see page 159) how to find your new home and give them to any workmen or friends who will be involved in you move. You will also need to give instructions to anyone who's delivering anything if your new home is difficult to find.
- Check (again) that the removers have all the instructions and information necessary – including maps and instructions how to find your old and new homes and the colour-coded floor plan (see page 162) of your new home – and confirm the moving date and time.
- Apply to the local council to suspend a parking bay (or two) or get the police to cone off a parking area on moving day.
- Obtain your pets' records from your vet.
- Give friends, relatives and business associates the address and telephone number of your new home or, if you're moving into temporary accommodation, an address (plus email) and telephone number (mobile?) where you can be contacted.
- Return any library books and videos or anything borrowed.
- Give your new address to all regular correspondents such as newspaper and magazine subscriptions, book clubs, social and sports clubs, and professional and trade journals. You can do this earlier, but it's advisable not to do so before the exchange of contracts, as your purchase could fall through.
- If you operate a business from home, arrange for the printing of new headed notepaper and business cards.
- Collect any dry cleaning, repairs or anything on loan.
- Obtain the forwarding address and telephone number of your sellers.
- Make sure that you've got a telephone number on the removal day where you can be contacted by the removers, your partner and anyone else who may need to contact you urgently. This could be your own or a borrowed mobile phone, or that of a friend who can relay messages.

Three Days Before Moving

By now you will be wondering whether you will ever get everything done in time, although you should be well on track if you've been following these guidelines!

- Before completion day it's important to check the general condition of the property you're buying and ensure that anything you purchased separately or which was included in the purchase price is present (see **Completion** on page 116). **Don't forget to do this in the chaos of moving.**
- Finish off cleaning the kitchen. Clear out the freezer if you're taking it empty, defrost the fridge and freezer and give them a thorough clean (make sure they're dry). If you're going to take your freezer full of food, turn it up to full power so that everything gets frozen solid over the next few days. Pack everything except your survival rations (see page 163).
- Prepare any plants that are you're taking with you; spray them with water, give them some nutrients if necessary and use canes to support them.
- Complete odd jobs such as finding and labelling spare keys, throwing away any junk you aren't taking with you, getting rid of sacks of rubbish, recycling bottles and newspapers, etc.
- Finish packing and labelling boxes and check that they're labelled correctly.
- Start cleaning the rest of the house.
- Confirm that meters will be read by utility companies before or soon after you move, and confirm that the meters will be read and services connected when you arrive at your new home.
- Do last minute laundry and pack any clothes you won't need before you move.
- Ensure that the keys for your new home are going to be available.
- Cancel any regular deliveries, e.g. milk, newspapers and magazines, and pay any outstanding bills.

The Day Before Moving

By now you should be almost finished and sitting around enjoying a well-earned rest, rather than running around like a headless chicken!

- If you haven't already done so, turn the fridge back on after it has been defrosted to keep your survival rations (see page 163) cool.
- Confirm that there's a parking area for the removal vehicle or hire van.
- Confirm that arrangement for your children and pets if they're being looked after by friends or relatives.
- Provide the shipping company with any last minute instructions regarding how to find your home from the nearest motorway or main road and how you can be contacted if they get lost.
- Make sure that you have all your survival rations (see page 163) – if not you may have to dash out and do a quick shop.
- Pack any remaining things that you've wanted to keep out until the last minute.
- Take down curtains and blinds if not done earlier.
- Check that you've the keys for your new home or when and where you can collect them.
- Finish cleaning the house.
- Disconnect the power and water from your washing machine and fit transit bolts if necessary.
- Disconnect your TV aerial or satellite dish if you're taking them with you.
- Have a final check over the home to see whether you've forgotten anything.
- Withdraw some cash from the bank to cover emergencies and out-of-pocket expenses.
- Get a good nights sleep – but don't forget to set the alarm (or two) if you're making an unusually early start!

Moving Out

There are certain unwritten rules when moving out:

- Don't remove door handles, light-bulbs or light fittings, fireplaces, fitted cupboards or anything planted in the garden or cemented down, unless it was specifically noted in the purchase contract.
- Leave a property in the condition in which the buyer first saw it, but cleared of items that weren't included in the purchase price or were purchased separately by the new owner.

- Do as you would be done by – clean the property and dispose of all rubbish and unwanted belongings.
- Don't forget to take everything with you, as the new owner could claim that any items you leave behind are now his and they could be hard to recover.

Moving Day

Hurrah – it's moving day at last! However, before you break open the champagne you've a long, exhausting day ahead of you, where anything and everything could go wrong. The following list assumes that you will be there to supervise the move at both ends. If this isn't the case, you must ensure that someone will be at the collection and delivery addresses to supervise the loading and unloading.

- Show the removal team's foreman around the house and give him any final instructions regarding the removal or packing of any special items.
- Ensure that the movers have the floor plan and colour-coded guide (see page 162) of your new home so that they know where to put items.
- Take the children and pets to their carers for the day or if they're staying with you, set aside a room with food, drink, toys, TV or computer.
- Provide ample tea, coffee and biscuits!
- Sedate the dog if you haven't found someone to look after it.
- Strip the beds and put the bedding into plastic bags for use that night.
- Pack up your toiletries and make a last check of bathroom cabinets.
- Check that wardrobes and cupboards are empty.
- Check that nothing is being taken that shouldn't be and that the packing inventory is accurate. This is the list that the remover will ask you to sign on departure and again after delivery.
- Check that all rooms are empty and the lights switched off.
- Switch off the fridge and boiler and disconnect any appliances that you're leaving. Ensure that the water, gas and electricity supplies are turned off at the mains and make a note of the final readings.
- Empty rubbish bins and leave rubbish bags for collection (or drop them off at the local rubbish dump).

- Close and lock all windows and doors. Leave all keys to internal doors, windows, garage, shed and other outbuildings (which should be clearly labelled).
- Once the van is loaded, check the complete house, garden and outbuildings with the foreman to ensure that all items to be moved have been loaded.
- Say goodbye to your old home, wipe away the tears and drive off into the sunset (taking one last backward glance in the mirror!).
- Drop the front door keys off at your solicitor.

On Arrival

On arrival at your new home you will need to do the following:

- Unload your survival rations and organise the children and pets. Pets should be kept in a quiet room from which they cannot escape.
- Make sure that you've protected the carpet in the hall and other rooms where it will get a lot of use from the removers, particularly if it's a wet day or the carpet is new or has just been cleaned.
- Ensure that everything is unloaded and stored in the appropriate rooms in your new home (and unpacked by the removers if applicable).
- Once you're satisfied that everything has been delivered (check them off against your inventory) and positioned in the appropriate place, you will be asked to acknowledge this by signing the delivery sheet. If you find that anything is damaged or missing later, contact the removal company immediately and make a claim.
- Make sure that your keys are returned by the removers.
- Have something to eat and drink (not forgetting to offer the removers a drink).
- Make the beds with the bed linen that you've brought with you.
- Plug in your fixed-line phone and any appliances that were left by the previous owners.
- If the house hasn't already been cleaned, start cleaning before you unpack and put everything away. This particularly applies to kitchen cupboards, fridge and freezer.
- Make a note of the meter readings and check that you aren't over-charged on your first utility bills.

After Moving

In the few days following your move you will need (or may wish) to do the following (some things will have been done already):

- Arrange to change the external locks (including the garage) as you've no idea how many keys are floating around. You may also wish to have an alarm system installed or the general security checked, e.g. are there locks on the windows?
- Photograph, measure and record the details of all period features and have them included in your household insurance.
- Contact the local council offices and organisations (e.g. CAB, tourist office) to obtain information about local amenities, sports facilities, clubs, educational establishments, etc.
- Make courtesy calls on your neighbours. This is particularly important in villages and rural areas if you want to become part of the local community.
- Register with the local council for council tax and the electoral roll.
- Register with a local National Health Service doctor and dentist.
- If you've oil or gas-fired central heating, you may need to order a delivery of oil or have the gas installation checked. You may also need to order logs or coal for open fires or boilers.
- Check with your local town hall regarding local regulations about such things as rubbish collection, recycling and on-road parking (you may need to obtain a resident's permit).
- If you've changed your bank account, you will need to ensure that all your direct debits or standing orders are switched to the new account or cancelled.
- Check that you've given everyone necessary your new address and telephone number.
- Make sure that you're receiving your post if it's being forwarded by the post office.
- Organise your house-warming party and invite your neighbours to it!

PREPARING YOUR NEW HOME

If you're lucky, you will have some time between taking over a new home and actually moving in. This will give you time to get your new home ready and to have any necessary work done before you move in.

After you move in it takes a while to get settled and the last thing you want is the disruption caused by renovation, repair or redecoration going on around you.

Cleaning

Whether you hire a professional cleaning firm or do it yourself, an empty house is far easier to clean than a full one.

Decoration

Doing any decorating before you move in means that you don't have to worry about rearranging rooms, putting dust covers on everything, getting paint spots on the carpet (if you're changing the carpets, do it after you've decorated) and living with the smell of wet paint.

Renovation & Repairs

Sometimes you must make some repairs to satisfy your lender or maybe your survey revealed a few nasty surprises that you want to get fixed. If you buy an old house it could need rewiring, new plumbing or eradication of damp. When a property is empty it's an ideal opportunity to get this work out of the way without having to live on a building site.

Improvements

Whether it's installing a new shower room, refurbishing the kitchen, installing new windows, before you move into a new home is the best time to get work done. Depending on how much time you have, you may also wish to convert the loft or add a conservatory or an extension. Even relatively straightforward jobs such as sanding floorboards, laying carpets or getting the existing carpets professionally cleaned is far simpler when you can entirely remove the contents of a room.

CHILDREN

Moving with young children can be highly stressful. Many parents find that it's best to get a relative or friend to look after them on moving day or allow older children to stay with friends. Failing this you should try to keep them occupied and out of the way by providing diversions in your survival rations (see page 163) such as a computer, TV, books, games and toys. If you're moving to a new area some way from your old home, you could invite some of their friends to stay once you're settled in, which will give them something to look forward to and help them feel less isolated. You could also suggest that they write to or email their friends if visiting them is difficult.

PETS

Cats and dogs become very attached to their familiar territory, so you should give them extra care and attention before and during a move. It may be possible to arrange for a friend or neighbour to look after them on moving day or arrange for them to go into a kennel/cattery for a few days. If they will be travelling with you they may need to be sedated, as many pets are frightened by the loss of their familiar surroundings and may run off and hide. On moving day it's best to keep them indoors in a quiet room well away from the hustle and bustle of workmen.

Cats should be transported in a vet-approved wire basket (an active cat can escape from a cardboard or wicker cage). Small animals such as guinea pigs, hamsters and rabbits are best transported in well-ventilated 'chew-proof' containers made of metal or rigid plastic. Give them plenty of bedding and a little food and provide lots of water in a non-spill container. Budgies travel best in a well-ventilated box with subdued lighting, which has a calming effect. If a budgie is travelling in its cage, make sure you remove any articles that could become dislodged. Keep a bird as quiet as possible during the trip – covering part of the cage with a cloth or blanket may help, but make sure that there's good ventilation.

Fish should be transported in clean, strong, polythene bags part-filled with tank water – not tap water. Make sure you seal the bags properly and leave a good air pocket above the water. Gently place the bags into a polystyrene container (available from fish importers and aquatic specialists) and label the containers with their contents and the words 'THIS WAY UP'.

Never move fish in their glass tank! Fish need to be transported as quickly as possible, particularly in extremes of weather. On a hot day the water will heat up quickly causing fish to overheat, while on a cold day the water will cool down to a very low temperature, both of which can prove fatal.

Many animals don't like travelling by car and can suffer from travel sickness, panic attacks and anxiety. To prevent travel sickness, it's advisable not to feed them for 12 hours before a journey. If you know that your pet suffers from travel sickness, ask your veterinary surgeon about anti-sickness pills and ensure that the car is well ventilated. Dogs need frequent stops for exercise, watering and toilet breaks. Ideally your dog should travel in a holding cage, but make sure that it's a suitable size.

Don't leave dogs alone in a car as the temperature can rise very quickly and they can die from heat exhaustion. If you do have to leave them for a short time, leave a window open and make sure that the car is parked in the shade.

Cats may take a little while to adjust to new surroundings. Give your cat a fresh litter tray, its favourite food and lots of attention. Let it rest quietly at least overnight, then when things have settled down let it explore the rest of the house. After two days or so, you can let your cat (on a lead ideally) have a short to let it get its bearings. However, note that if it becomes frightened or panicked it may try to go back to its old home. Give a cat only part of its normal feed just before it goes out alone for the first time, which will encourage it to come back to its new home. Dogs adapt quicker to new surroundings, although they still need to be left in a quiet room with food and water to recover from the journey. Take them dog on lots of walks to introduce them to their new surroundings. Fish need to be settled into their new home straight away. You should treat them as if they were new fish, de-chlorinating the water in the tank and ensuring that both the water in the tank and the bags in which they were transported is at room temperature.

Each year many animals are lost when their owners move house. Ensure that cats and dogs have a collar with your name and (new) address and telephone number. If they're registered on the national PetLog computer database this number should also be on the collar tag. Ideally a dog or cat should be microchipped, which allows vets and others to scan the chip to find the details of its owner. Contact your veterinary surgeon for further details.

6.

HOME IMPROVEMENTS

Each year we spend billions of pounds on home improvements, much of which is money down the drain. Shoddy work, eccentric taste and inappropriate extensions can actually devalue your home. The best improvements are those done for yourself, not for resale value, as the cost of improvements are rarely recovered when you sell (with certain exceptions), although they may make a house more saleable. Bear in mind that not all changes you wish to make may be considered as improvements by others and some could detract from a property's market value, particularly changes made to period properties (see below).

Trends have a huge impact on property prices and the rules regarding home improvements are continually changing. Generally any changes must be in keeping with the character and size of a house, for example adding a few bedrooms to a small cottage isn't much use if the space in the rest of the property (and garden) won't provide living space for extra people. Similarly, a property with four bedrooms should have at least two bathrooms. However, moving a bathroom from the ground floor to replace a small bedroom upstairs is usually more attractive to buyers.

See also **Chapter 8 – Selling Your Home**.

You must never start any work without obtaining planning permission (see below) – especially for a listed building – or ensuring that it isn't necessary.

PARKING

Note that if you live in an area with restricted or limited parking (i.e. anywhere in London), you will need to apply to the council to suspend a parking bay for a period or ask the police to reserve a parking area for tradesmen. Parking usually costs up to £70 per day in London and you need to apply around three to five days in advance, which isn't much good in an emergency! (Some London boroughs provide a system of prepaid parking vouchers that can be purchased in advance by residents.) In London and other cities, tradesmen may refuse jobs when there's nowhere to park.

THEFT

Bear in mind that the theft of period features from houses is at an all-time high, which isn't surprising when there's often little risk of being apprehended and period fixtures such as fireplaces (most at risk) can be worth tens of thousands of pounds. Fixtures and fittings are most at risk when a property is being renovated – almost every empty building with scaffolding is broken into in some areas. It's advisable to install a scaffold alarm and box off valuable features during building work. Unfortunately, the most likely culprits are often the very contractors that you engage to renovate a property!

SURVIVAL TIP
You should inform your builders that they're responsible for theft that occurs when they're working on a property.

DECORATION

Bear in mind that you will need to do any wiring, cabling, plumbing, plastering, etc. **before** you do any decorating. Unless you plan to live in a house for a long time or plan to re-decorate before you sell, it's advisable not to use too many bold colours when decorating. The décor should appeal to the widest possible market (not many people can live with orange or purple walls or garish flowered wallpaper!). This also applies equally to carpets and the colour of bathroom suites, which should be white if you're planning to sell. Home and property magazines (see **Appendix A**) are a wonderful source of inspiration for the DIY decorator.

BUDGET

If you're planning to buy a house requiring extensive renovation or which you plan to extend, find out exactly what you're letting yourself in for before buying. If you're planning on major work such as a loft conversion, extension or major structural work, you should obtain advice from a architect or builder at the earliest opportunity to ensure that your plans are feasible and affordable.

Budgets are invariably too low and work almost always takes longer than envisaged. You should add at least 10 per cent to the maximum you think any major work will cost and you will also need a reserve or contingency fund of a further 10 per cent of your total budget to allow for cost overruns.

Do your homework and get the costing right from the word go, otherwise you could be in for a nasty surprise.

Note that some jobs entail moving existing installations, such as the central heating boiler, drains and plumbing, which is expensive. You should obtain quotations (see below) from at least three builders or tradesmen for each separate job.

> **SURVIVAL TIP**
> **Unless your budget is really tight, you should employ someone to manage a large project (e.g. an architect or contractor) – trying to do it yourself is often a recipe for disaster!**

ALTERNATIVE ACCOMMODATION

Bear in mind that you may need alternative accommodation while renovating a property, as it may be impossible or unbearable to live there while work is in progress. If this is so, you will need to include the cost of accommodation in your budget.

FINANCING IMPROVEMENTS

If you need extra finance for home improvements, discuss this first with your mortgage lender. Re-mortgaging your home to pay for major improvements has never been better value with the lowest interest rates for some 50 years. If you don't have a mortgage you can obtain a low-interest loan secured on your home. Some local authorities provide home improvements grants, particularly to modernise older houses. Grants are also available from councils to help owners and tenants on low incomes pay for improvements and repairs. Check with your local council or a Citizens Advice Bureau.

PLANNING PERMISSION

If you wish to make improvements to a property immediately after moving in, you should check before completing the purchase whether you will need planning permission (see also page 79), and if so, whether it's likely to be approved. An architect can advise you about this or you can contact your local planning department. If you know or suspect that a property is listed (see page 202), you will need to obtain listed building consent (contact the local conservation officer for advice). You should also mention any planned improvements or repair work to your surveyor. If you're making improvements yourself, you must also ensure that you won't be contravening building regulations (see below). Your lender will also want to know of any changes you plan to make and will want to ensure that structural changes are carried out correctly and professionally.

To apply for planning permission first obtain a Planning Permission Application form from your local council. If a property is listed (see page 202) you will need a Listed Building/Conservation Area Consent Application form. Obtaining planning permission can be a lottery and some excellent traditional plans are refused, while other outlandish modern designs are approved. The speed with which applications are dealt with also varies hugely, although government guidelines are a maximum of two months. If you're planning on making exterior alterations or additions, look at similar properties in the area to see what precedents have been set regarding alterations, lofts and extensions. For major extensions or alterations, you should employ a good architect and discuss your plans (which should be complete!) with the planning authorities before applying for outline planning consent or full planning permission (if an application is refused you will incur the same costs again!). The cost of obtaining planning permission varies from a few hundred pounds for a small job where you're making your own drawings, to thousands of pounds for a large job requiring detailed architect's drawings.

Take care that your plans don't encroach on or overlook your neighbours' property, obstruct their light (light must be free to enter a home or business premises unimpeded by other buildings) or affect party walls. One of the most common reasons for the refusal of planning permission is objections by neighbours, therefore it's advisable to discuss your plans with your neighbours and try to allay their fears.

A small extension that doesn't increase the floor area by more than 247ft^2 (23m^2) or 10 per cent of the size of the total floor area of a property **doesn't** require planning permission. (However, this doesn't apply to properties in a conservation area or to listed buildings - see page 202.) This includes a garage or conservatory, although there are rules regarding the height and you mustn't reduce the size of the garden to less than 269ft^2 (25m^2). However, before planning any extension, it's wise to check with your local planning department. If you do any work without obtaining the necessary planning permission, you may need to demolish it or return the property to its original state.

BUILDING REGULATIONS

If you plan to make any structural alterations to a building, you will also need to make a Building Regulations application to your local authority before starting work. Work will need to be inspected by a building inspector at regular intervals to ensure that it complies with the approved plans. Don't do anything unless you're sure that you're doing it correctly or that it doesn't need approval, otherwise you may need to do it all over again (you could even be required to dig up foundations if it's suspected that they weren't laid correctly!).

ADDING VALUE

While certain improvements add value, others are a waste of money as an investment – creating a castle in a road of semi-detached houses (or the best house on the worst street) is a waste of money if you wish to recoup the cost! Examples of added value are listed below:

- Extensions (particularly those that add square footage to living spaces);
- Loft conversions;
- A conservatory;
- Extra (or new) bathrooms (with a walk-in wardrobe);
- Central heating (**essential**);
- A new or larger kitchen (preferably an eat-in kitchen with a utility room or larder);
- Landscaped gardens (a beautiful garden can sell an indifferent house);
- A garage (or double garage).

Adding a bedroom can increase the value of your home by up to 20 per cent, an extra bathroom or garage by 10 per cent (or as much as 20 per cent for a double garage), while central heating in the north-west of England can add as much as 20 per cent to the value (but less than 10 per cent in London). Other popular added-value improvements include new windows (e.g. double-glazing), painting and wallpapering, home security and insulation. Installing larger windows to let in more light is a way of improving many old buildings, provided you don't alter the character of a period house with inappropriate modern picture windows.

Other things to bear in mind when doing home improvements:

- Don't overdevelop a plot – the size of a house should be in proportion to the amount of land.
- Don't build an extension that's over 30 per cent of the size of the current house unless it can be done without spoiling the balance.
- Build in a complementary style rather than try to match the original craftsmanship of a period house and ensure that building materials match or compliment the existing style.
- Don't turn two large bedrooms into three small ones – more bedrooms is a big selling point – but, the difference in value between one and two bedrooms is much greater than the difference between a two and three-bedroom property.
- Utilise attic, garage and cellar space to its maximum.
- Make maximum use of natural light.

The most important question to ask yourself before lifting a paintbrush or choosing the wallpaper is exactly what is your motive for doing home improvements? How long do you plan to remain in the property? Do you expect to be there a few years or a decade? Are you doing improvements simply in order to sell a property or get a higher price? If you're planning to stay for the duration you can do whatever you like and simply enjoy it – you don't have to please anyone but yourself and can do as much or as little as you want. However, it would be wise to consider the impact of any major alterations, some of which could reduce the value of a property, such as reducing the number of bedrooms or bathrooms, or demolishing a garage to enlarge the garden. Of course, if you're confident that you will remain in a home for decades and its value doesn't concern you, go ahead. However, most of us will be concerned not to do anything that would reduce the value of our home; indeed most would much rather add value.

If you're only planning to stay for a few years before moving on, it would be wise not to be too extravagant or outlandish and do anything that won't add value or make a property easier to sell. Before doing anything it's wise to check the value of similar homes in your street or area. Is it a popular residential area, up-and-coming or downmarket and going nowhere? In hotspots you will see a return on almost any expenditure, while in depressed areas it won't be worth spending much money making a property more attractive if nobody wants to pay much to live there.

KITCHENS

Installing a luxury kitchen can add as much as 10 per cent to the value of a property, although it may not be cost-effective to choose a luxury range or a designer 'name'. More importantly, updating an old-fashioned, drab kitchen is considered essential to sell a home in a tough market, as it's the most important room in a house when selling and can clinch or scupper a sale. If you're a gourmet cook and fancy a state-of-the-art kitchen, it's advisable to employ a kitchen design service for a personal tailor-made kitchen. Most designers use high-tech computer programs that allow you to move units around and change the colour, finishes and fittings (such as handles) at the touch of a button.

BATHROOMS

Adding an en-suite bathroom or shower room is a great way to add value (most people want a second or even a third bathroom), although it can be expensive and cutting costs can put off prospective buyers. Enlarging a small bathroom by sacrificing a small bedroom can be a sure-fire winner, although the gain must be offset against the loss of the bedroom. A large bathroom (preferably en-suite) with corner bath (or Jacuzzi), twin basins, bidet and separate power shower is many buyers idea of heaven and can sell a house on its own! Although bidets are no longer considered 'fashionable', if you've ever used one for any length of time you'd probably consider them essential (as continental buyers do). It's advisable to employ a bathroom designer if you've got a large space.

Wet rooms, i.e. an open-plan shower within a bathroom with a waterproof floor and walls, are increasing popular and eliminate the need for shower cubicles or curtains and are easy to keep clean. However they aren't cheap and cost around £10,000 for an average-size bathroom. Although power showers are all the rage nowadays, you should bear in mind that there must be a bath in at least one bathroom; if you've got more than one bathroom a power shower alone is perfectly acceptable in a secondary bathroom.

A family bathroom should have a bath and a separate shower if there's room, while a separate toilet (perhaps downstairs) is a definite plus, particularly if a property has only one bathroom. An extra or larger bathroom is also likely to add double its cost to the value of your home.

ENLARGING YOUR HOME

If your family is out-growing your home, it may be possible to increase it's size. Bear in mind that it's usually **much** cheaper to increase the size of your current home, e.g. a loft conversion or an extension, than moving house.

> **SURVIVAL TIP**
> **Note that it's much easier to alter or extend a Victorian house than a Georgian house and you won't need permission to alter the interior, unlike a Georgian house which is likely to be listed (see below).**

There's no limit to what you can do provided that you've got the space, the money and can obtain planning permission and building regulation approval. The most common added-value extensions include the following:

- Conservatory;
- Loft conversion;
- Larger kitchen with dining area;
- Utility room;
- Extra bedroom;
- Extra (en-suite) bathroom;
- Downstairs toilet/shower room;
- Study;
- Granny flat or nanny studio;
- Workshop;
- Garage (double);
- Walk-in wardrobe;
- Playroom;
- Extra sitting room.

Bear in mind, however, that an extension must be in keeping with the rest of the house and look natural – not added-on. In this respect it's essential to employ a good architect (employing an architect to manage the project will cost around 15 per cent of the total budget) and first-class builders and tradesmen. It isn't advisable to try to save money by using inferior materials, accepting the cheapest quote simply because it's the lowest, or reducing the size of an extension – it's better to wait until you can afford it. Increasing the size of a kitchen and adding a dining area will allow you to convert a formal dining room into a office, playroom or extra sitting room. A double-height extension is even better if you've the space, although it's generally much more expensive than doing just one floor. A bungalow can easily be extended if you've a large garden and can dramatically increase its value.

Most people like large rooms and many people reduce the number of bedrooms to make larger rooms or a larger bathroom. Bear in mind, however, that reducing the number of bedrooms can significantly reduce the value when you sell. However, although it isn't usually advisable to reduce the number of bedrooms, turning a tiny two-bedroom apartment into a spacious one-bedroom apartment can add value. A nanny studio, which can be built over a garage, can add serious value to a home and there are also considerable benefits and savings from having a live-in nanny or au pair.

CONSERVATORIES

A conservatory is one of the best added-value extensions you can make and it's also one of the cheapest. A good conservatory can transform a fairly ordinary house into something special (it usually quickly becomes the favourite and most used room in the house) and can add twice its cost or more to the value of a house. A basic conservatory can be purchased from a DIY store and built by a competent DIY builder, while a more elaborate bespoke design will cost much more and needs professional installation – but will add much more to the value of a property. Modern conservatories are designed to be used as dining and family/sitting rooms, and can be open to the elements by adding floor to ceiling folding doors. Before deciding on a design don't just read brochures, but check your friends' and neighbours' conservatories to see whether you like them. Bear in mind that it's generally essential to install central heating, blinds and air-conditioning (they can get very hot in summer).

LOFT CONVERSIONS

A loft extension is one of the best ways to extend your house without increasing its footprint. In a town or city you can recoup the cost of a loft conversion within a year depending on how much house prices are increasing in the area (although in the countryside it isn't guaranteed to make money). The cost could be recouped immediately if you plan to sell and may also make a property much easier to sell. A loft extension can have a variety of uses from additional bedrooms and bathrooms to a study, (nanny) studio or granny flat – and it can be changed as your family grows or reduces and your lifestyle changes.

You must ensure that the space will be habitable, is large enough with sufficient roof space, that the floor joists are strong enough to support the structure, and that it complies with building and fire regulations. A fixed (spiral) staircase should be installed rather than a ladder and it's advisable to spend money on a dormer window (if permitted) and add extra height to the roof space. Don't scrimp on windows (modern roof windows admit up to 40 per cent more light) as good lighting and ventilation are a must. You should install plenty of power points and air-conditioning may be necessary in summer. If you're adding a bedroom, it always advisable to add an en-suite bathroom or shower room.

BASEMENTS & CELLARS

In London, wealthy property owners are tunnelling beneath their homes to build swimming pools, spas and saunas, garages and entertainment areas. A basement can also be turned into a self-contained apartment (e.g. for letting), provided you can build a separate entrance. For information contact Cellar Conversions (☎ 020-7244 8585, 💻 www.cellarconvert.co.uk) or the London Basement Company (☎ 020-8847 9449, 💻 www.tlbc.co.uk).

CREATING MORE SPACE

In small apartments and houses, owners are ditching kitchens to free up valuable space and hiding kitchen apparatus (such as the fridge/freezer, dishwasher and oven) in a cupboard or behind a partition. However, bear in mind that when you plan to sell having no kitchen may reduce the price. A glass partition can be used to turn a small studio into a one-bedroom apartment and won't reduce the light and is just as good as partition walls when it come to sound-proofing. Removing walls to create a large dining/living room or kitchen/dining room can be a real winner in a relatively modern home.

DIY OR PROFESSIONALS

One of the first decisions you will need to make regarding home improvements is whether to do all or most of the work yourself or have it done by professionals. You shouldn't attempt to do a major job (or any job) that's beyond your capabilities (although many people do), as it usually ends up costing far more to put right than it would to employ professionals in the first place! If you're a keen but hopeless DIY enthusiast, leave it to the experts. When renovating a period property, it's important to have a sensitive approach to restoration and you shouldn't tackle jobs by yourself or with friends unless you're sure you're doing it right. In general, you should aim to retain as many of a property's original features as possible and stick to traditional building materials such as wood and stone reflecting the local style. It's important not to over-modernise an old property so that too much of its natural charm and attraction is lost.

EMPLOYING A BUILDER

It's difficult to find good builders and craftsmen and the UK has a severe shortage of plumbers, electricians and other tradesmen, all of whom charge heavily for their services. A good builder or tradesman is likely to be booked up for months ahead and you should be suspicious of someone who appears to have little or no work.

You must be very (very) careful whom you employ to do your home improvements and avoid the crooks and cowboys (one in five homeowners fall victim to them).

This applies to all work around the house, whether it's an extension or conversion, new windows (e.g. double-glazing), a new kitchen, plumbing, electrical work, carpets - anything. The building industry in the UK is almost totally unregulated and anyone can call themselves a builder or tradesman without any qualifications, experience or registration. The prices charged can be astronomical and complaints about shoddy workmanship are commonplace (tens of thousands a year). Many building contractors also work 'on the black' without paying tax or social security (they should charge VAT only if they're VAT registered).

A professional builder should be a member of a reputable trade association such as the Federation of Master Builders (FMB), the National Federation of Builders (NFB) or the Guild of Master Craftsmen (GMC) - check if someone claims to be a member - which offer an arbitration service should things go wrong. Further protection is offered when a builder is covered by a warranty such as the National Register of Warranted Builders (NRWB), which is a Masterbond Warranty scheme offered by the Federation of Master Builders, or the Building Guarantee Insurance Scheme. The Masterbond Warranty provides clients with a two-year insurance plan (the fee is 1 per cent of the total cost of a project) covering defective workmanship and materials for all registered builders and tradesmen. Note that not all members of the FMB are members of the NRWB. You should also have a industry-recognised warranty for jobs such as wiring, plumbing, roofing, timber treatment and work to eradicate rising damp.

It's very important to ensure that all tradesmen you hire are ensured for third party claims.

The best builders or tradesmen to hire are those who are personally recommended by someone you can trust. Ask your neighbours, friends, relatives and colleagues if they can recommend someone. Failing this, ask local builders if they can provide the names of previous customers as a reference (but make sure that they aren't relatives or friends!) and speak to them and inspect the work that has been done.

Quotations

Always obtain at least three quotations (not estimates) in writing and when comparing prices make sure that all quotes are for the same quality of materials and workmanship, and that everything is included (the 'cheapest' quote may turn out to be the most expensive). Note that for quotations to be accurate, you must detail exactly the work that's required, e.g. for electrical work this would include the number of lights, points and switches, and the quality of the materials to be used. If you've only a vague idea of what you want, you will receive a vague and unreliable quotation. Avoid adding to a job or changing your mind halfway through and if problems arise, discuss and resolve them immediately. Better still, rather than rely on quotations for essential work from a builder, you should have a survey done by a member of the Association of Building Engineers (☎ 01604-404121, 💻 www.abe.org.uk). An engineer will provide an independent survey for a few hundred pounds, which can save you spending thousands of pounds unnecessarily.

A common ploy by 'cowboy' builders is to give a rough oral estimate and increase (e.g. double) the price later. Obtain a written agreement (including dates when work will start and finish) and have your solicitor check the small print. Check whether sub-contractors will be used and who's liable if things go wrong. You should ask whether the builder will be doing other jobs at the same time – if so it could lead to problems with labour shortages.

Don't pay anything in advance apart from a small deposit, as it's quite possible that a builder will disappear with your money (it happens regularly).

On the other hand, always pay a builder on time, as he may not turn up if you haven't paid him!

For a large job you should agree in writing any staged payments before work starts, avoid paying cash and be wary of workmen who insist on it – pay by cheque or credit card if you can, as it provides added protection, and get a receipt. Although there are many reputable and excellent builders and craftsmen in the UK, you simply cannot take too many precautions. Everything should be put into writing and included in an 'agreement' (or a formal JCT contract for a large job), two to three pages should cover most domestic work, which should include the following:

- When the work will start?
- How long it should take (but expect it to take much longer)?
- How and when payments are to be made?
- What standards of workmanship, materials and cleanliness are required?
- What date will the materials or equipment will be required (if you're supplying them)?
- A penalty for finishing late and a bonus for early completion. You should also include a clause stating that the contract may be terminated if the builder disappears for an unreasonable period. If the timetable slips by more than a few days you should obtain an explanation in writing. However, if delays or extra work are due to your mistakes, you cannot blame the builder and may need to pay extra.
- On a large job you should agree a retention (say 10 per cent of the total cost) with the builder that will ensure that if any problems arise within six months of completion, they will be fixed before you make the final payment. The builder is responsible for ensuring that work is carried out in accordance with the local building regulations (as detailed by the district surveyor) and the final payment should be withheld until you receive a copy of the building regulation certificate from the local planning department.

The job description should be detailed and include the quality and/or make of materials to be used. When you've agreed on the total cost and the schedule you should make two copies, both of which must be signed by both parties. If any changes need to be made at a later date, they must be agreed and appended to the schedule (or written on the back of the original schedule) and initialled by both parties. Bear in mind that problems invariably arise on a large job – which is why it's recommended that you employ an architect to oversee major work (see below) – which should be discussed and resolved amicably with your builder.

> **SURVIVAL TIP**
> **If you want a job done on time and properly it's imperative to maintain good relations with your builder at all costs and avoid acrimonious disputes, particularly in front of his employees.**

Employing An Architect

If you're planning on making major structural changes, such as a loft conversion, extension or major structural work, you should obtain advice from an architect at the earliest opportunity to ensure that your plans are feasible and affordable. An architect's drawings for an extension may cost from £1,000 to £2,500 for an average house, depending on the complexity of the job. It's also advisable to have your architect manage a substantial job, which will cost around 15 per cent of the total budget. If you employ an architect, you should give him your specifications and budget in writing. If he accepts your budget and discovers later that he cannot complete the project on budget, you shouldn't be required to pay for his services. This also applies if the cost spirals for reasons beyond your control and you're unable to complete the job.

RESTORATION & MODERNISATION

Modernisation of old houses should be done carefully and with sensitivity, as what you decide to do away with may constitute the very features that give a house its character.

> **SURVIVAL TIP**
> **Don't over-restore and bear in mind that an old building is supposed to look old.**

You should be wary of removing period features, as they're what attracts people to old houses in the first place and many people won't buy a period property that has been 'over-modernised' – many would say vandalised!

> **SURVIVAL TIP**
> **If you decide to remove or replace original period features such a doors, windows, fireplaces or baths, bear in mind that there's a huge market for them and you shouldn't let a builder take them away for free.**

Some things you shouldn't even think about doing include stone cladding, which most buyers will hate and which can be disastrous if water gets trapped between the bricks and tiles. In general you should never replace wooden windows with uPVC ones, particularly in a period property (wood windows may also be cheaper).

Old houses can be **very** expensive to maintain or renovate, particularly if they haven't been cared for. Typical problems may include dry rot, rising damp, woodworm or other infestations, a leaking roof, rotting window frames, frost damage to stone and brickwork, subsidence or land-slip, rusty pipes and gutters, old electrical (possible dangerous wiring) and plumbing (lead pipes?) installations, and poor insulation. The most important things to do in a old building after restoring or renovating the structure (roof, walls, flooring, windows, doors, etc.) are to install central heating, good-size bathrooms, a modern kitchen, good insulation, a (double) garage and to re-decorate.

Don't let the potential problems deter you, as it's generally a labour of love restoring a period property to its former glory and many people become serial restorers – bringing out the character and features of an old property is never wasted money and can increase its value many fold. When restoring a period property you should restore it as closely as possible to its original splendour and if you need to replace something you should fit like with like and not mix and match period and modern features. You should restore period features such as dado rails, skirting boards and picture rails, but shouldn't put them in where they never belonged as they will look out of place. If you're thinking of re-installing a fireplace make sure that there's a working chimney, as a working fireplace is one of the best features in a period home and a huge selling point. Note that restoring a listed property (see page 202) should be handled with kid gloves and obtaining planning permission can be a nightmare.

Architectural Salvage

Recycled building materials, fixtures and fittings from old houses has become a lucrative business and nowadays you can find (or have made to order) virtually any period feature, including fireplaces, mantelpieces, doors, window frames, stained glass, mouldings, floorboards, tiles, porcelain, porches, ironwork, beams, bricks, flint, skirting boards and chimney pots. You can use a architectural salvage dealer to find reclaimed building materials and fixtures and fittings for a period house.

Salvo (PO Box 333, Cornhill-on-Tweed, Northumberland TD12 4YJ, ☎ 01890-820333, 💻 www.salvo.co.uk) is an organisation of architectural salvage companies that can provide a list of approved merchants to subscribers and send a tailored email (for a fee) to over 150 dealers on its database to search for a particular item. Salvo publishes the *Salvo News* (available on subscription) and the *Salvo Guide*, a 240-page guide to architectural antiques, reclaimed building materials and antique garden ornaments that's essential reading for anyone restoring a period property. It also organises an annual 'Salvo' exhibition in London.

Other useful contacts for anyone restoring a period home include Original Features (💻 www.originalfeatures.co.uk), which specialises in supplying and installing products for the restoration of 19th and early 20th century properties, and Architectural Heritage (💻 www.heritage.co.uk), which provides links to many useful websites. Owners of period properties may also be interested in the Society for the Protection of Ancient Buildings (☎ 020-7377 1644, 💻 www.spab.org.uk), English Heritage (☎ 020-7973 3000, 💻 www.english-heritage.org.uk), the Georgian Group (☎ 020-7529 8920, 💻 www.georgiangroup.org.uk), the Victorian Society (☎ 020-8994 1019, 💻 www.victorian-society.org.uk) and the Twentieth Century Society (☎ 020-7250 3857, 💻 www.c20society.demon.co.uk), all of which are dedicated to preserving buildings of historic importance.

SWIMMING POOLS & TENNIS COURTS

In general a pool, even a heated indoor spa, isn't a value-added improvement. A concrete in-ground pool can cost as much as £60,000 when all the costs are included and is also expensive to maintain (the same amount spent on a conservatory, extension or loft conversion would add double their cost to the value of your home). However, it may help sell a luxury home and add value if you install an indoor swimming pool (perhaps with a sauna and Jacuzzi).

On the other hand, if you've got the money and plan to remain put for some time, an outdoor pool can be a good investment in your family's quality of life; it will also save you time and money running the kids to the local pool and on trips to the seaside. You don't usually need planning permission for a pool provided it isn't within five metres of the house or a party wall, doesn't involve walls over two metres high and doesn't take up more than half your garden. It takes around 20 weeks to install an in-ground pool (an above ground pool takes just a week to install). For information and a list of suppliers contact the Swimming Pool and Allied Trades Association (☎ 01264-356210, 💻 www.spata.co.uk).

A tennis court will add value to a large family house with sufficient (expansive) gardens for it to be unobtrusive. It must usually be invisible from the house and mustn't encroach on the garden. The cost depends on the size and finish – tarmac (from around £15,000) or artificial grass (from around £25,000) are best for low maintenance. It takes around three or four weeks to clear and prepare the ground and install a court.

ORGANISATIONS

The Office of Fair Trading (☎ 020-7211 8000, 💻 www.oft.gov.uk) publishes a free booklet entitled *Home Improvements* that contains excellent advice for home improvers and a list of national associations, many of which provide warranty schemes. The National Home Improvement Council (☎ 020-7828 8230, 💻 www.nhic.org.uk) is an umbrella organisation for builders, surveyors and architects, and publishes the *Home Improvement Directory* which lists 'reliable' specialists. The National Home Improvement Advisory Service (NHIAS), 18 Lord Mayor's Walk, York YO31 7HA (☎ 0800-028 5809, 💻 www.nhias.org) is a consumer organisation that provides free independent advice regarding building, extending or improving your home.

BOOKS & MAGAZINES

There are many books available for those planning home improvements, including *Getting Work Done on Your House* and *The Which? Book of Home Maintenance*, both published by the Consumers Association, *Getting the Builders in . . . and Staying in Control* by Paul Grimaldi (Elliot Right Way Books) and *The Home Front Directory* by Alison Reynolds & Sarah Childs-Carlile (BBC). See **Appendix B** for a comprehensive list of building and renovation books. *Homebuilding & Renovating* magazine (☎ 01527-834435, 💻 www.homebuilding.co.uk) is essential reading for homebuilders and renovators, and organises shows for self-builders throughout the UK (💻 www.homebuildingshow.co.uk).

INTERNET

There are also many excellent Internet sites for DIY enthusiasts, including the Federation of Master Builders (🖳 www.fmb.org.uk), the Guild of Master Craftsmen (🖳 www.thegmcgroup.com), the National Register of Warranted Builders (🖳 www.fmb.org.uk/about/nrwb/index.asp), the Building Centre (🖳 www.buildingcentre.co.uk), the Building Information Warehouse (🖳 www.biw.co.uk) and Buildstore (🖳 www.buildstore.co.uk). Building Control (🖳 www.buildingcontrol.org) provides information on all aspects of building control in England, Wales and Northern Ireland, plus a complete database of all building control offices and officers. You can also make an online building regulations application via their website. See also **Appendix C** for a list of other useful websites.

WHEN THINGS GO WRONG

If, in spite of your precautions, things go wrong, you should try to resolve the problem with the tradesman or company concerned or, failing this, their trade organisation. If you've got a dispute with an architect you can refer it to the reconciliation service of the Royal Institute of British Architects (☎ 020-7580 5533). If you require advice regarding your legal position, you can obtain advice from your local trading standards or consumer protection department, a Citizens Advice Bureau (CAB) or a consumer advice centre. Depending on the amount involved, you may be able to take your case to the Small Claims Court, which is an inexpensive and relatively simple way of resolving disputes involving a maximum of £5,000. Information and an application form can be obtained from any court (see the Court Service website, 🖳 www.courtservice.gov.uk, for your nearest court).

DIY & BUILDING SUPPLIES

DIY is extremely popular (it saves you from cowboy builders!) and there's a wide range of DIY equipment, tools and building supplies available. Ask your neighbours about where to buy fittings and materials, as they usually know the best places locally. There are many DIY hypermarkets and superstores such as B&Q Superstores (🖳 www.diy.com), Focus Do It All (🖳 www.focusdoitall.co.uk) and Homebase (🖳 www.homebase.co.uk), which in addition to stocking most DIY requirements usually also have a wide range of tools and machinery for hire. Most DIY stores carry a large selection of goods, keep most items in stock and have helpful staff – look out for special promotions (even if nothing appears to be on offer it's worth asking, as offers aren't always advertised). Most towns have a hardware store, handy for tools and small items, and builders' yards which are good for plumbing parts, porcelain, fireplaces and doors.

LISTED BUILDINGS

Listed buildings (see page 56) are buildings of special architectural or historic interest which are protected throughout the UK. In England, the most common listed buildings (over 90 per cent of the total) are classified as grade II and owners must obtain special permission from English Heritage (☎ 020-7973 3000, 🖳 www.english-heritage.org.uk) to make any changes. You must obtain planning permission or listed planning consent to make alterations to a listed building.

Obtain advice from the planning department of the local council or the relevant organisation (e.g. English Heritage in England) if you're planning to make changes to a listed building. Any building work must comply with building regulations – your local library should have a copy of the 'Planning Policy Guidance. Note 15', which contains (in annexe C) a detailed guide to what you can do to a listed building and the materials to use.

With a listed building you cannot even change the colour of your front door without permission and will be unlikely to be able to attach a satellite dish to the side of a listed building!

No structural changes are permitted with grade I (mostly churches and public buildings) and grade II* (star) buildings (of outstanding interest but usually in a local context). Note that in Scotland and Northern Ireland Grades I, II* and II are replaced by the grades A, B and C.

Grade I and II* buildings may be eligible for English Heritage grants for urgent major repairs, although you're extremely unlikely to get any sort of grant for a Grade II listed building. Restoration costs are exempt from VAT when the work has been granted listed building consent, although the work must not be repairs or maintenance. Grants are also available from English Heritage and the Heritage Lottery Fund to restore derelict Grade I and Grade II* properties (or install indoor sanitation) and in conservation areas to repair things as old iron railing or sash windows.

Other organisations of interest to owners of listed building are the Listed Buildings Information Service (☎ 020-7208 8221), the Listed Property Owners Club (☎ 01795-844939), Save Britain's Heritage (☎ 020-7253 3500, 💻 www.savebritainsheritage.org), The Society for the Protection of Ancient Buildings (☎ 020-7377 1644, 💻 www.spab.org.uk) the Georgian Group (☎ 020-7529 8920, 💻 www.georgiangroup.org.uk) and the Victorian Society (☎ 020-8994 1019, 💻 www.victorian-society.org.uk). For more information about listed buildings, see page 202.

7.

LETTING

Property has always been a good long-term investment, particularly when the stock market has been in a slump and interest rates are at an all-time low, as in the last few years. The proliferation of buy to let mortgages in recent years has encouraged many more people to buy investment property, which has helped fuel the booming UK property market, particularly in London. Many people now invest in property as an alternative to a pension (or to supplement a pension), as it provides both capital growth and a regular income – even a low yield of 5 per cent per annum is better than a pension fund! Note, however, that buying property for investment should be seen as a medium to long-term investment, say a minimum of 10 to 15 years. There was a high demand for rental property in autumn 2003, although rents fell dramatically in London and the south-east as people flocked to invest in property rather than save money in pension schemes. This lead to a glut of rental properties that drove down rents as owners competed to let their properties.

Some people run courses in how to get rich by playing the property market, although the information you need is widely available for free and nobody will tell you exactly which properties to buy or where! Many 'amateur' investors have built up substantial property portfolios in the last few decades buying property to let.

This chapter includes both buying to let (below) – where a property is purchased for letting and is let permanently for periods of 6 to 12 months as a condition of the mortgage – and short-term holiday lets (see page 218), usually for a period of weeks or months (but usually for less than six months). Short lets (e.g. in cities and resorts) can generate up to 30 per cent more rent than long-term lets, but are harder to secure.

See also **Buying For Investment** on page 70.

Note that if you decide to let a property, whether short-term (e.g. holiday lets) or long-term, you must obtain the consent of your lender.

BUYING TO LET

Since the introduction of the 1988 Housing Act and the amendments in the 1996 Housing Act, landlords have had far greater security when letting their properties. These acts introduced two new kinds of tenancy, assured and assured shorthold, whereby the length of the tenancy and an open market rent are agreed at the outset, and landlords have a guaranteed right in law to possession of their property at the end of the fixed term. These acts had a positive effect on revitalising the private rental sector, which had previously been in a slump for decades.

In recent years buy to let mortgages have revolutionised the letting market and it has been an excellent investment for tens of thousands of people. In 1998 there were under 30,000 buy to let mortgages, while in the first six months of 2003 there were over 250,000. Many new developments are snapped up by large investors who sell them on to smaller investors. Some buy to let properties are sold with tenants in situ which can be an advantage provided they're good tenants paying a market rent.

Most people make a yield of between 5 and 10 per cent (the gross profit on your capital investment after all expenses, but before taxes) and capital growth (the value of the property) has been up to 25 per cent or more a year in many areas. It's a win-win investment – no other investment comes close – and is apparently risk-free! On the down side, buy to let investors have contributed to spiralling property prices in recent years, which has led to a dearth of first-time buyers (who cannot afford to buy) that is threatening the whole property market.

SURVIVAL TIP
Although it seems like the dream investment, don't be tempted to dump your pension and rush into the buy to let market without giving it serious thought!

Where To Buy

When buying property to let – whether it's a buy to let or a holiday home – location is critical! It's important to buy the right property in the right area to maximise both rental income and capital growth. Ask advice from letting agents who will generally offer unbiased advice as they have no hidden agenda (unlike an estate agent trying to sell to you). Your best chance of maximising your profit is to buy a property that needs complete renovation, do it up yourself and let it for a good rent. Buying a large house and converting it to apartments can also pay handsomely. If income rather than capital growth is your major concern, you may be better off buying in an unfashionable area where prices are low and yields are high, but capital growth is relatively low.

The buy to let phenomenon has meant that many towns and city suburbs have become saturated with property to let, which has put pressure on landlords to lower rents – you need to do your sums very carefully and choose the location carefully. Before buying a property to let, it's important to identify your ideal tenant and to ensure that there's a demand for rental properties in the area where you plan to buy. You must be emotionally detached (you won't be living there) and not buy something that appeals to you, but to your target market. Wherever you buy, it must usually be close to public transport (e.g. a railway station or a tube station in London) and in an area of high employment.

You can get good yields letting to students sharing a property, but you will need to put up with a lot of problems; they will almost certainly ruin the decoration and may even trash the place! Most landlords prefer to let to a business or to professionals with steady jobs. Up-market homes near foreign and international schools command high rents from itinerant foreigners who pay vast rents (actually their employers usually pay the rent). Properties close to large office blocks, factories, hospitals and universities also have good letting potential. The corporate rental market has traditionally been a lucrative sector of the market, particularly in London, although there has been a big turndown in the corporate rental market since 2001. Corporate lets represent some 30 per cent of the London markets, but only 6 to 12 per cent of regional markets.

Books such as, *Property Hotspots: Where and How to Buy and Let Property for Profit*, that profess to tell you where and what to buy need to be taken with a pinch of salt, as areas change rapidly from hot to cold and no book can keep up. Plus, of course, everyone else who buys the book will also know the best areas, which means that the information will be worth little or nothing almost as soon as it's published. It's probably better to keep your eyes and ears open and to follow the trends highlighted in newspaper and magazine articles, which are more up to date. Note that in autumn 2003, the top ten property hotspots (where property prices had risen fastest in the previous year) were all outside the south of England, i.e. in the north of England, Wales or Scotland.

What To Buy

One-bedroom apartments (but not studios) are the easiest to rent in cities (where most renters are singles), while large houses are best in country areas. Houses are better than apartments for long-term tenants – the average stay of a tenant in an apartment is around six months to a year, whereas in a house it's around two and a half years. Don't buy a very expensive property as the rent won't cover the costs. Buying resale rather than new usually provides better value – glossy new developments are expensive and the extra cost isn't usually reflected in the rent you can charge (although capital growth may be higher).

If you're buying an apartment off-plan, buy one that will appeal to both owner-occupiers and renters, so that on completion you have the option to sell it at a profit or let it. Be wary of investing in a development where most owners are investors – a 60-40 ratio of owner-occupiers to tenants is considered the best split. A good apartment in a city (where competition is usually fierce) must usually be modern (or with all mod cons), well equipped, well decorated and very well furnished (see below) to command a high rent. Rooms should be well-proportioned (big enough for 'proper' furniture), well-lit and preferably south facing. Low-maintenance gardens with paved surfaces or decking rather than lawns and flowerbeds are best (if you've got a large garden you will need to employ a gardener).

SURVIVAL TIP

Avoid pokey apartments and houses with tiny living rooms and 'joke' box rooms masquerading as bedrooms. Make sure that it has the right attributes such as being a good area, close to public transport and major roads, off-road parking (preferably a lock-up garage), a peaceful and secure location, and close to amenities such as shops, restaurants, pubs, parks and sports facilities.

Buy (or create) a property with a killer selling point such as a vast lounge/dining room, a good-sized terrace, a garage or off-road parking (e.g. in a city where it's expensive or non-existent!), great views, a beautiful garden (could be shared), a stunning kitchen or a fabulous bathroom with a Jacuzzi and power shower. It's advisable to make your place look different (i.e. desirable), as there are far too many places that look exactly the same.

LETTING TO BUY

In recent years an increasing number of people have been letting (rather than selling) their family home in order to fund their next move; let to buy rather than buy to let. If you plan to do this you must ensure that your home meets the necessary requirements for letting (see below) and the rent should be at least 130 per cent of your mortgage payments. You should consider re-mortgaging to free equity for a deposit on your next home.

Note that capital gains tax is payable when you sell if you've let a property for three years.

YIELD

The yield on a property is the gross profit on your capital investment (after the deduction of expenses, but before tax), which varies depending on how much you pay for a property and the rent. Generally the cheaper the property the higher the yield. For example, if you buy a property for £100,000 and let it for £700 per month (gross income £8,400 a year), your gross yield is 8.4 per cent (8,400 divided by 200,000 = 0.084 x 100). If you buy a property for £200,000 and let it for £1,200 a month (£14,400 a year) your gross yield is 7.2 per cent. This is a simple example to illustrate that yields are usually higher on cheaper properties and it doesn't take into account your costs.

Costs may include purchase costs, furniture and furnishings, service charges, ground rent, insurance, wear and tear, agent's fees, cleaning, maintenance and decorating, void periods, council tax (when a property is empty), etc. – but not your mortgage payments. These must to be deducted from your gross income in order to calculate your net income and net yield. For example, if you buy a £200,000 property, earn £15,000 a year in rent and have costs of £5,000, you've a net income of £10,000. Your net yield is therefore £10,000 divided by £200,000 = 0.05 x 100 = 5 per cent – but bear in mind that you still have to pay tax on your net income! Note that you should always use the current market value of a property to calculate the yield.

SURVIVAL TIP

It's important that you know the net yield you can expect to earn before embarking on a buy to let scheme.

Yields vary and can be less than 5 per cent and as high as 15 per cent or more. In 2003 yields were historically very low with returns in London in autumn 2003 between 3.5 and 7 per cent, while northern cities had higher yields of up to 10 per cent (the average is around 5 per cent). Rents have fallen in the last few years while house prices have risen, although by mid-2003 rents had levelled off in most areas. (Due to the low rental returns on residential property, some professional investors were turning to commercial property in 2003.) Buying to let isn't a good idea if your maximum rent will barely cover your mortgage and you've little other disposable income and are relying on 100 per cent occupancy. However, if you buy off-plan and rental returns aren't sufficient to pay your mortgage, you can usually sell quickly and make a nice profit.

Take care - with the property market stagnating in the south of England (particularly London), many people were struggling to attract tenants in mid-2003 and house prices were flat or fell in most of London in 2003.

FINANCE

Buy to let mortgages (see page 148) are relatively easy to obtain from a large number of lenders, with interest rates typically around 1 per cent higher than for standard residential loans. Fixed-rate, interest-only mortgages are favoured by many buy to let investors, which allows you to keep the rent competitive while watching the capital value grow. Most lenders will lend a maximum of 75 or 80 per cent of the value of a property, although it's advisable not to borrow more than 50 to 60 per cent of the value. It's important not to be too heavily geared by having too high a mortgage - and you will also need a cash reserve for maintenance, repairs and void periods. Some experts recommend that you don't buy if you need to rely solely on rental income to pay your mortgage, although this depends on your mortgage payments.

SETTING THE RENT

You must set a realistic rent that compares with similar properties in the area and that will also give you a decent return on your investment. You can check the rents of similar properties in local newspapers (e.g. *Loot* in London - see page 261 - which includes a table of rental rates by area). Alternatively you can use a letting agent (see below) to calculate the right price band and find your own tenants or market a property yourself. However, you must be flexible and be prepared to lower the rent (particularly for an excellent long-term tenant) or pay higher fees to an agent when tenants are thin on the ground.

Bear in mind that the last resort, you may have to sell if you cannot find a tenant!

If you've got a long let (minimum 12 months) and a desirable property in a good area, you may be able to budget for 45 to 50 weeks income a year, although in an area that's saturated with rental properties you may have to make do with 40 weeks or less. Note that it's often better to lower the rent than have a property empty for a number of weeks. For example, if your rent is £800 per month and a property is empty for two months, it would have been better to reduce the rent to £700 per month for a quick let. This would bring in £8,400 for 12 months (12 x £700) compared with £8,000 for 10 months (10 x £800) – and you'd have spared yourself the agony of not having a tenant! A void of one month is equivalent to a loss of 8.3 per cent of one year's rent. In general, you're rental income should cover your mortgage repayments plus another 25 to 50 per cent. You must pay tax on your rental income, but can deduct mortgage repayments and costs before paying tax on the profits.

Tenants pay one month's rent in advance plus a deposit equal to four to six weeks' rent, which is held by the letting agent (if applicable) in a bonded account – not by the landlord. You can also get a solicitor to hold the deposit and have the inventory prepared by an inventory clerk and signed by the tenant, which should prevent any disputes. Wear and tear is taken into consideration, but breakages, damage and missing items are deducted from the deposit when a tenancy ends. Some landlords charge up front for wear and tear, although this simply invites tenants to trash the place.

A property must be spotless when vacated and the contract may stipulate that it must be professionally cleaned. Some landlords are prone to use tenants' deposits to refurbish their properties, while claiming that tenants left the place in a mess – even a third party holding the deposit doesn't protect tenants as the deposit holder simply accepts what the landlord tells him (unless you get a solicitor to hold the deposit)! Tenants also usually pay for utility services such as gas, electricity, water, telephone, TV licence, cable TV service and council tax.

EXPENSES

When calculating your budget, don't forget to take into account all your costs such as mortgage repayments, agency and management fees, service charges (leasehold apartment), stamp duty, land registry fees, council tax (when a property is empty), cleaning, gas safety certificate, redecorating, repairs, replacing equipment and furniture, inventory fee, advertising and tax on any profit.

FURNISHED OR UNFURNISHED

Discuss with an agent whether you should let a property furnished or unfurnished. Most properties are let furnished, although the gap is narrowing. In cities (where the majority are renters) people generally want furnished properties, particularly luxury apartments, while in rural areas unfurnished houses are more common. It also depends on the standard – at the lower end of the market the demand is generally for furnished properties, while at the top end it's for unfurnished. Many landlords prefer to let properties furnished as the property looks better (even bigger) and they can charge a slightly higher rent, although many are (wisely) flexible and will let a property furnished, unfurnished or even part-furnished.

Furnishings must be appropriate for your target tenants, whether they be students, single professionals, a family or the corporate market. If you want to market a property at the top end of the market it must be beautifully, even luxuriously, furnished and equipped. This includes top-of-the-range finishes, bed linen, deluxe fully-equipped kitchen (dishwasher, microwave, etc.), television, DVD player, cable or satellite TV, power shower, off-road parking and resident concierge (caretaker, porter, gardener or maid service). The property should be fresh, light, spacious and be perfectly decorated in neutral colours (white, cream, etc.), with modern, hard-wearing furniture and a well-presented garden. You need to provide quality appliances, but shouldn't go overboard with chic design or kitchen gadgets (most people don't want them).

Carpets in neutral colours and resilient materials are best and must be regularly cleaned, while sofas and armchairs should have machine-washable covers (two sets). Don't install cheap or coloured bathroom suites (white is best) and don't carpet bathroom floors (use tiles, cork or vinyl). There should be no clutter and only a few pictures and ornaments as most tenants will want to provide their own. Don't buy second-hand furniture unless you're letting to students (if you do, make sure that it meets fire regulations – see page 227), don't over-clutter the kitchen and keep spare electrical items handy such as a kettle or toaster. Other things to avoid are cheap handles, knobs, curtain rails or anything else that will get a lot of hard use, and don't use workmen (such as electricians and plumbers) who haven't been highly recommended. The furniture and décor must be spotless and in excellent condition each time a property is let. Replace bedding and mattresses (which should be turned between tenants) frequently and bin appliances that are well past their best.

Use the 'house doctor' approach (see page 238) when deciding how to furnish and present a property. If you plan to let a luxury property for a premium rent you may wish to call in professional 'house doctors' such as Final Touch (☎ 020-7228 4233, 💻 www.thefinaltouch.co.uk), although their fees can be very high (if they do a complete makeover you can reckon on a fee of from £3,000 to £6,000 for an average two-bedroom property!). However, any letting agent should be able to tell you what's required or you can watch the *House Doctor* TV programme a few times or buy *The House Doctor* book (see **Appendix B**).

You will need an inventory for a furnished apartment, which must be taken before a tenant moves in and after he has left. The inventory will be drawn up by your management company (see below) if you have one.

FINDING TENANTS

It may pay you to market your own property and vet clients yourself. An agent may be marketing a glut of properties in your area, whereby you won't be competing with all the other properties on the agent's books. You must have somewhere to advertise (such as *Loot* – see page 261 – or a local newspaper) and time to show clients around. You will need to do a good selling job and also sell transport, restaurants, supermarkets, specialists shops (a superb deli is a winner), general shops, gyms, sports facilities, etc. It's best to avoid pets (which may be prohibited in some apartment blocks by the managing agents), young children and smokers – although tenants may lie about being smokers and there's little you can do about it.

The quality of tenants is paramount and long-term tenants are much better than short-term. Good tenants are too precious to be mistreated or taken for granted and model tenants need to be pampered. (If a good prospective tenant is wavering, it may help to throw in an extra appliance or upgrade to snare him.) Don't scrimp on getting things repaired or providing equipment, as if you lose a tenant through petty meanness you could lose thousands of pounds in rent. In some areas you may be able to let to the local council, who will guarantee your rent (usually lower than in the private sector) for an agreed period, whether or not there are any tenants, and return the property in good order. Note that without any voids, you can actually earn more with council tenants. Most experienced landlords advise newcomers to use a letting agent (see below) to manage a property, even when they find their own tenants.

Checking References

The first things you need to confirm are their identity, where they work, whether they have sufficient income to pay the rent (ask to see bank statements) and their previous address.

It's vital to check a prospective tenant's references carefully, as the number of nightmare tenants has risen in recent years as owners have become more desperate to let their properties.

References usually include one from a bank or accountant to establish a prospective tenant's financial standing, an employer's reference and a character reference, which can be from a previous landlord, employer or solicitor. Don't be taken in by a prospective tenant's appearance as even the most presentable and seemingly trustworthy people can prove to be a nightmare once you hand over the keys. The following organisations can help you check references:

- **Companies House** (www.companieshouse.gov.uk/info) – to check out a limited company that a prospective tenant claims to work for (ensure that they're a bona fide company with a good reputation).
- **192.com** (www.192.com) – if the prospective tenant doesn't work for a limited company, you can check on 192.com whether his employer exists and whether the tenant and his previous landlord are on the electoral roll. This is a subscription service, but new users can make limited free searches.
- **Land Registry** (www.landreg.gov.uk) – for a fee of £2, the Land Registry can confirm who owns the previous house where a prospective tenant claimed to live.
- **Experian** (www.tenantverifier.com) – this is a credit reference agency that provides an online credit check for £9.89.
- **Caddell's** (www.caddells.co.uk) – this company provides a similar service to Experian, but will make more in-depth checks for a fee of £35.
- **Homelet** (www.homeletuk.com) – make a standard credit check for a fee of £15 and, provided the prospective tenant has a clean record, will provide legal expenses insurance.
- **Court Service** (www.courtservice.gov.uk/mcol/index.htm) – if things go wrong you can sue the tenant for rent owed via the online Court Service.
- **Landlord Action** (020-7906 3838, www.landlordaction.co.uk) – for an initial fee of £98 plus VAT, Landlord Action will start proceeding against a bad tenant and follow it up with court action and bailiffs if necessary.
- **Small Landlords Association** (020-7828 2445, www.landlords.org.uk) – SLA protects and promotes the interests of private landlords operating in the private rented sector.

It's better to be safe than sorry, as if you end up with a tenant from hell who pays nothing after the initial rent and deposit, he will take months to evict and it may end up costing you thousands of pounds.

If a tenant stops paying the rent or becomes a problem you should seek immediate legal advice, as it can take three months or longer to evict someone. You can insure against bad tenants by signing up to a 'landlords legal protection scheme' (most agents offer this) which covers the cost of legal expenses if you need to evict or take legal proceedings against a tenant, and it may also cover you for loss of rent.

LETTING AGENTS

You can use a letting agent to find tenants and manage a property, which is advisable if you work and have little spare time (or don't live close to where your rental property is situated). A letting agent will give your property the once over and tell you what you need to do in order to let it for a good rent. An agent will do the following:

- Advise you on the open market rent;
- Market the property;
- Arrange viewings and vet clients (you can reserve the right to approve tenants);
- Check references;
- Compile an inventory;
- Prepare the tenancy agreement;
- Collect and hold the deposit;
- Notify service companies (electricity, gas, water, telephone);
- Pay bills (e.g. ground rent, insurance premiums, service charges);
- Authorise emergency repairs and collect the rent;
- Carry out regular inspections (usually once every six months);
- Deal with tenants' problems;
- Arrange maintenance, repairs, the replacement of damaged or faulty items and obtain estimates for redecoration or major work;
- Deal with insurance claims;
- Arrange cleaning (between lets) and gardening.

You can place a property with more than one letting agent when looking for a tenant. Most agents charge a 10 to 12 per cent introduction fee for finding clients, which increases to 15 per cent or more if they also manage a property (fees are tax deductible).

The introduction fee may remain the same for the period of the lease, whether it's six months or a number of years, although some agents lower it after the first year.

The landlord usually pays for drawing up the rental agreement (which costs from around £60 plus VAT) and the tenant pays for the inventory (from around £40 plus VAT depending on its size). If you use an agent, make sure that you provide a contingency fund (say £1,000) to cover any problems and that he has a telephone number where you can be contacted.

There are a wide choice of agents which vary from small one-office outfits to vast chains such as Foxtons (☎ 0800-138 6060, 💻 www.foxtons.co.uk), who dominate the market in London, and Prime Location (💻 www.primelocation.co.uk). The best way to find an agent is via a personal recommendation, failing which you can check the yellow pages or use the Internet. Choose an agent who's a member of the Association of Rental and Letting Agents (☎ 0845-345 5752, 💻 www.arla.co.uk), whose members are bonded and fully insured and have a professional code of conduct.

Note that letting agents' employees work mostly on commission and they can be relentless (pushy) in getting your business.

MANAGING YOUR OWN PROPERTY

You can save money by managing your own property, but be warned, it can be a nightmare and may be impossible if you don't live nearby.

Managing your own property isn't recommended for most people, who simply aren't up to it, and it isn't usually worth the hassle.

However, you will save around 5 to 10 per cent on management fees and will know exactly what's happening with your property - something an agent may not know or tell you. If you're managing a property yourself you will need to be well organised and have a team of servicemen, including a plumber, electrician, handyman, decorator, gardener (possibly), window cleaner and a cleaner. You also need to keep records of such things as when your gas safety certificate needs renewing or your inventory updating.

There are a number of associations for private landlords, including the National Federation of Residential Landlords (☎ 0845-456 0357, 💻 www.help4landlords.org), the Southern Private Landlords' Association (☎ 01273-600847, 💻 www.spla.co.uk) and the Small Landlords' Association (☎ 020-7828 2445, 💻 www.landlords.org.uk).

SHORT-TERM HOLIDAY LETS

Many people planning to buy a second or holiday home are interested in owning a property that will provide them with an income to cover the running costs and help meet the mortgage payments. Note, however, that with short-term letting you're highly unlikely to meet your mortgage payments and running costs from rental income.

⚠ **Buyers who over stretch their financial resources often find themselves on the rental treadmill, constantly struggling to find sufficient income to cover their running costs and mortgage payments.**

Most experts recommend that you don't purchase a holiday home if you need to rely heavily on rental income to pay the mortgage.

⚠ **Note that burglars target second homes – the risk of burglary is three times greater in rural areas – and if you own a property that's empty for long periods you will pay much higher contents insurance. Make sure that you have adequate security and that you remove or secure all valuables when a property is unoccupied.**

Finance

Mortgages for second homes (see page 150) aren't easy to obtain as most lenders require buyers to be able to afford the repayments without the necessity of earning any rental income, and most will only lend a maximum of 75 per cent of the value of a property. It's important not to be too heavily geared by having too high a mortgage and you will also need a cash reserve for maintenance and repairs and void periods.

⚠ **Most experts recommend that you don't buy a second home if you need to rely heavily on rental income to pay your mortgage!**

Where To Buy

If you wish to let a second home, you must ensure that it's in the right location. Most holiday homes are let for no more than 20 weeks a year, mainly during summer and the Christmas/New Year and Easter periods, although you can do better in popular short-break destinations, major cities, and holiday resorts/areas. If you want year-round letting potential and high rents, you need to choose a property in or close to tourist magnets such as Bath, Brighton, Chester, Edinburgh, London, Stratford-upon-Avon, Windsor and York. Short lets can generate up to 30 per cent more rent than long-term lets, but are harder to secure. The hot spots for traditional holiday homes are the West Country (Cornwall, Devon, Dorset, Somerset), East Anglia (Norfolk Broads), the Cotswolds and the Lake District. In recent years buyers have been looking at cheaper alternatives such as west Wales and the Norfolk and Yorkshire coasts, although prices have risen considerably everywhere in the last five years (in some areas they've doubled in less than two years!).

To maximise rental income, a property should be located as close as possible to main attractions, a major city and/or a beach, be suitably furnished and professionally managed. If there are important local events such as international sports events (e.g. Wimbledon), you may be able to earn a small fortune for a few weeks of the year. A swimming pool is a big advantage in summer, when properties with pools are much easier to let, and you can charge a higher rent for a property with a pool (you may also be able to extend the letting season by installing a heated or indoor pool).

What To Buy

The best property to buy for holiday letting is usually a cottage with two bedrooms that sleeps four or five with a sofa bed. A photogenic, old property with lots of character is usually best, with access to the coast, in a picturesque country location or near a lake, river (with fishing) or popular golf course (etc.). A property needs to be clean, have central heating, decent furniture and ideally should have a special features such as a hot tub, Jacuzzi or an indoor heated swimming pool.

Rents

Rental rates vary considerably depending on the time of the year, area, size and quality of a property. They tend to be stable and to increase in line with inflation (around 2.5 per cent a year). The rent for a typical two-bedroom property varies from around £500 to £700 per week in high season, while out of season rents fall to as low as £200 per week. At the other extreme, a luxury property in a popular area with a pool and accommodation for 8 to 12 can be let for up to £2,000 a week in the high season, which generally includes the months of July and August. The mid season usually comprises May, June and September (and possibly Easter), when rents are around 25 to 30 per cent lower than the high season; the rest of the year is the low season.

If you live in major city or a popular tourist destination you will have year-round letting potential and will be able to let a (serviced) apartment by the day at a higher rate. There are generally no seasonal variations in rent in a major city. High quality properties can expect to get more lettings than others. If you've got an average two-bedroom property sleeping four to six, you shouldn't expect to make more than £5,000 to £6,000 a year. Bear in mind that tax must be paid on rental income (see **Taxation Of Property Income** on page 228).

It may be possible to increase rental income outside the high season by offering special interest or package holidays, which can be organised in conjunction with other local businesses in order to broaden the appeal and cater for larger parties. These may include activity holidays such as golf, tennis, cycling or hiking; cooking and local gastronomy; and arts and crafts such as painting, sculpture, photography and writing courses. You don't need to be an expert or conduct courses yourself, but can employ someone to do it for you.

Season

It's difficult to make much money from self-catering holiday accommodation in most areas, as the season is too short. Most holiday homes are let for no more than 20 weeks a year, mainly during summer and the Christmas/New Year period. However, you can do better in popular short-break destinations, major cities and holiday resorts and areas (such as the Lake District). Properties in or close to tourist magnets such as Bath, Edinburgh and York tend to attract the highest rents and attract tenants year-round (like most city properties). If you live in a popular tourist destination you may have year-round letting potential and will be able to let a (serviced) property by the day. You may be able to let long-term during the winter, although central heating is essential.

Furniture & Furnishings

If you let a holiday property, don't fill it with expensive furnishings or valuable personal belongings. While theft is rare, items will certainly get damaged or broken over a period of time. When furnishing a property for letting, you should choose hard wearing, dark coloured carpets (which won't show the stains), and buy durable furniture and furnishings that can be washed rather than dry-cleaned. Simple inexpensive furniture is best in a modest property, as it will need to stand up to hard wear. Small one or two-bedroom properties usually have a settee in the living room which converts into a double bed. Properties should be well equipped with cooking utensils, crockery and cutlery, and it's also advisable to provide bed linen and towels. You may also need a cot and high chair for young children. Depending on the price and quality of a property, your guests may also expect central heating, a washing machine, dishwasher, microwave, covered parking, a barbecue and garden furniture. Some owners provide bicycles, and badminton and table tennis equipment.

Keys

You will need several sets of spare keys, which will inevitably get lost at some time. If you employ a management company, their address should be on the key fob and not the address of the house. If you let a home yourself, you can use a 'keyfinder' service, whereby lost keys can be returned to the keyfinder company by anyone finding them. You should ensure that 'lost' keys are returned, otherwise you may have to change the locks (in any case it's advisable to change the external locks periodically if you let a home). You don't need to provide clients with keys to all external doors, only the front door (the others can be labelled and left in the property). If you arrange your own lets, you can send keys to clients or they can be collected from a local caretaker. It's also possible to install a security key-pad entry system.

LETTING AGENTS

If you're letting a holiday home, the most important decision is whether to let it yourself or use a letting agent (or agents). If you don't have much spare time you're better off using an agent, who will take care of everything and save you the time and expense of advertising and finding clients. Letting agents charge around 10 per cent for letting only and between 15 and 20 per cent for full management (some specialist companies may charge more, some of which can usually be recouped through higher rents). Most agents charge extra for drawing up a tenancy agreement, inventories and looking after a property between lets. Management contracts usually run for a year.

If you want your property to appear in an agent's catalogue, you must contact them by the summer of the previous year (the deadline is usually September). Note that although agents may fall over themselves to take on luxury properties, in the most popular areas the leading agents turn down as many properties as they accept. Most agents don't permit owners to use a property during the peak letting season (July and August) and may also restrict your use at other times.

Take care when selecting a letting agent and make sure that your income is kept in a bonded (escrow) account and paid regularly, or even better, choose an agent with a bonding scheme who pays you the rent **before** the arrival of guests (some do). It's essential to employ an efficient, reliable and honest company, preferably long-established. Always ask a management company to substantiate rental income claims and occupancy rates by showing you examples of actual income received from other properties. Other things to ask a letting agent include:

- How do they market properties?
- Do they have tie-ins with holiday and travel companies?
- How many weeks the property is likely to be let each year?
- When is letting income paid?
- What extras fees are levied and what for?
- Do they provide detailed accounts of income and expenses (ask to see samples)?
- Who they let to (what nationalities, families, young children, singles, smokers, people with pets, etc.)?
- Are you free to let the property yourself (e.g. to friends and family) and use it when you wish?

A management company's services should include:

- Arranging routine and emergency repairs;
- Routine maintenance of house and garden, including lawn cutting and pool cleaning;
- Cleaning and linen change between lets;
- Advising guests on the use of equipment;
- Providing guest information and advice (24-hours in the case of emergencies);
- Reading meters (if utilities are charged as an extra).

Agents may also provide someone to meet and greet clients, hand over the keys and check that everything is in order. The actual services provided usually depend on whether a property is a basic cottage or apartment or a luxury mansion costing thousands of pounds a week. A letting agent's representative should also make periodic checks when a property is empty to ensure that it's secure and that everything is in order.

It's best to let a holiday home using a specialist holiday rental company such as Cottages Direct (☎ 01305-250151, 🖳 www.cottagesdirect.com), Cottages 4 You (☎ 08700-782100, 🖳 www.cottages4you.co.uk), English Country Cottages (☎ 08700-781100, 🖳 www.english-country-cottages.co.uk), Hoseasons Holidays (☎ 0800-754657, 🖳 www.hoseasons.co.uk), Landmark Trust (☎ 01628-825920, 🖳 www.landmarktrust.co.uk), National Trust Holiday Cottages (☎ 01225-791199, 🖳 www.nationaltrustcottages.co.uk), Rural Retreats (☎ 01386-701277, 🖳 www.ruralretreats.co.uk) and Vivat Trust (☎ 0845-090 0194, 🖳 www.vivat.org.uk). Agents' commission is usually between 20 and 35 per cent of the rental for letting and management. You can obtain catalogues from these and other agents from travel agents and also look them up on the Internet.

DOING YOUR OWN LETTING

Some owners prefer to let a property to family, friends, colleagues and acquaintances, which allows them more control (and hopefully the property will be better looked after). In fact, the best way to get a high volume of lets is usually to do it yourself, although many owners use a letting agency in addition to doing their own lets. If you wish to do your own letting there's a wide range of newspapers and magazines in which you can advertise, including *Dalton's Weekly* and newspapers such as the *Sunday Times* and *Sunday Telegraph*. You will need to experiment to find the best publications and days of the week or months to advertise. You can also advertise your property with local tourist boards, who will inspect it and give it a grading.

There are also a number of companies that produce holiday accommodation magazines (sold by newsagents such as WH Smith), including *Country Holidays* (☎ 0870-781200, 🖳 www.country-holidays.co.uk), *Holiday Cottages Magazine* (☎ 01448-274447, 🖳 www.holidaycottages.cc) and *Stilwell's Independent Country Cottages* (☎ 01305-250151, 🖳 www.stillwell.co.uk). You pay an annual fee to have your property included in magazines and handle enquiries and bookings yourself, thus saving on agents' fees.

You pay for the advertisement but handle bookings yourself. Local tourist offices can put you in touch with local letting agents. You can also advertise among friends and colleagues, in company and club magazines (which may even be free), and on notice boards in company offices, stores and shopping centres. The more marketing you do, the more income you're likely to earn. It also pays to work with other local people in the same business and send surplus guests to competitors (they will usually reciprocate). It isn't necessary to just advertise locally or stick to the UK and you can also extend your marketing abroad or advertise via the Internet (see below). It's necessary to have a telephone answering machine and a fax machine.

You can get an idea of the rent you should charge, by simply ringing a few agents and asking them what it would cost to rent a property such as yours at the time of year you plan to let. They're likely to quote the highest possible rent you can charge. You should also check the advertisements in newspapers and magazines. Set a realistic rent as there's a lot of competition. Add a returnable deposit (£100 or £200) as security against loss of keys and breakages. A deposit should be refundable up to six weeks before a booking. You will need a simple agreement form that includes the dates of arrival and departure and approximate times. If you plan to let to non-English speaking clients you will need a letting agreement in other languages. You will also need to decide whether you want to let to smokers or accept pets or young children (some people don't let to families with children under five years of age due to the risks of bed-wetting).

If you want to impress your guests, you may wish to arrange for fresh flowers, fruit, a bottle of wine and a grocery pack to greet them on their arrival. It's little touches like this that ensure repeat business and recommendations. If you go 'the extra mile' it will pay off in recommendations and you may find that you rarely need to advertise after your first year or two in business. Many people return to the same property each year and you should do an annual mail-shot to previous clients and send them some brochures.

SURVIVAL TIP
Word-of-mouth advertising is the cheapest and always the best!

Leaflets

If you don't have a website (see below) containing photographs and comprehensive information, you should produce a coloured brochure. This should contain external/internal pictures, comprehensive details, the exact location, local attractions and details of how to get there (with a map). You should enclose a stamped addressed envelope when sending out leaflets and follow up within a week if you don't hear anything. It's necessary to make a home look as attractive as possible in a brochure without distorting the facts or misrepresentation - advertise honestly and don't over-sell your property.

Internet

Advertising on the Internet is an increasingly popular option for property owners, particularly as a personalised website is an excellent advertisement and can include photographs, brochures, booking forms and maps of the area, as well as comprehensive information about your property. You can also provide information about flights, ferries, car rental, local attractions, sports facilities and links to other useful websites. A good website should be easy to navigate (don't include complicated page links or indexes) and must include contact details, preferably via email. It's also advisable to subscribe to a company that will submit your website to all the popular search engines, such as Altavista, Google and Yahoo. You can also exchange links with other websites.

Pre-Arrival Information

After accepting a booking, you should provide guests with a pre-arrival information pack containing the following:

- A map of the local area and instructions how to find the property;
- Information about local facilities and attractions (available free from tourist offices);
- Emergency contact numbers if guests have any problems or plan to arrive late;
- The keys (if you send them) or instructions about where to collect them on arrival.

It's an advantage if you can arrange for someone to be on hand to welcome your guests when they arrive, explain how things work and deal with any special requests or minor problems.

Instructions & Local Information

You should also provide an information pack in your home for guests explaining the following:

- How things work such as kitchen appliances, TV/video, heating and air-conditioning;
- Security measures;
- What not to do and possible dangers (for example, if you allow young children and pets, you should make a point of emphasising dangers such as falling into the swimming pool);
- Local emergency numbers and health services such as a doctor, dentist and hospital/clinic;
- Emergency assistance such as a general repairman, gardener, plumber, electrician and pool maintenance (you may prefer to leave the telephone number of a local caretaker who can handle any problems);
- Recommended shops, restaurants and attractions (you can also provide a visitor's book where guests can write their comments and recommendations regarding local restaurants and attractions).

Caretaker

It's generally advisable to let a property yourself only if you live close by or have someone (e.g. a friend or family member) who can look after it for you. Otherwise you will find it essential to employ a local caretaker and you may also need to employ a gardener. You can have your caretaker prepare the house for your family and guests, in addition to looking after it when it isn't in use. It's advisable to have your caretaker check it periodically (e.g. weekly) and to give him authority to authorise routine maintenance and repairs. If you let a property yourself, your caretaker can arrange (or carry out) cleaning, linen changes, maintenance and repairs, gardening and the payment of bills. Ideally you should have someone on call seven days a week who can repair broken appliances or arrange any necessary maintenance or repairs.

Closing A Property For The Winter

If you close a property for the winter, you should turn off the water at the mains and drain all pipes, remove all the fuses (except the fuse for a dehumidifier if you leave it on while you're away), and empty the food cupboards, refrigerator/freezer and dustbins. You should also leave the interior doors and a few small windows with grills or secure shutters open to provide ventilation. Many people keep their central heating on a low setting during the winter (which can be controlled via a master thermostat) during absences to prevent freezing and pipes bursting.

Lock all the doors and shutters and secure anything of value against theft, leave it with a neighbour or remove it. Check whether any essential work is necessary before you leave and arrange for it to be done in your absence. Most importantly, leave a set of keys with a neighbour and have a caretaker check your home periodically.

Safety Requirements

Safety is paramount when letting a property and includes electrical wiring, sockets, appliances, gas appliances, smoke alarms and extinguishers, flame-retardant furniture and textiles. Your local trading standards office can provide details. A gas safety certificate is required for a gas boiler and gas appliances and costs around £50 a year (you may need to have appliances serviced before a CORGI engineer will issue the certificate). It must be renewed annually (even when the same tenant is renting a property) and your agent must keep a copy in his office. If you let a property furnished, all furniture and furnishings must comply with the Furniture and Furnishing (Fire and Safety) Regulations 1988 (emended 1989 and 1993). There are large fines (up to £5,000) and even prison sentences for non-compliance. All curtains, upholstery, sofas and mattresses must pass flammability tests and be labelled as such (so take care if you're buying second-hand furniture). It's also advisable to install smoke detectors and fire extinguishers, although they aren't compulsory in building built before 1992. Contact the Letting Centre (☎ 01395-271122, 💻 www.letlink.co.uk) for more information.

Insurance

If you let a property you must notify your insurance company (both building and contents) and must usually have special public liability insurance of at least £1 million. There are usually restrictions when a property is let or left empty for long periods and many insurance companies insist that a property is inspected regularly. If you let a property, either long or short-term, you should take out rent and legal indemnity insurance (premiums are around 3 per cent of the monthly rental), which covers the cost of legal expenses if you need to evict or take legal proceedings against a tenant and the loss of rent. There are a number of specialist insurers such as LetSure, whose policies are sold through letting agents. Europea-IMG (☎ 01403-263860) and Winter Richmond (☎ 01628-470470) offer policies for homes that are either left empty for long periods or let, and both cover accidental damage caused by tenants. Long-term tenants require their own contents insurance to cover their possessions.

TAXATION OF PROPERTY INCOME

Income tax is payable in the UK on rental income from a second home or an investment property, even if you live abroad and the money is paid there. All rental income must be declared to the tax authorities (except for the Rent-a-Room scheme - see below), whether you let a property for a few weeks to a friend or 52 weeks a year on a commercial basis. You must pay income tax on the net profits (after expenses) at your highest rate of income tax (if you pay higher rate income tax, tax is payable at 40 per cent). Before buying property, a married couple should decide whose name it will be registered in order to take advantage of personal allowances and the lower tax bands (if applicable). After personal allowances and expenses have been deducted, you may find that there's little or no tax to pay on rental income.

Deductions

You're permitted to make deductions from your income for expenses, which may include all or some of the following:

- Management and letting expenses, including inventory and tenancy agreement fees and advertising;
- Financial fees and loan interest payments;
- Repairs and maintenance to the building and fixtures (excluding improvements);
- Renewal costs for appliances and furnishings (unless wear and tear is being claimed - see below);
- Security (such as a monitored alarm system);
- Cleaning and gardening;
- Council tax;
- Buildings, contents and other insurance;
- Accountant's and book-keeping fees;
- Legal fees;
- Service charges and ground rent for an apartment;
- Bills for mains' services;
- Miscellaneous expenses such as stationery, telephone calls, and travel expenses to and from the property, e.g. when collecting rent or carrying out inspections.

You aren't permitted to claim capital costs such as the initial outlay on furniture and kitchen appliances. You should seek advice from an accountant to ensure that you're claiming everything to which you're entitled.

Furnished Lettings

If a property is let **unfurnished**, the cost of repairing or replacing fixtures and fittings is tax deductible. If a property is let **furnished**, you can claim on the 'renewals basis', where you claim for items that need to be replaced, or use an alternative method called the 'wear and tear allowance'. This allows you to claim an annual depreciation equal to 10 per cent of the net rent (i.e. less council tax, water rates, etc.), which is usually more beneficial. Under the wear and tear allowance scheme, when items such as soft furnishings are replaced no additional claim is available against tax, as this has been covered by the 10 per cent allowance. However, you can still claim the cost of renewing or repairing fixtures that are an integral part of a building. Whatever basis is chosen must be followed consistently; you cannot chop and change between the wear and tear method and the renewals allowance from year to year.

SURVIVAL TIP
The most beneficial method will depend on your rental income and should be discussed with your accountant.

Furnished Holiday Letting

The inland revenue has a special set of rules for property let as 'furnished holiday lettings'. These are defined as properties that are let for at least 70 days (ten weeks) of the year, are available to let for 140 days (20 weeks) and aren't let to the same person for more than 31 days in any period of seven months. You can offset the cost of a loan and the running costs (but not when you occupy it yourself) against your other income and if you make a loss, which is likely in the first few years, you can offset this against other income thus reducing your income tax bill. However, you must intend to make a profit in the future. Under the special rules you may also qualify for capital gains tax reliefs such as roll-over relief and retirement relief (ask you tax advisor or an Inland Revenue office for information).

Letting A Room

Homeowners can take in a lodger (i.e. someone who's treated as a member of the family) under the 'Rent-a-Room' scheme, where the first £4,250 of rent is tax-free. However, it isn't compulsory to take part in the scheme if it isn't to your advantage and you can simply declare all your letting income and claim expenses and (where applicable) capital allowances in the normal way. **Note that it's important to check that your lease or mortgage lender allows you to take in lodgers.** For more information see the Inland Revenue (IR) booklet *Letting and your home* (IR87).

Non-Resident Landlords

If you're a UK resident, tax on property income is paid on account twice a year on 1st January and 1st July, in the same way as those who are self-employed. If you're a non-resident and don't have a UK letting agent, income tax must be deducted from rental income by your tenant(s) and paid to the IR each quarter on 31st March, 30th June, 30th September and 31st December. If you've a UK letting agent you can apply to have your rental income (which must be over £100 a week) paid gross and pay tax annually in arrears. If an agent provides a full management service, you should apply to the Financial Intermediaries and Claims Office (FICO), Non-Resident Landlord (NRL) section of the IR to have your rental receipts paid gross of tax. Under the NRL scheme, this relieves the agent of the responsibility of deducting basic rate income tax at source from rental income.

The advantages of registration are that you pay your tax annually in arrears after deduction of your expenses and allowances (which helps your cash flow), and aren't required to reclaim money from the IR. **Note that if you change agents or tenants, you must re-register with FICO.** More information is provided in a booklet, *Non-resident landlords, their agents and tenants* (IR140), or you can contact FICO (Non-Residents), St. John's House, Merton Road, Bootle, Merseyside L69 9BB (☎ 0151-472 6208/9).

Landlords (including expatriate or foreign landlords) must complete an annual self-assessment tax return from April after letting commences. If applicable, the return is sent to the address given on the FICO application form, which should be a private address (preferably your UK accountant). If you don't receive a return you must apply for one, as this isn't accepted as an excuse not to file.

If you fail to file a return, your application to pay tax in arrears will be revoked by FICO and a penalty could be imposed.

Some accountants advise that you file a return even if you make a loss, as it could be offset against future tax.

The Inland Revenue (IR) also publishes a comprehensive guide to letting income, *Taxation of Rents: A Guide to Property Income* (IR150), available from tax offices. Further information and leaflets can be obtained from the IR (☎ 08459-000444, 🖳 www.ir.gov.uk).

8.

Selling Your Home

In recent years the UK property market has been booming with one in ten homes selling within a week, a third within three weeks, and three in five within ten weeks or less. However, in 2003 the market slowed, particularly in London, the south-east and the south-west. Lead times were getting longer and properties needed to be competitively priced and to offer something special to sell quickly. In mid-2003 the number of unsold properties was the highest for three years.

SURVIVAL TIP

It's crucial when selling a home to show it in its best light and to make any necessary improvements that will either help you sell it quickly and/or increase the price you can ask.

If your home doesn't sell within three to six months, it's generally either **very** badly presented, in an area that isn't in demand or over-priced (unless the market is in a slump and nothing is selling). Between March and July is usually the best time to sell a house, although if the market is buoyant anytime is good. Certain homes will always sell, even in a depressed market, for example a roomy period house with a good location and outlook is almost 'bomb-proof' as far as the general market is concerned. Having decided to sell your home, your next decision will be when to put it on the market.

See also **Chapter 6 – Home Improvements**.

WHEN TO SELL

Before offering your home for sale, you should investigate the state of the property market. For example, unless you're forced to sell, it isn't advisable during a property slump when prices are depressed or when it needs essential work doing. It may be wiser to let your home long-term and wait until the market has recovered. If you're relocating abroad for a few years, it's better to maintain a foothold in the property market and let your home rather than sell it. Selling your home at the same time as a neighbour also isn't a good idea, as too many 'for sale' boards in the street may ring alarm bells with prospective buyers. You also need to check your mortgage to make sure that you don't incur a huge redemption penalty.

Having made up your mind to sell, make absolutely certain that you're ready to sell before putting it on the market. There's nothing more frustrating for a buyer than setting his heart on a house (and paying for a survey and other fees) only for the owner to decide that he's not going to sell after all! Spring is usually the best time to sell (e.g. between January and April), although autumn can also be good. However, a good property can be sold anytime, although it may take a bit longer in mid-winter.

SURVIVAL TIP
If your home isn't selling, it generally means that there's something wrong with it, it's too expensive or your agent is useless!

It's advisable to start planning and preparing around three months in advance, including contacting estate agents, measuring rooms, taking photographs, designing brochures, advertising, etc. All this can take much longer than you think and you need to work closely with your estate agent. Agents may charge extra (in addition to their commission) for taking photographs, drawing up details and floor plans, advertising, marketing, producing a coloured brochure, putting a property on their website, providing a 'for sale' board, etc.

LEGAL MATTERS

Note that when selling a house there are certain things that you must disclose by law. For example, if you've a long-running dispute with a neighbour or there are any problems that aren't apparent, you must inform a prospective buyer. Estate agents or owners must disclose any history of flooding when selling a house. If you've made any changes without obtaining planning permission, you must also inform a prospective buyer (a survey would in any case, bring to light any illegal alterations).

PREPARATION

The secret to selling a home quickly lies in its presentation - always assuming that it's competitively priced. First impressions are vital when marketing your home and it's important to make every effort to present it in its best light and make it as attractive as possible to potential buyers. After location the most important selling point is light, which can be increased by putting in stronger light bulbs, cleaning the windows, removing the curtains and painting your home white. Simple things that may help seduce prospective buyers include the smell of fresh flowers, house plants, potpourri, scented candles, aromatherapy oils (such as lavender), furniture polish, baking bread or cakes, and the smell of fresh brewed coffee (**you can also place a few coffee beans under the grill just before viewers arrive!**). These may be well-worn clichés but they actually work – also use air-fresheners and avoid creating unpleasant smells. Ensure that a home is warm in winter and well-ventilated in summer (a home that's too hot or too cold won't seem so enticing).

You should reduce the clutter and furniture to create more space, and keep the décor and soft furnishings light and neutral – check how developers present their show homes and copy them. It may pay to invest in new interior decoration, carpets, exterior paint and landscaping.

SURVIVAL TIP

Note that when decorating a home for resale, it's important to be conservative and not to do anything radical (such as paint the walls red or orange!).

Bear in mind, however, that complete redecoration may arouse suspicions. It may also pay you to do some modernisation such as installing a new kitchen or bathroom, as these are of vital importance when selling a home. A good kitchen often sells a house and an attractive garden will help sell an indifferent home, although it isn't necessary to spend a fortune.

Although modernisation may be required to sell an old home, you shouldn't overdo it as it's easy to spend more than you could ever hope to recoup on its sale. If you're using an agent, you should ask him what you should do (or need to do) to help sell your home. If it's in poor repair this should be reflected in the asking price and if major work is needed that you cannot afford, you should obtain a quotation (or two) and offer to deduct it from the asking price. Some of the things you need to do before putting a property on the market are listed below:

- **Clear away all unnecessary clutter (and then de-clutter again!)** and remove **everything** that doesn't enhance the appearance of a room or the garden;
- De-personalise and reduce your personal and family items to the minimum such as framed photographs on walls and cupboard tops, posters and collections of knickknacks;
- **Rigorously spring clean** the house from top to bottom (including windows inside and out), taking special care that the kitchen and bathrooms are spotless;
- **Replace badly worn carpets** (or polish the floorboards) and cover or replace unsightly furniture;

- **Get rid of any animal smells** – dogs can be particularly smelly (owners are often blissfully unaware), although cats may be okay and an asset when showing to cat lovers (but don't leave litter trays on view);
- **Maximise light** by ensuring that all the light bulbs are working, open the doors (wedge them open if necessary) and windows, and turn on the lights;
- **Carry out non-essential repairs** that may put off a prospective buyer, such as repointing brickwork, replacing broken tiles, and filling and painting over cosmetic cracks in walls (but not if it means hiding a more serious problem);
- **Tidy up the décor**, e.g. touch up chipped woodwork and fix or replace loose wallpaper;
- **Finish any incomplete DIY jobs** and replace broken handles, knobs, window latches, locks, hinges and light switches;
- **Fix things** such dripping taps and make sure that everything works properly;
- **Redecorate** where necessary such as painting the front door and painting over any garish colours;
- **Camouflage unsightly radiators** by fitting radiator covers (you can buy ready-made units);
- **Spruce up the garden**, which should look as smart as the house – if necessary mow the law, trim the borders and hedges, replant barren areas and fix/paint the garden gate (etc.);
- **Change the name** – you may find that changing the name of your house will help it sell – don't call a manor a cottage or vice versa – and make sure that the name or number is prominently displayed on your door and visible from the road;
- **Have quality interior/exterior photographs taken** – or take them yourself – on a sunny day when the flowers are in bloom.

You should have all relevant papers and receipts to hand such as a copy of the deeds, warranties for major work and systems, inspections or survey reports, guarantees for appliances, planning permission certificates (e.g. for extensions), bills for electricity, gas, heating, insurance, council tax, and ground rent and service charges for an apartment. You should also have a list of all the fixtures and fittings plus anything else (appliances, furniture, garden ornaments, etc.) that's included in the price.

Things **not** to do include the following:

- Don't spend money on expensive fittings, equipment, decorative finishes, carpets and curtains;
- Don't redecorate using strong colours;
- Don't leave the house untidy or dirty;
- Don't simply stuff everything haphazardly into cupboards as prospective buyers are likely to want to look inside them (put clutter in a garage or leave it with a friend or put it in storage).

House Doctoring

Employing the 'House Doctor' principle (the term comes from the TV programme of the same name) when selling a property simply means presenting it in the best possible light in order to maximise its sales potential and price. In general you should be prepared to spend 1 or 2 per cent of the asking price to prepare a property for sale. This can easily be recouped by obtaining a quick sale or increasing the price or – where before there may have been no prospective buyers at all! However, it isn't necessary to go overboard with chic design. A new, high-tech kitchen may help sell a penthouse and is generally essential, but it may not help sell the average semi and will be a waste of money – particularly if prospective buyers don't like it. The same applies to fancy bathroom fittings. A house or apartment to let must look the part, depending on who your target buyer is. When selling to a couple, it's invariably the woman who decides what to buy and a feminine house will sell better than a masculine one (a stylish bachelor pad has only a limited market).

Kerb Appeal

First impressions are vital and a property must have kerb appeal – many would-be purchasers drive by to see whether a house appeals to them and if it doesn't they don't even bother to get out of their car! Spending lots of money improving the interior is wasted if the exterior puts most people off before they even get inside the door. Many builders and building suppliers specialise in transforming the exterior of houses and adding external character to a modern house can reap huge dividends and greatly enhance its value.

Road noise, unsightly neighbouring buildings and plots, electricity pylons, derelict cars and skips are all turnoffs and difficult or impossible to disguise; all you can do is ensure that your property is immaculate. If you've a huge satellite dish hanging off your home, you'd be advised to remove it or at least replace it with something less obtrusive. A gravel driveway (edged by bricks or stone) is relatively cheap to install and easy to maintain, while a paved driveway is a definite plus. Paint the front door (blue doors sell the most properties) and polish the letterbox and knocker. Sprucing up the front garden - relaying turf is inexpensive and has immediate impact - and installing a tub of blooming flowers on your doorstep adds immediate appeal.

Maximising Space

Floor to ceiling mirrors are a good way to make a room look twice its size and much brighter. A large mirror over a fireplace is essential and large mirrors can also be usefully employed in small kitchens and bathrooms. If the sitting/living room doesn't have a real fireplace or an attractive gas fire, it's important to create a focal point with an attractive piece of furniture. Most houses contain too much furniture and it's worth removing some of it, particular in small rooms or a small apartment. However, bear in mind that an empty room actually looks smaller and a furnished property is usually easier to sell than an empty one. If a house is empty it may be worthwhile hiring furniture (a common practice in the US), particularly to sell an up-market property. Painting walls and ceilings a pale neutral shade will also enhance the feeling of space (and light). Using the same shade and texture when decorating unifies the space and makes it seem larger and allows rooms to flow into one another.

Maximising Light

A property should have a light and bright entrance - a bright, attractive hallway is vital if you want immediate impact. Where possible, remove curtains and drapes leaving only net curtains or blinds in order to let in more light - and clean the windows thoroughly. If you cannot remove the curtains, draw them well back. Install spotlights or uplighters to illuminate dark corners and switch on the lights in dark areas (check that the bulbs are working and if it still seems dim, fit higher wattage bulbs). Painting walls and ceilings a pale neutral shade and fitting a light coloured carpet will also enhance the light (and space).

Kitchens

The kitchen is the most important room in a house when selling and can clinch or scupper a sale on its own. **Above all it must be spotless and**

uncluttered. It isn't usually worthwhile splashing out on a new kitchen to sell a home, unless it's really terrible and beyond redemption. A lot can be done to spruce up a dull kitchen, including:

- Staining or painting kitchen units;
- Replacing doors, drawer fronts and/or handles;
- Fitting new marble-effect or granite work surfaces;
- Installing good quality, second-hand appliances;
- Replacing the hob/oven if it's beyond cleaning;
- Painting the walls white or a pale shade that compliments the units;
- Replacing chipped/cracked tiles and covering a dark or old-fashioned tiled splash back with white tiles or painting it white;
- Replacing dark vinyl flooring or linoleum with light coloured vinyl, wood laminate or stone-effect vinyl flooring;
- Replacing curtains with blinds;
- New lighting (it's essential that a kitchen is brightly lit – if you've a kitchen/dining room, dimmer lights will provide both bright light for cooking and mood lighting for dining);
- Replacing some cupboards with open racks and shelves (which will also give an impression of more space).

A kitchen should be in tune with the character of the house, for example wood and an Aga for a traditional country home and modern with sleek surfaces, chrome and stainless steel for a loft-style apartment. There are also many neutral kitchen designs that look equally well in either. A large kitchen with dining area is a **huge** bonus and an added-value improvement (see below) that will easily pay for itself when selling. If you're planning to completely remodel or enlarge your kitchen, you will find that it pays to employ a kitchen designer.

Bathrooms

The bathroom is the second most important room after the kitchen and (like the kitchen) **it must be spotlessly clean.** You may need to replace obnoxious coloured (brown, blue, green, avocado, etc.) suites with a white one (as Henry Ford **didn't** say – you can have any colour provided it's white!). Go for non-designer names for the best value for money, avoid expensive showrooms and buy direct or from a small plumber's merchant. It's best to avoid fibre glass unless it's all you can afford – better to buy a second-hand porcelain suite. A huge bathroom (preferably en-suite) with a bath and separate power shower is a definite winner and can sell a house. To spruce up boring bathrooms you can:

- Remove clutter, most toiletries (or reduce to a minimum), reading material and toys;
- Install a new or second-hand bathroom suite (modern taps can dramatically improve the look of a serviceable suite) or repair chips in the bath/basin with enamel paint;
- Fit new flooring – cork or vinyl tiles are inexpensive or you can use mosaic ceramic tiles if you want an exotic look;
- Paint the walls white or a pastel shade;
- Replace gaudy tiles or paint them white and re-grout/reseal where necessary;
- Fit new curtains or blinds;
- Install a large mirror (which will make a small bathroom appear larger) and new lighting;
- Install cupboards or added storage;
- Replace a feeble shower head with a power shower attachment;
- Fit a new toilet seat (replace a brown seat with a white one) and make sure it smells and looks hygienic (blue loo);
- Buy a new shower curtain, a white cotton mats and white fluffy towels.

Make sure that you don't neglect the following:

- **Walls And Ceilings** – These are one of the easiest and cheapest things to improve – they should be painted in neutral colours such as white, cream or magnolia. Remove or disguise artex ceilings or special paint effects, which aren't popular. Expensive wallpaper doesn't add value and is a very personal statement.
- **Floors** – Carpets should be in neutral colours and in good condition. If they look worn and are a sickly colour or 'swirly' pattern they will need replacing. Fancy vinyl (which has come a long way from the '50s) and seagrass matting are good inexpensive floor coverings, while polished wooden floors are a good selling point (but may not be permitted in an apartment). Ceramic tiles, marble and stone are wonderful for kitchens.
- **Woodwork** – Touch up woodwork or repaint scruffy woodwork and replace cheap and flimsy door handles.

- **Windows** – These must be appropriate for the period and in good condition – wooden window frames may need repainting. They should be sparkling clean and not blocked by furniture or clutter – it's often worthwhile removing curtains and fitting plain blinds to maximise the light. However, good curtains can be the making of a room and highlight a beautiful window.
- **Lighting** – Subtle lighting (e.g. concealed ceiling lighting or skirting lights on stairs) can be used to highlight the finest points of a room and hide flaws. Installing a high-tech lighting system usually adds value in an up-market property and may clinch a sale. Lighting is the most important element for creating atmosphere and can be magical. To do it properly you may need to employ a lighting expert and it will be expensive.

Garden

A glorious garden will add value to your home and may be the clincher when it comes to a sale – provided a house is presentable and in good order. A neglected overgrown and unkempt garden is an immediate turnoff for buyers, most of whom attach huge importance to how well the garden has been maintained. If a garden is really bad it's worth spending money on landscaping and plants to sell an up-market property – if the size of a garden is a good selling point, it must look the part. Numerous things can be done to make a boring garden more attractive, including:

- New fencing;
- A patio, paving or decking;
- Climbing plants, hanging baskets and terracotta pots;
- New turf;
- Screens;
- A pergola;
- Garden furniture (add chairs and a table to a patio area);
- Attractive statues and other ornaments;
- A pond incorporating the sound of running water – which adds a touch of magic that can tip the scales.

ADDING VALUE

The best way to make money when selling property is not to pay too much in the first place! However, many people buy a property with a view to adding value (see page 188) through renovation or adding an extension, conservatory or loft conversion. Other examples of added value are an extra (or new) bathroom/shower room, central heating (which is a must), a new or larger kitchen, landscaped gardens (a beautiful garden can sell an indifferent house), and a garage or double garage. Adding a bedroom can increase the value of your home by up to 20 per cent, an extra bathroom by 10 per cent and a garage by 10 per cent.

Even if you don't plan to have work (such as an extension) done yourself, obtaining planning permission can increase the value of a property considerably. If a property has planning permission for an extension it can add up to 15 per cent to its value. Architect's drawings for an extension may cost £1,000 to £2,500 for an average house, but can add as much as £25,000 to its value. However, if you can afford to have the work done and wait for a sale, it may pay you to extend before putting a house on the market. If a house has a very large garden or plot of land, you could make a substantial profit by selling part of it to a developer (or neighbour) and then sell the house with a smaller garden (although you must make sure that the remaining garden isn't too small in proportion to the size of the house).

VIEWING

In most parts of the UK it takes 10 to 15 viewings before a property is sold, although this varies considerably depending on the state of the local property market. In 2003, homes were selling faster in the north of England and Scotland than in London and the south of England (in the south of England the number of viewings doubled between 2002 and 2003). **The favourite viewing day is Saturday.** It may be worthwhile holding an open day (or days) for an up-market property and renting furniture if necessary.

SURVIVAL TIP

Note that while the average viewing lasts for 20 minutes, prospective buyers tend to make their minds up in the first few minutes – so first impressions are vital.

Bear in mind when selling to a couple that it's invariably the woman who decides what to buy, so concentrate your selling efforts on the female partner! Be friendly and co-operative and answer any questions honestly – they're more likely to make an offer if they like you and think you will be a good person to do business with.

It advisable to keep pets outside when showing your home or house them with a friend (the same also applies to noisy children!).

Beware displaying too many valuables – it might also be a good idea to mention your fort Knox security and dangerous rottweiler – as some viewers may be casing the joint! Don't leave small valuables or jewellery lying around if you allow viewers to inspect a property at their leisure without close supervision (viewers should be free to wander on their own or with an agent).

Before showing a property you can enhance its ambience by doing the following:

- Put away clutter (newspapers, magazines, toys, etc.), make up the beds, empty waste bins and put down toilet seats;
- Doing a quick tidy (fluff up cushions and pillows, etc.) and vacuum rooms;
- Making sure that the kitchen and bathrooms are spotless (they can never be **too** clean);
- Turning on lights to brighten rooms and enhance dark corners;
- Brightening rooms by drawing back curtains;
- Putting fresh flowers in the living room and a bowl of fruit in the dining room or kitchen;
- Lighting a fire if it's winter or anytime when it's cold;
- Making sure that the house smells fresh and pleasant.

CHOOSING AN AGENT

Most people prefer to use an estate agent (see also **Agents** on page 39) rather than sell a home themselves, particularly when selling a second home. If you purchased a property through an agent, it's often advisable to use the same agent when selling, as he will already be familiar with it and may still have the details on file. You should take particular care when selecting an agent as they vary considerably in their professionalism, friendliness (some have a decidedly superior manner unless you look and sound like a millionaire), expertise, experience and honesty. The best way to investigate agents is by posing as a buyer (you can also get a friend to do this). It's preferable to choose an agent who's a member who's a member of a professional organisation, such as the National Association of Estate Agents (NAEA, ☎ 01926-496800, 💻 www.naea.co.uk).

You should use a local agent unless you're planning to market a property internationally – small and friendly agents generally try harder than huge impersonal chains. Most agents cover a relatively small area, so you should take care to choose one who regularly sells properties in your area and price range. You should obtain valuations from at least three agents. Ask to see a contract and details of other properties and compare them with other agents. When comparing agents' commission and other costs, make sure that you know exactly what a standard agreement includes and what any extras will cost, and obtain the agreement in writing.

Property Details

Make sure that the property description is correct in every detail, particularly the room dimensions, and ensure that all special features and positive points are listed. Include a list of local amenities and distances to shops and supermarkets, schools, local towns (if situated in the country), public transport (railway station), local attractions, etc. Have your utility bills to hand so that prospective buyers can see what they will have to pay for electricity, gas and water. You should also make it clear what's included in the price (e.g. carpets, curtains, appliances, etc.) and what's negotiable – either for an extra cost or which could be included if the price is right.

Fees

Agents fees vary considerably from around 2 to 3 per cent, depending on the agent, the area, the price of the property, the state of the local property market and the type of agreement (see below). Fees are negotiable and you should try to negotiate a lower fee, particularly when selling a desirable property. Fees in London and the south-east are generally higher than other regions, although sole agency usually includes a 'for sale' board, photographs, information brochures/leaflets (with a floor plan) and may also include some advertising (other than in the agent's window or on his website). Elsewhere all of these could cost extra, particularly advertising (e.g. in local newspapers). Fees are usually due when contracts are exchanged (or on conclusion of missives in Scotland), but you don't pay until the sale is completed.

Contracts

Before offering a property for sale, an agent must have a signed authorisation from the owner or his representative. There are the following types of agreement:

- **Sole Agency** – All agents offer this option, although it isn't always the best deal from the seller's point of view. The advantage is that fees are lower and an agent usually makes more effort to sell your property and may include 'extras' such as advertising and printing a colour brochure. Agents will try to get you to sign a contract for three to six months which you should avoid, as you may wish to change agents if he turns out to be useless. Some agents offer cash inducements to obtain the 'sole agency' rights to sell a property. The fee for sole agency is usually 2 to 2.5 per cent.

⚠ **Take care not to sign two sole agency agreements; if you do you must pay both agents' fees if one of them finds a buyer.**

- **Joint Sole Agency** – With this type of agreement you sign up with two agents only, both of whom agree to the arrangement and decide between them how they will split the commission. It is, however, rare and usually just as expensive as having multiple agency (see below) and therefore generally a waste of time. The fee for joint sole agency is usually between 2.25 to 2.75 per cent.
- **Multiple Agency** – You instruct as many agents as you like and the one who sells your property receives the commission, i.e. no sale, no fee. This is generally the best deal, as it gives you a wider audience, which may mean you receive a better price (and can therefore afford to pay a higher commission). However, marketing material is usually inferior to other options and you may need to pay for extra marketing. It pays to use more than one agent when selling to avoid dirty tricks (see page 39) – usually three is considered the maximum. The fee for multiple agency is usually 2.5 to 3 per cent.

- **Flat Fee** – Some 'property shops' charge a flat fee to sell a home, although this is non-returnable if they fail to sell it. Make sure that you know exactly what they will do for their money before paying anything. Some agents also charge a flat fee, e.g. £1,500 plus VAT (VAT at 17.5 per cent is always added to bills) for properties costing over £150,000 for a standard package, although this arrangement is rare.
- **Ready, Willing And Able** – Under this agreement you must pay an estate agent if he finds a buyer who's prepared and able to buy your property and exchange unconditional contracts (conclude unconditional missives in Scotland). Note that if you have this sort of agreement, you must pay the agent's fees if a suitable offer is made, even if you decide not to accept it.

Generally you should avoid a contract that states that fees will be payable for introducing a buyer who's 'ready, willing and able' to buy, otherwise you could be liable to pay commission if you pull out of a sale before contracts are exchanged (which can happen for a variety of reasons).

- **Sole Selling Rights** – You must avoid giving an agent sole selling rights, which means that you must pay him a fee even if you sell your home to a friend or relative. You should only pay an agent a fee if the buyer was introduced by him.

You're under no obligation to sign an agreement with an agent and you should take care before signing one. Note that you must still pay an agent's fee if you sell to someone introduced by him within a certain period (e.g. one year) of the expiry of an agreement. Check the contract and make sure that you understand what you're signing.

Total Costs

The costs when selling a property include the selling agent's commission, an agent's additional fees (advertising, marketing, etc.), solicitor's fees and a seller's pack (if applicable). You also need to budget for any work that needs to be done to prepare a property for sale and the cost of moving to your new home (if applicable).

SETTING THE PRICE

It's important to bear in mind that (like everything) property has a market price and the best way of ensuring a sale is to ask a realistic price – a property doesn't have a fixed market value and is 'worth' precisely what someone is willing to pay for it! During the recession in the early '90s many properties remained on the market for years because owners asked absurd prices and refused to acknowledge that their homes were no longer worth what they had been in the late '80s before the bottom fell out of the market. However, don't undervalue your home. In a seller's market when prices are soaring and houses are in demand, you should test the market first before accepting an offer. If you've an unusual property that's in high demand, such as a converted mill or barn or an outstanding period property, it may pay you to set a closing date and invite sealed bids or to sell it at auction (see page 123).

If your home's fairly standard for the area, you can find out its market value by comparing the prices of other similar homes on the market or those that have recently been sold. Most agents provide a free appraisal of a home's value in the hope that you will sell it through them. However, don't believe everything that they tell you as they often deliberately over-value properties simply to encourage you and obtain your business – bear in mind that valuations by different agents can vary by tens of thousands of pounds or as much as 10 or 20 per cent. After a few weeks an agent may persuade you to lower the price after you're locked into a sole agency contract! You should obtain around three valuations and pitch the asking price close to (or just above) the highest valuation or just above or below a stamp duty threshold, if applicable.

Depending on where a property is situated and the state of the local property market, you should be prepared to drop the price slightly (e.g. 5 or 10 per cent) and should set it accordingly, but you shouldn't grossly over-price it as this will deter buyers. If you're in no hurry to sell, you could price it higher than the highest valuation – and lower it later if you get little or no interest. Don't reject an offer out of hand unless it's ridiculously low, as you may be able to get a prospective buyer to raise his offer. If you're selling in a falling market and **really** want to sell, you should think long and hard before turning down an offer. If you sell – even at a reduced price – you can then rent and wait for prices to fall lower before buying. Alternatively you may be able to let a property and borrow against it to buy a new home – and sell your home later when the market has recovered.

When selling a home, you may wish to include some appliances and furnishings (such as carpets and curtains) in the sale, particularly when selling a relatively inexpensive property with modest furnishings. You could add an appropriate amount to the price to cover the value of any extras you include or alternatively you can use them as an inducement to prospective buyers.

SELLING PRIVATELY

Most property sold in the UK is sold via estate agents, with just 5 per cent sold privately. However, selling a property privately is a viable option for many people and is particularly recommended when you're selling an attractive home at a **realistic** price in a favourable market (or any home in a booming market).

⚠ **Note that selling your own home isn't for the fainthearted – it's time-consuming and a lot of work. However, it may allow you to offer it at a more appealing price, which could be an important factor if you're seeking a quick sale.**

Marketing is the key to selling your home. The first step is to get a professional looking 'For Sale' sign made showing your telephone number and display it in the garden or in a window. Do some market research into the best newspapers and magazines for advertising your property, and place an advertisement in those that look most promising. Make your advertisement short and snappy using emotive words such as beautiful, stunning, enchanting, etc. (but don't oversell it) and make it stand out by putting it in a box or bold type. If you've got the space (and can afford it) your advertisement should include:

- The location;
- Period of the property or building;
- Size and number of bedrooms;
- Number of reception rooms if it's a large house;
- Any special features or attractions (huge garden, double garage, gym, sauna, Jacuzzi, hot tub, etc.);
- Whether it's freehold or leasehold;
- The asking price;
- Your telephone number.

It may be worthwhile advertising in a specialist property magazine if you're selling a very desirable (i.e. expensive) property, such as a large period house or a penthouse. The best place to advertise include the property section of national and local newspapers and specialist newspapers such as *Dalton's Weekly* and *Loot*. *Loot* is a daily newspaper that publishes various north-west and south-east (England) editions, devoted to selling most goods and services, including property (plus rentals). Advertisements in *Loot* are free, although *Loot* also offers a special service (☎ 0870-701 7171, 💻 www.loot.com) for property sellers costing from £60 in the north-west of England or from £100 in the south-east. This includes a listing for 12 weeks in regional *Loot* newspapers, a website listing, a 'For Sale' board, and a 'home information pack'. *Loot* claims that most of the properties it advertises are sold within three weeks – it's hassle free and almost as simple as selling a car!

You could also have a leaflet printed (with colour pictures and a floor plan) extolling the virtues of your property, which you could drop into local letter boxes or have distributed with a local newspaper (many people buy a new home in the immediate vicinity of their present home). You may also need a 'fact sheet' printed if your home's vital statistics aren't included in the leaflet mentioned above and could offer a finder's fee (e.g. £500 or £1,000) to anyone finding you a buyer.

SURVIVAL TIP
Don't forget to market your home around local companies, schools and organisations, particularly if they have many itinerant or foreign employees. It may also be worthwhile holding an open house for prospective buyers.

You should have all the papers and receipts to hand such as a copy of the deeds, warranties for any work carried out, inspections or survey reports, guarantees for major systems (such as central heating) and appliances, planning permission certificates (e.g. for extensions), bills for any work carried out and utility, insurance and council tax bills. You may also wish to make a list of all fixtures and fittings plus anything else (appliances, furniture, garden ornaments, etc.) that's included in the price. You may benefit from having a survey (see page 99) done on your home, although prospective buyers may not believe that it's impartial. You need to find out as much as possible about a prospective buyer, particularly their finance (do they have cash or a mortgage approval) and whether they need to sell first (and if so, whether they already have a buyer). Be careful not to sell to someone who was introduced to you by an estate agent. When selling a home yourself, you will need to engage a solicitor or licensed conveyancer to complete the sale.

SURVIVAL TIP
If you're a single female, you should be accompanied by a friend (preferably a man) when showing the property.

With a bit of effort and practice you may make a better job of marketing your home than an agent! Unless you're in a hurry to sell, set yourself a realistic time limit for success, after which you can try an agent. Once you've found a buyer and the price has been agreed, all you need to do is contact your solicitor and let him do the rest.

SELLING VIA THE INTERNET

You may also be able to sell your own home via the Internet, although it's still in its infancy and you shouldn't rely on selling a property this way as it has a relatively poor success rate. The leading websites include House Web (💻 www.houseweb.co.uk), the Property Broker (💻 www.propertybroker.com), DIY House Sales (💻 www.diyhousesales.com), Home Pages (💻 www.homepages.co.uk), Use The Mouse (💻 www.use-the-mouse.com), Internet Homes (💻 www.internethomes.co.uk), My Property For Sale (💻 www.mypropertyforsale.co.uk) and Private House for Sale (💻 www.privatehousesforsale.co.uk). Ugly properties (💻 www.uglyproperties.com) specialise in selling vandalised and just plain ugly-looking properties. (See also **Appendix C**.) Websites charge a flat fee of around £30 to £125 (or around £300 for a virtual tour) plus VAT and they may offer various levels of service which generally include an advertisement, a number of photographs and a 'for sale' sign. Some websites claim to attract over 100,000 visitors a month and ads may remain online until a property is sold.

HOME INFORMATION PACK

To speed up the home buying process (to around six weeks in trials) and reduce the risk of gazumping, the government plans to introduce a new law requiring vendors to produce a 'home information pack' (HIP), at a cost of between £500 and £1,000, before putting a property on the market. The HIP is expected to include:

- Ownership details;
- Details of guarantee and warranties in force;

- Details of any relevant planning or listed building regulations;
- A survey report (possibly a full structural survey);
- Local authority searches;
- A draft sales contract.

Leasehold properties would also require details of the lease, service charge details, a building insurance policy and any regulations made by the landlord.

However, among the reservations voiced are fears that buyers and lenders wouldn't trust a survey commissioned by the vendor, who could bribe a surveyor to overlook certain matters (of course, no surveyor would ever accept a bribe!), and most people may still commission their own survey. Another problem is that surveyors are currently responsible only to the person who commissions a survey, and the buyer would have no come back if a major fault was discovered, which would be disastrous and could lead to costly legal disputes.

Inconclusive trials have been carried out and there was considerable doubt about whether the scheme would ever be introduced; however, in late 1993 the government announced that the HIP would become law in 2006. (Most experts agree that the government should simply introduce a deposit scheme, such as is common on the continent).

SELLING AT AUCTION

A property auctioneer (a member of the MRICS/FRICS) will advise you whether a property is suitable to sell at auction (see page 123). Usually a property must be exceptional and have broad appeal to sell for a good price at auction. Other properties commonly sold at auction are houses requiring renovation or complete restoration or properties for conversion (such as barns) with planning permission.

SWAPPING OR PART-EXCHANGING

If you're having trouble selling your home, you could try swapping it with another property, where the party with the most valuable house is paid the difference. Before going through with a swap, it's important to have a structural survey carried out on the other property and to engage a conveyancer to carry out the usual checks. Stamp duty is paid only on the higher value property and you also save on estate agent's fees. There are 'house exchange' agencies in some areas, some of which have a national list of clients.

Part-exchange is a lucrative business for developers and relieves vendors of the hassle of selling their home and paying agents' and other fees. Many developers offer a part-exchange deal when you're buying a more expensive new home – usually the property you're buying must be worth 30 per cent more than the one you're offering in part exchange.

> **SURVIVAL TIP**
> **Make sure that you receive the market price for your house (have it valued independently) and that the price of the new house hasn't been inflated.**

Most developers will knock 10 per cent off the value of your home to cover their expenses and the original valuation is also likely to be on the low side. Some even agree a price for your home and then reduce the offer a week before you're due to move, which is a form of 'gazundering' (see page 93).

> **SURVIVAL TIP**
> **Bear in mind that you may be able to negotiate a lower price if you aren't part-exchanging – like buying a new car, you usually get a better deal when you aren't trying to trade in your old one!**

CAPITAL GAINS TAX

Capital Gains Tax (CGT) is applicable whenever you sell or otherwise dispose of real estate in the UK (e.g. lease, exchange or give away) other than your principal home, although you must live in it for the whole time you own it or you could be liable for CGT.

Note that if you build a home or renovate a property and plan to sell it when the work is completed, to avoid paying CGT it must be your principal home (i.e. you cannot own another home in the UK) and you must usually occupy it for one year before selling it (there's no fixed period).

If you let part of your principal home to someone who isn't treated as a member of the family (i.e. who doesn't eat with the family or share the family rooms), you may have to pay some capital gains tax (see page 253) when you sell the property. For more information see the Inland Revenue booklet *Letting and your home* (IR87).

Second Homes Or Investment Property

If a property was acquired **before** 31st March 1982, no capital gains tax is usually payable. When you sell a second home purchased after 31st March 1982 and make a gain that's above your annual CGT allowance – £7,900 in 2003/2004 – you're liable for CGT. However, if your second home qualifies as a furnished holiday letting (see page 212) and you re-invest the proceeds of a sale in another qualifying property within three years, you can avoid CGT. If you're married, you can share ownership with your spouse and you both qualify for the annual CGT allowance. If you pay tax at the higher rate and your spouse is a basic-rate taxpayer, it makes sense for her to own a second home or the lion's share (but you need to be sure that she won't run off with the milkman).

CGT is payable at your highest rate of income tax (companies pay corporation tax at their normal rate) and liability must be included in your income tax return. However, before you're liable for CGT you can deduct any expenses incurred during the purchase and sale, plus the cost of improvements and maintenance during the period of ownership. You may also qualify for indexation allowance and/or taper relief, described below.

Indexation Allowance

This is an allowance that adjusts gains for the effects of inflation up to April 1998. The value of a property purchased after 31st March 1982 and before 1st April 1998 is adjusted for the increase in the Retail Prices Index (RPI). After 1st April 1998 a new taper relief system (see below) was introduced and this may also apply to disposals after this date. When a property is disposed of, its cost is adjusted for the increase in RPI between the date of purchase and its sale, and the adjusted cost is deducted from the net sales proceeds to arrive at the gain or loss. This calculation is termed the indexation allowance (RPI tables are provided). This is a complicated subject and you should ask a tax office or accountant for help in making the calculation.

Taper Relief

Taper relief reduces the percentage of a gain on which CGT is payable, depending on how long you've owned a property before disposing of it.

On 6th April 1998 a new taper relief system was introduced which applies to assets disposed of on or after this date:

- **Non-Business Asset** – The percentage of capital gains payable on a non-business asset reduces to 95 per cent after three years and to a maximum of 60 per cent after ten or more years.
- **Business Asset** – A property use for letting qualifies for business taper relief, which is more generous than non-business taper relief. When you've owned a property for one year, only 50 per cent of a gain is taxable and after two years, three-quarters of any gain on its sale is exempt from CGT. If your second home is classed as a 'furnished holiday letting' (see page 212) it qualifies as a business asset.

  For more information about taper relief see Inland Revenue helpsheet, *Taper Relief* (IR279).

Owners Of Two Homes

If you have two homes, living part of the year in one and part in another, you can choose (elect) which is your principal residence for capital gains tax purposes, but you must live in it some of the time (so you cannot elect a buy to let property as your principal home). It's best to choose the one on which you think you will make the largest profit as your main home. You should inform the Inland Revenue of your choice of principal home within two years of buying a second home, otherwise they may decide which property is your main home (although you can change your mind at any time afterwards).

SURVIVAL TIP

You don't pay tax for the period that a property was regarded as your principal home or for the final three years of ownership. Therefore, if you owned a property for four years and elected it as your main home for the first year, you wouldn't pay any CGT on a gain.

Your choice of main residence for capital gains tax purposes doesn't affect your choice for council tax purposes. The cost of improvements made to a property can be offset against CGT, but not repair and maintenance. An unmarried couple can legally own two 'principal' homes, whereby each claims a property as his or her main home, but if they get married only one home qualifies as a principal home (the other becomes a second home and is liable for CGT).

If you live in a home for a number of years and also let it for a number of years before selling it, the Inland Revenue looks at the total gain from the date of the purchase to the date of the sale. It then divides the gain in proportion to the years the property was used as a primary residence (which are exempt from CGT) and the years it was let (for which CGT is payable). For example, if you owned a property for ten years and let it for three of those ten years, CGT would be payable only on three tenths of any gain.

> **SURVIVAL TIP**
> **If you're liable for CGT, you should obtain advice from a tax office or an accountant, as you may be able to reduce your tax liability.**

The Inland Revenue (☎ 08459-000444, 💻 www.ir.gov.uk) publishes a number of leaflets about capital gains tax, including *Capital Gains Tax* (CGT1), most of which are available via its website.

DUNROBBIN'

Jim Watson

APPENDICES

Appendix A: Useful Addresses

Publications

BBC Good Homes, Woodlands, 80 Wood Lane, London W12 0TT (☎ 020-8576 2391, 💻 www.goodhomes.beeb.com). Monthly magazine.

Build It, Inside Communications Media Ltd., Isis Building, Thames Quay, 193 Marsh Wall, London E14 9SG (☎ 020-7772 8300, 💻 www.buildit-online.co.uk). Monthly magazine for self-builders.

Complete Guide to Homebuying, Charterhouse Communications Group Ltd., Arnold House, 36-41 Holywell Lane, London EC2A 3SF (☎ 020-7827 5454, 💻 www.home buying.co.uk). Bimonthly magazine.

Country Homes & Interiors, IPC Magazines, King's Reach Tower, Stamford Street, London SE1 9LS (☎ 01622-778778, 💻 www.ipc.co.uk/pubs/counthom.htm). Monthly magazine.

Country Life, 21st Floor, Kings Reach Tower, Stamford Street, London SE1 9LS (☎ 01444-445555, 💻 www.countrylife.co.uk). Monthly magazine.

Country Living, 72 Broadwick Street, London W1V 2BP (☎ 020-7439 5000, 💻 http://magazines.ivillage.com/countryliving). Monthly magazine.

Home, SPL, Berwick House, 8-10 Knoll Rise, Orpington, Kent BT6 0PS (☎ 01689-887200). Monthly magazine.

Homebuilding & Renovating, Sugar Brook Court, Aston Road, Bromsgrove, Worcs. B60 3EX (☎ 01527-834400, 💻 www.home building.co.uk). Monthly magazine for homebuilders and renovators.

Home Buyer & Mortgage Advisor, 14 Northfields, London SW18 1UU (☎ 020-8875 5600, 💻 www.homebuyermag.co.uk). Monthly magazine.

Homes & Antiques, BBC Magazines, Woodlands, 80 Wood Lane, London W12 0TT (☎ 020-8433 3490, 💻 www.bbchomes andantiques.com).

HomeStyle, Essential Publishing Ltd., 1-4 Eaglegate, East Hill, Colchester, Essex CO1 2PR (☎ 01206-796911). Monthly magazine.

House Beautiful, National Magazine House, 72 Broadwick Street, London W1F 9EP (☎ 020-7439 5000, 💻 www.house beautuful.co.uk). Monthly magazine.

House & Garden, Vogue House, 1 Hanover Square, London W1R 0AD (☎ 020-7499 9080, 💻 www.houseandgarden.co.uk). Monthly magazine.

Hot Property, Sherlock Publications, 16-21 The Quadrant, 135 Salisbury Road, London NW6 6RJ (☎ 020-8964 7400, 💻 www.hotproperty.co.uk). Weekly magazine.

Ideal Home, Freepost CY1061, Haywards Heath, West Sussex RH16 3ZA (☎ 01622-778778). Monthly magazine.

International Homes, 3 St Johns Court, Moulsham Street, Chelmsford, Essex CM2 0JD (☎ 01245-358877, 💻 www. international-property.co.uk). Monthly magazine for UK and overseas property.

Livingetc, IPC Magazines, King's Reach Tower, Stamford Street, London SE1 9LS (☎ 01444-445555, 💻 www.living etc.co.uk). Monthly style magazine.

The London Property News, London Property News, 9 Milner Street, London SW3 2QB (☎ 020-7388 1744, 💻 www.london propertynews.co.uk). Weekly newspaper.

Loot, Loot House, 24/32 Kilburn High Road, London NW6 5TF (☎0870-701 7171, 💻 www.loot.com). Daily newspaper for buying/selling properties privately (and just about everything else) and property rentals.

Mortgage Advisor & Home Buyer, Gainsborough House, 2 Sheen Road, Richmond-upon-Thames, Surrey TW9 1AE (☎ 020-8334 1600, 💻 www.mortgageadvisormag.co.uk). Monthly magazine.

Mortgage Magazine, MSM International Ltd., Thames House, 18 Park Street, London SE1 9ER (☎ 020-7407 1795). Monthly magazine.

Mortgage Matters, The Essential Guides Ltd., Devonshire House, Devonshire Road, Bexleyheath, Kent DA6 8DS (☎ 020-8301 6666). Monthly magazine.

What House?, Blendon Communications Ltd., 207 Providence Square, London SE1 2EW (☎ 020-7939 9888, 💻 www.whathouse.co.uk). Monthly magazine.

What Mortgage, Charterhouse Communications Group Ltd., Arnold House, 36-41 Holywell Lane, London EC2A 3SF (☎ 020-7827 5454). Monthly magazine.

Which? magazine, Castlemead, Gascoyne Way, Hertford SG14 1LH (☎ 01992-822800, 💻 www.which.net). Monthly consumer magazine, available on subscription only.

World of Interiors, Vogue House, 1 Hanover Square, London W1R 0AD (☎ 020-7499 9080, 💻 www.worldofinteriors.co.uk). Monthly magazine.

Your Mortgage, Matching Hat Limited, 143 Charing Cross Road, London WC2H 0EE (☎ 020-7478 4600, 💻 www.yourmortgage.co.uk). Monthly magazine.

Your New Home, NCG Media, Devonshire House, Devonshire Road, Bexleyheath, Kent DA6 8DS (☎ 020-8301 9259, 💻 www.yournewhome.co.uk). Bimonthly magazine.

Property-Related Organisations

Association of Relocation Agents (ARA), PO Box 189, Diss, Norfolk IP22 1PE (☎ 08700-737475, 💻 www.relocationagents.com).

The Association of Residential Managing Agents, 178 Battersea Park Road, London SW11 4ND (☎ 020-7978 2607, 💻 www.arma.org.uk).

Council for Licensed Conveyancers, 16 Glebe Road, Chelmsford, Essex CM1 1QG (☎ 01245-349599, 💻 www.theclc.gov.uk).

Council of Mortgage Lenders, 3 Saville Row, London W1X 1AF (☎ 020-7440 2255, 💻 www.cml.org.uk).

National Association of Estate Agents (NAEA), Arbon House, 21 Jury Street, Warwick CV34 4EH (☎ 01926-496800, 💻 www.naea.co.uk).

Ombudsman for Estate Agents (OEA), Beckett House, 4 Bridge Street, Salisbury, Wilts. SP1 2LX (☎ 01722-333306, 💻 www.oea.co.uk).

Royal Town Planning Institute, 26 Portland Place, London W1N 4BE (☎ 020-7636 9107, 💻 rtpi.org.uk).

Architects & Surveyors

Architects and Surveyors Institute (ASI), St Mary House, 15 St. Mary Street, Chippenham, Wilts. SN15 3WD (☎ 01249-444505, 💻 www.asi.ork.uk).

Architects Registration Council of the United Kingdom, 75 Hallam Street, London W1N 5LQ (☎ 020-7580 5861).

Association of Self-Build Architects (☎ 0800-387310 or 0131-319 1329, 💻 www.asba-architects.org).

Royal Incorporation of Architects in Scotland (RIAS), 15 Rutland Square, Edinburgh EH1 2BE (☎ 0131-229 7205, 💻 www.rias.org.uk).

Royal Institute of British Architects (RIBA), 66 Portland Place, London W1N 4AD (☎ 020-7580 5533, 💻 www.riba.org.uk).

Royal Institute of Chartered Surveyors (RICS), 12 Great George Street, Parliament Square, London SW1P 3AD (☎ 020-7222 7000, 💻 www.rics.org.uk).

Royal Institute of Chartered Surveyors in Scotland, 9 Manor Place, Edinburgh EH3 7DN (☎ 0131-225 7078, 💻 www.rics-scotland.org.uk).

Royal Society of Architects in Wales, Bute Building, King Edward VII Avenue, Cathays Park, Cardiff CF10 3NB (☎ 029-2087 4753, 💻 www.architecture-wales.com).

Royal Society of Ulster Architects, 1 Mount Charles, Belfast BT7 1NZ (☎ 01232-323760, 💻 www.rsua.org.uk).

Contractors & Trade Associations

Association of Building Engineers, Lutyens House, Billing Brook Road, Weston Favell, Northants. NN3 8NW (☎ 01604-404121, 💻 www.abe.org.uk).

Association of Plumbing and Heating Contractors (APHC), 14/15 Ensign House, Ensign Business Centre, Westwood Way, Coventry CV4 8JA (☎ 02476-470626, 💻 www.licensedplumber.co.uk).

The Association of Selfbuilders, 13 Laburnum Drive, Porthcawl, South Wales, CF36 5UA (☎ 0704-154 4126, 💻 www.self-builder.org.uk).

British Association of Landscape Industries (BALI), Landscape House, 9 Henry Street, Keighley, West Yorks. BD21 3DR (☎ 01535-606139, 💻 www.bali.co.uk).

British Bathroom Council, Federation House, Station Road, Stoke-on-Trent ST4 2RT (☎ 01782-747074).

British Security Industry Association, Security House, Barbourne Road, Worcester WR1 1RS (☎ 01905-21464, 💻 www.bsia.co.uk).

British Wood Preserving and Damp-Proofing Association, 1 Gleneagles House, Vernon Gate, Derby DE1 1UP (☎01332 225100, 💻 www.bwpda.co.uk).

Building Centre, 26 Store Street, London WC1E 7BT (☎ 020-7692 4000, 💻 www.buildingcentre.co.uk).

Building Employers' Confederation, 66 Cardiff Road, Glan y Llyn, Cardiff CF15 7PQ (☎ 029-2081 0681).

Building Guarantee Insurance Scheme UK Ltd., 143 Malone Road, Belfast, N. Ireland BT9 6SU (☎ 028-9087 7148, 💻 www.cefni.co.uk).

Building Merchants Federation, 15 Soho Square, London W1V 5FB (☎ 020-7439 1753).

Centre for Alternative Technology, Machynlleth, Powys, SY20 9AZ (☎ 01654-705950, 💻 www.cat.org.uk).

Chartered Institute of Building Services Engineers, Delta House, 222 Balham High Road, London SW12 9BS (☎ 020-8675 5211, 💻 www.cibse.org).

Conservatory Association, 2nd Floor, Godwin House, George Street, Huntingdon PE18 6BU (☎ 01480-458278).

The Construction Federation, 56-64 Leonard Street, London EC2A 4JX (☎ 020-7608 5000, 💻 www.constructionconfederation.co.uk).

Construction Resources, 16 Great Guildford Street, London SE1 0HS (☎ 020-7450 2211, 💻 www.constructionresources.com).

Constructive Individuals, 70A Holgate Road, York YO24 4AB (☎ 01904-625300, 💻 www.constructiveindividuals.co.uk).

Council for the Registration of Gas Installers (CORGI), 1 Elmwood, Chineham Business Park, Crockford Lane, Basingstoke RG24 8WG (☎ 01256-372200, 💻 www.corgi.gas.co.uk).

Draught Proofing Advisory Association Limited, PO Box 12, Haslemere GU27 3AH (☎ 01428-654011, 💻 http://dubois.vital.co.uk/database/ceed/wall.html).

Electrical Contractors' Association (ECA), ECA House, 34 Palace Court, London W2 4HY (☎ 020-7313 4800, 💻 www.eca.co.uk).

Electrical Contractors' Association of Scotland, Bush House, Bush Estates, Midlothian EH26 0SB (☎ 0131-445 5577, 💻 www.select.org.uk).

Energy Saving Trust (☎ 0845-727 7200, 💻 www.est.org.uk).

Federation of Master Builders (FMB), Gordon Fisher House, 14/15 Great James Street, London WC1N 3DP (☎ 020-7242 7583, 💻 www.fmb.org.uk).

Fire Protection Association, Bastille Court, 2 Paris Garden, London SE1 8ND (☎ 020-7902 5301, 💻 www.thefpa.co.uk).

Glass and Glazing Federation, 44-48 Borough High Street, London SE1 1XB (☎ 020-7403 7177, 💻 www.ggf.org.uk).

Guarantee Protection Trust, 27 London Road, High Wycombe, Bucks. HP11 1BW (☎ 01494-447049, 💻 www.gptprotection.co.uk).

Guild of Builders & Contractors, Crest House, 102-104 Church Road, Teddington, Middlesex TW11 8PY (☎ 020-8977 1105, 💻 www.buildersguild.co.uk).

Guild of Master Craftsmen, 166 High Street, Lewes, East Sussex BN7 1XU (☎ 01273-478449, 💻 www.thegmcgroup.com).

Heating and Ventilation Contractors Association (HVCA), 34 Palace Court, London W2 4JG (☎ 020-7229 2488, 💻 www.hvca.org.uk).

House Builders Federation, 56-64 Leonard Street, London EC2A 4JX (☎ 020-7608 5100, 💻 www.hbf.co.uk).

Institute of Electrical Engineers, Savoy Place, London WC2R 0BL (☎ 020-7240 1981, 💻 www.iee.org).

Institute of Plumbing, 64 Station Lane, Hornchurch, Essex RM12 6NB (☎ 01708-472791, 💻 www.plumbers.org.uk).

Kitchen Bathroom Bedroom Specialists Association, 12 Top Barn Business Centre, Holt Heath, Worcester WR6 6NH (☎ 01905-726066, 💻 www.kitchen-specialists.co.uk).

National Approval Council for Security Systems (NACOSS), Queensgate House, 14 Cookham Road, Maidenhead, Berks. SL6 8AJ (☎ 0870- 205000, 💻 www.nacoss.org.uk).

National Association of Plumbing, Heating and Mechanical Services Contractors, 14 Ensign House, Ensign Business Centre, Westwood Way, Coventry CV4 8JA (☎ 01203-470626).

National Conservatory Advisory Service, PO Box 163, Bangor, County Down, Northern Ireland BT20 5BX (☎ 0500-522525, 💻 www.nrwas.com).

National Federation of Builders, Construction House, 56-64 Leonard Street, London EC2A 4JX (☎ 020-7608 5150, 💻 www.builders.org.uk).

National Federation of Roofing Contractors, 24 Weymouth Street, London W1N 4LX (☎ 020-7436 0387, 💻 www.nfrc.co.uk).

National House Building Council (NHBC), Buildmark House, Chiltern Avenue, Amersham, Bucks. HP6 5AP (☎ 0845-845 6422, 💻 www.nhbc.co.uk).

National Register of Warranted Builders, Gordon Fisher House, 14-15 Great James Street, London WC1N 3DP (☎ 020-7242 7583, 💻 www.fmb.org.uk).

New Homes Marketing Board (NHMB), 82 New Cavendish Street, London W1M 8AD (☎ 020-7580 5588, 💻 www.new-homes.co.uk).

Painting & Decorating Association, 32 Coton Road, Nuneaton CV11 5TW (☎ 024-7635 3776, 💻 www.paintingdecoratingassociation.co.uk).

Scottish and Northern Ireland Plumbing Employers' Federation (SNIPEF), 2 Walker Street, Edinburgh EH3 7LB (☎ 0131-225 2255, 💻 www.snipef.org).

The Solar Trade Association (☎ 01908-442 290, 💻 www.solartradeassociation.org.uk).

Swimming Pool and Allied Trades Association Ltd. (SPATA), 1A Junction Road, Andover, Hants. SP10 3QT (☎ 01264-356210, 💻 www.spata.co.uk).

Timber and Brick Homes Information Council, Gable House, 40 High Street, Rickmansworth, Herts. WD1 3ES (☎ 01923-778136).

Worshipful Company of Builders Merchants, 4 College Hill, London EC4R 2RB (☎ 020-7329 2189, 💻 www.wcobm.co.uk).

Zurich Municipal, Galaxy House, 6 Southwood Crescent, Farnborough, Hants. GU14 0NJ (☎ 01252-522000, 💻 www.zurichmunicipal.com). New homes warranty.

Letting

Association of Residential Letting Agents (ARLA), Maple House, 53-55 Woodside Road, Amersham, Bucks. HP6 6AA (☎ 0845-345 5752, 💻 www.arla.co.uk).

Landlord Action, Concorde House, Grenville Place, London NW7 3SA (☎ 020-7906 3838, 💻 www.landlordaction.co.uk).

The Letting Centre, Old Vicarage, Withycombe Village Road, Exmouth, EX8 3AG (☎ 01395-271122, 💻 www.letlink.co.uk).

National Federation of Residential Landlords, PO Box 4840, Wimborne BH21 3WZ (☎ 0845-456 0357, 💻 www.help4landlords.org).

Small Landlords Association, 78 Tachbrook Street, London SW1V 2NA (☎ 020-7828 2445, 💻 www.landlords.org.uk).

Southern Private Landlords' Association, PO Box 2883, Brighton BN1 1PB (☎ 01273-600847, 💻 www.spla.co.uk).

Retirement Homes

Age Concern England, Astral House, 1268 London Rd, London SW16 4ER (☎ 020-8679 8000, 💻 www.ageconcern.org.uk).

Age Concern Scotland, 113 Rose Street, Edinburgh EH2 3DT (☎ 0131-220 3345, 💻 www.ageconcernscotland.org.uk).

Elderly Accommodation Counsel, 3rd Floor, 89 Albert Embankment, London SE1 7PT (☎ 020-7820 1343, 💻 www.housingcare.org).

Help The Aged, 207-221 Pentonville Road, London N1 9UZ (☎ 020-7278 1114, 💻 www.helptheaged.org.uk).

Retirement Homesearch, Queensway House, 11 Queensway, New Milton, Hants. BH25 5NR (☎ 0870-600 5560, 💻 www.retirementhomesearch.co.uk).

Miscellaneous Property-Related Organisations

Auctioninfo Ltd., PO Box 62, Daventry NN11 3ZY (☎ 01327-361732, 💻 www.auctioninfo.co.uk).

The British Association of Removers (BAR), 3 Churchill Court, 58 Station Road, North Harrow, Middx. HA2 7SA (☎ 020-8861 3331, 💻 www.bar.co.uk).

British Holiday and Homes Parks Association (BHHPA), Chichester House, 6 Pullman Court, Great Western Road, Gloucester GL1 3ND (☎ 01452-526911, 💻 www.parkhome.co.uk).

The Building Societies Association/Council of Mortgage Lenders, 3 Savile Row, London W1X 1AF (☎ 020-7437 0655, 💻 www.bsa.org.uk).

Cadw (Welsh Heritage), Cathays Park, Cardiff CF10 3NQ (☎ 029-2050 0200, 💻 www.cadw.gov.uk).

English Heritage, 23 Saville Row, London W1S 2ET (☎ 020-7973 3000, 💻 www.english-heritage.org.uk).

The Final Touch London Ltd., 12 St. John's Hill Grove, London SW11 2RG (☎ 020-7228 4233, 💻 www.thefinaltouch.co.uk).

The Financial Ombudsman Service, South Quay Plaza, 183 Marsh Wall, London E14 9SR (☎ 0845-080 1800, 💻 www.financial-ombudsman.org.uk).

The Georgian Group, 6 Fitzroy Square, London W1T 5DX (☎ 020-7529 8920, 💻 www.georgiangroup.org.uk).

Historic Scotland, Longmore House, Salisbury Place, Edinburgh EH9 1SH (☎ 0131-668 8600, 💻 www.historic-scotland.gov.uk).

HM Land Registry, Lincoln Inn Fields, London WC2A 3PH (☎ 020-7917 8888, 💻 www.landreg.gov.uk).

Homelands of England, PO Box 7003, Oakham, Rutland LE15 6WH (☎ 01572-723626, 💻 www.homelandsplots.co.uk). Building plots.

Land Registers of Northern Ireland (☎ 0290-251756, 💻 www.lrni.gov.uk).

The Leasehold Enfranchisement Advisory Service, 70-74 City Road, London, EC1Y 2BJ (☎ 0845-345 1993, 💻 www.lease-advice.org/newintro.htm).

The Listed Property Owners Club, Freepost, Hartlip, Sittingbourne, Kent ME9 7TE (☎ 01795-844939, 💻 www.lpoc.co.uk).

The Location Company, 1 Charlotte Street, London W1P 1HD (☎ 020-7637 7766, 💻 www.thelocation.co.uk).

The National Improved Lettings Scheme, PO Box 1843, Warwick CV34 4ZA (☎ 01926-496683, 💻 www.nalscheme.co.uk).

The National Home Improvement Advisory Service (NHIAS), 18 Lord Mayor's Walk, York YO31 7HA (☎ 0800-0285 809, 💻 www.nhias.org).

The National Home Improvement Council, Carlyle House, 235 Vauxhall Bridge Road, London SWIV 1EJ (☎ 020-7828 8230, 💻 www. nhic.org.uk).

The National Land Finding Agency, Rood End House, 6 Stortford Road, Great Dunmow, Essex CM6 1DA (☎ 01371-876875).

The Northern Ireland Housing Executive, The Housing centre, 2 Adelaide Street, Belfast BT2 8PB (☎ 01232-317000, 💻 www.hihe.gov.uk).

Office for the Supervision of Solicitors, Victoria Court, 8 Dormer Place, Leamingtom Spa, Warks. CV32 5AE (☎ 01926-820082, 💻 www.lawsociety.org.uk).

Registers of Scotland, Erskine House, 68 Queen Street, Edinburgh EH2 4NF (☎ 0845-607 0161, 💻 www.ros.gov.uk).

The Society of Garden Designers, The Institute of Horticulture, 14-15 Belgrave Square, London SW1X 8PS (☎ 020-7838 9311, 💻 www.sgd.org.uk).

The Society for the Protection of Ancient Buildings, 37 Spital Square, London E1 6DY (☎ 020-7377 1644, 💻 www.spab.org.uk).

The Twentieth Century Society, 70 Cowcross Street, London EC1M 6EJ (☎ 020-7250 3857, 💻 www.c20society.demon.co.uk).

The Ulster Architectural Heritage Society, 66 Donegall Pass, Belfast BT7 1BU (☎ 028-9055 0213, 💻 www.uahs.co.uk).

The Victorian Society, 1 Priory Gardens, London W4 1TT (☎ 020-8994 1019, 💻 www.victorian-society.org.uk).

Miscellaneous

The Association of British Insurers, 51-55 Gresham Street, London EC2V 7HQ (☎ 020-7600 3333, 💻 www.abi.org.uk).

The Chartered Institute of Arbitrators, 24 Angel Gate, City Road, London EC1V 2RS (☎ 020-7837 4483, 💻 www. arbitrators.org).

The Consumers Association, 2 Marylebone Road, London NW1 4DF (☎ 020-7770 7000, 💻 www.which.net).

Department for Environment, Food and Rural Affairs (DEFRA), Room 320, Nobel House, 17 Smith Square, London SW1P 3JR (☎ 08459-335577, 💻 www.defra.gov.uk).

The Environment Agency (☎ 0845-9333 111, 💻 www.environment-agency.gov.uk).

Floodgate Ltd. (flood defences), 49/51 Lammas Street, Carmarthen SA31 3AL (☎ 01267-234205, 💻 http://floodgate.ltd.uk).

The Good Housekeeping Institute, National Magazine House, 72 Broadwick Street, London W1V 2BP (☎ 020-7439 5000).

HM Customs and Excise, New King's Beam House, 22 Upper Ground, London SE1 9PJ (☎ 020-7620 1313, 💻 www.hmce.gov.uk).

Inland Revenue, Somerset House, Strand, London WC2R 1LB (☎ 020-7438 6622, 💻 www.ir.gov.uk).

The Insurance Ombudsman Bureau (IOB), c/o Financial Ombudsman Service, South Quay Plaza, 183 Marsh Wall, London E14 9SR (☎ 0845-080 1800, 💻 www.theiob.org.uk).

The Law Centres Federation Duchess House, 18-19 Warren Street, London W1T 5LR (☎ 020-7387 8570, 💻 www.lawcentres.org.uk).

The Law Commission, Conquest House, 37-38 John Street, Theobalds Road, London WC1N 2BQ (☎ 020-7453 1220, 💻 www.lawcom.gov.uk).

The Law Society, 113 Chancery Lane, London WC2A 1PL (☎ 020-7242 1222, 💻 www.lawsoc.org.uk).

The Law Society of Scotland, 26 Drumsheugh Gardens, Edinburgh EH3 7YR (☎ 0132-226 7411, 💻 www.lawscot.org.uk).

The Legal Services Ombudsman, 3rd Floor, Sunlight House, Quay Street, Manchester M3 3JZ (☎ 0845-601 0794/0161-839 7262, 💻 www.olso.org).

The National Association of Citizens Advice Bureaux, Myddelton House, 115-123 Pentonville Road, London N1 9LZ (☎ 020-7833 2181, 💻 www.nacab.org.uk).

The National Consumer Council, 20 Grosvenor Gardens, London SW1 0DH (☎ 020-7730 3469, 💻 www.ncc.org.uk).

The National Solicitors' Network, 156 Cromwell Road, London SW7 4EF (☎ 020-7244 6422, 💻 www.tnsn.com).

The Office of Fair Trading (OFT), Fleetbank House, 2-6 Salisbury Square, London EC4Y 8JX (☎ 08457-224499, 💻 www.oft.gov.uk).

Appendix B: Further Reading

The books listed below are just a small selection of the many books written for those planning to buy, sell, let or improve property. Some titles may be out of print, but you may still be able to find a copy in a bookshop or library. Books prefixed with an asterisk (*) are recommended by the author.

Buying, Selling & Letting Property

Affordable Housing in London, C.M.E. Whitehead & D.T. Cross (Pergamon)

***Building Surveys of Residential Property** (RICS Books)

***Buying Bargains at Property Auctions**, Howard Gooddie (Wyvern Crest)

Buying a Home, Sarah Pennells & Marc Robinson (Dorling Kindersly)

Buying a Home When Your Single, Donna G. Albrecht (John Wiley)

Buying a Home on the Internet, Robert Irwin (McGraw-Hill)

Buying a Manufactured Home, Kevin Burnside (Van der Plas)

Buying & Selling Your Home, Richard Newell (Longman Law)

***Buying Your Home with Other People**, Dave Treanor (Shelter)

The Complete Idiot's Guide to Buying and Selling a Home, Shelley O'Hara & Maris Bluestein (Prentice Hall)

Daily Mail Guide to Buying or Selling a House or Flat, Margaret Stone (Kogan Page)

Essential Guide How to Buy & Sell Your Home, Keith Carlton (Prentice Hall)

***'Good Housekeeping' Consumer Guide: Buying and Selling Your Home** (Ebury Press)

The Good Web Guide to Property: The Essential Guide to Buying, Selling and Renting Property Online, Mike Miller (The Good Web Guide)

***Home Ownership: Buying and Maintaining**, Nicholas Snelling LLB (Guild of Master Craftsmen)

Homes and Property on the Internet, Philip Harrison (International Briefings)

House Buying, Selling & Conveyancing and Buying Bargains at Property Auctions, Joseph Bradshaw & Howard Goodie (Law Pack)

***How to Make Money from Your Property**, Fiona Fullerton (Piatkus)

***Location Location Location**, Fanny Blake (Channel 4 Books)

The Mirror Guide to Buying a House, Diane Boliver (Prentice Hall)

Moving In: buying, selling & renting your home, Sara McConnell (Prentice Hall)

***New London Property Guide: The Only Guide to Buying, Selling, Renting and Letting Homes in London**, Carrie Seagrave (Mitchell Beazley)

Save Money Buying and Selling Your Home, David Orange (Foulsham)

A Straightforward Guide to Buying, Selling and Renting a Property, Frank Worth (Straightforward Publishing)

The Unofficial Guide to Buying a Home, Ion Perlis (John Wiley)

***Which? Way to Buy, Sell and Move House** (Which? Books)

Your First Home: Buying, Renting, Selling and Decorating, Niki Chesworth (Kogan Page)

Building & Renovation

***The Book of Lofts**, Suzanne Rozensztroch & Daniel Stafford (Thames & Hudson)

***'Build It' Guide to Building Your Own Timber Frame Home**, Rosalind Renshaw (Dent)

Building Your Home, Susan Heal (HarperCollins)

***Building Services Thesaurus**, G. A. Beale (BSRIA)

Building Surveys of Residential Property (RICS Books)

***Building Your Own Home**, Murray Armor & David Snell (Ebury Press)

Choosing Colours: an expert choice of the best colours to use in your home, Kevin McCloud (Quadrille)

***Collins Care & Repair of Period Houses**, Albert Jackson & David Day (HarperCollins)

***Collins Complete Home Restoration Manual**, Albert Jackson & David Day (HarperCollins)

A Fine Restoration, Kitty Ray (Little, Brown)

***Getting the Builders in . . . and Staying in Control**, Paul Grimaldi (Elliot Right Way Books)

Home Extensions, Paul Hymers (New Holland)

***The Home Front Directory**, Alison Reynolds & Sarah Childs-Carlile (BBC)

***House Doctor: Instant Makeovers**, Ann Maurice (Collins)

***House Doctor Quick Fixes: 100 Top Tips to Help You Make That Sale**, Ann Maurice (HarperCollins)

***Illustrated Dictionary of Building Terms**, Tom Philbin (McGraw)

***Lofts**, Marcus Field & Mark Irving (Laurence King)

***Penguin Dictionary of Building**, John S. Scott & James Maclean (Penguin)

Renovating Your Own Home: A Step-by-Step Guide, David Caldwell (Stoddart)

Miscellaneous

ABC of Gardening, Sally Maltby (Kyle Cathie)

The Best of British Architecture 1980-2000, Dennis Sharp & Noel Moffett (E&FN Spon)

Concise Dictionary of Interior Design, Frederic H. Jones (Crisp)

***Concise Encyclopaedia of Interior Design**, A. Allen Dizik (John Willey)

Creating Space, Elizabeth Wilhide (Pavillion)

Creative Interiors: A Complete Practical Course in Interior Design, Wren Loasby (David & Charles)

***Easy Living**, Terence Conran (Conran Octopus)

***The Family Home**, Joanna Copestick (Conran Octopus)

***'Gardener's World' Practical Gardening Course**, Geoff Hamilton (BBC)

***'Good Housekeeping' Traditional Garden Hints** (Ebury Press)

Guide to Good Living in London (Francis Chichester)

***The Home Plans Book**, Murray Armor & David Snell (Ebury Press)

***Interior Design**, Philip Graham (Prentice Hall)

Interior Design Ideas, Norman Sullivan (Lock Ward)

***London Living,** Lisa Lovett Smith & Paul Duncan (Phoenix)

New British Architecture (Architecture Foundation)

***The New Natural House Book,** David Pearson (Conran Octopus)

***One Space Living,** Cynthia Inions (Ryland)

Rooms to Remember, Barbara & Rene Stoeltie (Francis Lincoln)

A Straightforward Guide to Letting Property for Profit, G. J. Hardwick (Straightforward Publishing)

***The Sunday Times Personal Finance Guide to Your Home,** Diana Wright (HarperCollins)

Top Towns (Guinness Publishing)

Appendix C: Useful Websites

Professional Associations

Building Societies' Association (www.bsa.org.uk): Central representative body for building societies.

Council For Licensed Conveyancers (www.theclc.gov.uk): Alternative conveyancers to solicitors.

Council Of Mortgage Lenders (www.cml.org.uk): Trade association for mortgage lenders.

Federation of Master Builders (www.fmb.org.uk): Includes a directory of members.

Land Registry (www.landreg.gov.uk): Practical information about registering land and land registry archives.

Land Registers Of Northern Ireland (www.lrni.gov.uk): The Land Registry in Northern Ireland.

The Law Society (www.lawsoc.org.uk): Professional body for solicitors in England and Wales.

The Law Society, Scotland (www.lawscot.org.uk): Professional body for solicitors in Scotland.

National Association Of Estate Agents/NAEA (www.naea.co.uk): The main organisation for Estate Agents.

Ombudsman For Estate Agents (www.oea.co.uk): Independent arbitration for property buyers with complaints about registered estate agents.

Registers Of Scotland (www.ros.gov.uk): The Land Registry in Scotland.

Mortgages

Charcol Online (www.charcolonline.co.uk): Online mortgage brokers.

Council Of Mortgage Lenders (www.cml.org.uk): The trade association for mortgage lenders.

Finance For Professionals (www.f4p.com): Finance for members of certain professions, e.g. architects, engineers and teachers.

Home Buyer & Mortgage Advisor magazine (www.homebuyermag.co.uk): The UK's most popular mortgage magazine. Good general information about buying and selling property.

Market Place (www.marketplace.co.uk): Search for the best mortgage deals.

Money Extra (www.moneyextra.co.uk): Financial services, including best mortgage deals.

Money Net (www.moneynet.co.uk): Financial services, including best mortgage deals.

Money Quest (www.moneyquest.co.uk): Mortgage brokers.

Money Supermarket (www.moneysupermarket.com): General finance including mortgages.

Mortgage Next (www.mortgage-next.com): Financial advisers.

This Is Money (www.thisismoney.co.uk): Data and statistics on money matters as well as useful money guides.

Virgin Money (http://uk.virginmoney.com): The Virgin Group's financial services online.

What Mortgage Magazine (www.whatmortgageonline.co.uk): Mortgage information and comprehensive advice on buying a property.

Your Mortgage Magazine (www.yourmortgage.co.uk): Provides a wealth of information about mortgages and all aspects of buying and selling property.

Neighbourhood Information

Environment Agency (www.environment-agency.gov.uk): Check the occurrence of flooding in an area.

Enviro Search (www.home-envirosearch.com): Check whether a property is adversely affected by environmental factors.

Get A Map (www.getamap.co.uk): Free downloadable Ordnance Survey neighbourhood maps.

Home Check (www.homecheck.co.uk): Local information about the risks of flooding, landslip, pollution, radon gas, landfill, waste sites, etc. Also provides general information about neighbourhoods.

Hometrack (🖳 www.hometrack.co.uk): Online property reports.

Knowhere (🖳 www.knowhere.co.uk): An alternative look at over 2,000 UK towns.

My Village (🖳 www.myvillage.com): Community sites for London and 20 other cities.

Neighbourhood Statistics (🖳 http://neighbourhood.statistics.gov.uk): Contains a wide range of statistics for neighbourhoods in England and Wales.

Provisor (🖳 www.proviser.com)Local property prices and street maps for England and Wales.

UK Online (🖳 www.ukonline.gov.uk) Comprehensive information about local services and neighbourhoods, including local schools, health, housing and crime statistics.

Up My Street (🖳 www.upmystreet.co.uk): Information about neighbourhoods, including property prices, local services, schools, local government etc.

Estate Agents

Asserta Home (🖳 www.assertahome.com): Large database of properties for sale around the country.

Find A Property (🖳 www.findaproperty.com): Property for sale in London and surrounding counties.

Fish 4 Homes (🖳 www.fish4homes.co.uk): Selection of properties and directory of estate agents around the UK.

Foxtons (🖳 www.foxtons.co.uk): London's largest chain of estate and letting agents.

Home Sale (🖳 www.home-sale.co.uk): National network of over 700 estate agents.

Hot Property (🖳 www.hot-property.com): The Hot Property magazine website featuring property in London and the south-east.

House Web (🖳 www.houseweb.co.uk): Independent property website that contains comprehensive advice and tips for the homebuyer.

London Property Guide (🖳 www.londonpropertyguide.co.uk): Buy, sell or rent in London.

My Property (🖳 www.mypropertyforsale.co.uk): Internet estate agent.

New-Homes (🖳 www.new-homes.co.uk): Comprehensive database of new home developments throughout the UK.

Number One For Property (🖳 www.numberone4property.co.uk): Property website.

Property Finder (🖳 www.propertyfinder.co.uk): Internet estate agent.

Property Live (🖳 www.propertylive.co.uk): The National Association of Estate Agents' property website.

Prime Location (🖳 www.primelocation.com): Consortium of estate agents advertising properties.

Right Move (🖳 www.rightmove.co.uk): Buying, selling and letting.

Smart Estates (🖳 www.smartestates.com): Independent property website selling new and resale property.

Smart New Homes (🖳 www.smartnewhomes.co.uk): Search for new homes.

Vebra (🖳 www.vebra.com): One of the UK's most visited property sites run by a consortium of estate agents.

Ugly Properties (🖳 www.uglyproperties.com): Specialists in selling vandalised and empty properties, 'brownfield' development land and just plain ugly-looking homes.

Winkworth (🖳 www.winkworth.co.uk): Property database for London and Yorkshire.

Private Sales

The following websites are online property agents who advertise property for sale, usually for a modest one-time fee (many also contain comprehensive general information):

4 Sale By Owner (🖳 www.4salebyowner.co.uk).

DIY House (🖳 www.diyhousesales.com): Property for sale in Northern Ireland.

Estate Agent (💻 www.estateagent.co.uk): Advertise free of charge.

Home Pages (💻 www.homepages.co.uk).

Home Sale Network (💻 www.home-sale.co.uk).

House Web (💻 www.houseweb.co.uk).

Internet Homes (💻 www.internethomes.co.uk).

My Property For Sale (💻 www.mypropertyforsale.co.uk).

Private House for Sale (💻 www.privatehousesforsale.co.uk).

Property Broker (💻 www.propertybroker.co.uk).

Property Finder (💻 www.propertyfinder.co.uk).

Smart Estates (💻 www.smartestates.com).

Use The Mouse (💻 www.use-the-mouse.com).

Home Improvements & Renovation

BBC Homes (💻 www.bbc.co.uk/homes): Home improvements and makeovers.

Build It magazine (💻 www.buildit-online.co.uk): Comprehensive information for self-builders.

Building Centre (💻 www.buildingcentre.co.uk): The worlds largest permanent exhibition and single source of information for the construction industry.

Building Conservation (💻 http://www.buildingconservation.com): For the conservation and repair of historic buildings.

Building Control (💻 www.buildingcontrol.org): Information on all aspects of building control in England, Wales and N. Ireland.

Building Information Warehouse (💻 www.biw.co.uk): You can register with this website for the latest information on building products and supplies.

Buildstore (💻 www.buildstore.co.uk): Comprehensive advice and information for the self-builder and renovator.

Federation of Master Builders (💻 www.fmb.org.uk): The largest association in the UK construction industry.

Homebuilding & Renovating (💻 www.homebuilding.co.uk): Comprehensive information on self-build homes plus a useful 'Beginners Guide' from *Homebuilding & Renovating* magazine.

Home Pro (💻 www.homepro.com): Directory of home improvement professionals.

House Builders Federation (💻 www.hbf.co.uk): The principal trade federation for private sector house builders and the voice of the house building industry in England and Wales.

Improve Line (💻 www.improveline.com): Advice on home improvements.

National Home Improvement Advisory Service (💻 www.nhias.org): Aims to provide quotations for high quality products and services at the most cost-effective price.

National Home Improvement Council (💻 www.nhic.org.uk)): The NHIC represents the most important body of companies and organisations working in the home improvement sector.

National Register Of Warranted Builders (💻 www.fmb.org.uk/about/nrwb/index.asp): Members of the Federation of Master Builders who provide a warranty scheme.

Plotfinder.net (💻 www.plotfinder.net): Plots for self-builders.

Property Medics (💻 www.thepropertymedics.com): DIY, home improvements and general property information.

Salvo (💻 www.salvo.co.uk): Architectural salvage, including a guide to sources of antique and reclaimed building materials.

Moving Resources

British Association of Removers (💻 www.bar.co.uk): Association of removal companies offering a professional service with a conciliation and arbitration service.

I Am Moving (💻 www.iammoving.com): Will inform companies on your behalf that you are moving.

Really Moving (💻 www.reallymoving.com): Excellent information about property including home-moving services and a property finder.

The Move Channel (💻 www.themovechannel.com): General property website containing everything you need to know about moving house.

General Information

BBC Homes (💻 www.bbc.co.uk/homes): Lifestyle homes from the BBC.

Homes Online (💻 www.homes-on-line.com): Useful information about buying, selling, home improvements and financing a property.

Home Pages (💻 www.homepages.co.uk)Comprehensive property database and information about buying and selling.

The Move Channel (💻 www.themovechannel.com): Comprehensive information on all aspects of buying and selling property.

Plot Finder (💻 www.plotfinder.net): Land and renovations for sale.

Property Investor (💻 www.propertyinvestor.co.uk): Buying, selling and letting property for profit plus information about Property Investor shows..

Property Seeker (💻 www.property-seeker.co.uk): Complete home-move service run by a consortium of estate agents.

PropertySpy Group (💻 www.propertymarket.co.uk): Specialises in land for sale in England.

Property Telegraph (💻 www.property.telegraph.co.uk): Comprehensive property information including advice, prices and latest news and developments.

Save Britain's Heritage (💻 www.savebritainsheritage.org): Conservation of historic buildings.

Scoot (💻 www.scoot.co.uk): Find essential services for homeowners.

Shelternet (💻 www.shelternet.co.uk): The website of Shelter, a charity for the homeless, the leading provider of independent housing advice in the UK.

Your New Home Magazine (💻 www.yournewhome.co.uk): The magazine for new homebuyers.

Appendix D: Checklists

The way to ensure a smooth move is to make a number of checklists of jobs to be done before moving day, split into periods of from four weeks before the move to the actual moving day itself. These checklists relate solely to the task of moving your family and belongings from one home to another. They don't include other activities involved in the buying or selling process, therefore you should bear in mind that there will be many other things going on that could affect your schedule. To help you plan a move, the jobs to be completed before moving day have been divided into the timeframes shown below.

- Four weeks before moving;
- Two weeks before moving;
- One week before moving;
- Three days before moving;
- The day before moving;
- Moving day;
- On arrival;
- After moving.

Note that the checklists below are only a guide and you may prefer to do some things earlier or later than indicated.

Four Weeks Before Moving

There are a number of things you need to do well in advance of a move. Some jobs can be left until one or two weeks before your move, but you should at least be aware of them and make sure that they're on your 'jobs to do' list.

☐ You need to start of the process of cancelling services or insurance at your old address and re-arranging them at the new address, possibly with a different company.

- [ ] Book a removal company or van or reconfirm the moving date with the removal company or van hire company.
- [ ] Notify your landlord if you live in rented accommodation. Obviously this will need to done in accordance with your rental contract, so check your notice period well in advance.
- [ ] Let your employer know when you're moving and arrange to take time off work, if necessary. Some employers give employees a day of two off work to move house.
- [ ] If you will need a bridging loan (see page 132) until the sale of your current home goes through, discuss this with your bank manager well in advance.
- [ ] Arrange alternative accommodation if you're selling your home before buying a new one, or if you don't plan to stay in your old or new home amidst the chaos of moving. If you will need hotel or self-catering accommodation you should book well in advance, particularly if you're moving during the summer months.
- [ ] You may wish to arrange for a few friends to help you move, which you will need to organise well in advance, particularly if they need to get time off work.
- [ ] If you require a residents' parking permit or special permission from the council or police for the removals van to park outside your current or new house, you will need to make an application for a permit around a week in advance.
- [ ] Arrange for a friend or neighbour to look after your pets on moving day or book them into a kennel/cattery for a few days. If they will be travelling with you they may need to be sedated – contact your vet for advice.
- [ ] Find a babysitter or someone to look after your children for the day of the move.
- [ ] Contact your insurance companies, for example private health, car, buildings and home contents. You should insure your new home from the day you exchange contracts. Check whether you're entitled to a rebate on your car, buildings and home contents insurance, which will apply if you're moving to a cheaper home or to an area with a lower insurance rating for car and home contents insurance, e.g. when moving from

a city to the country. However, if you're moving from a rural area to a city, you will usually have to pay more! Shop around for new insurance as moving home is a good opportunity to save money.

☐ Contact government agencies such as the Department of Social Security, Child Benefit Agency, Department of Pensions, etc. If you're self-employed you will need to contact your local DSS office and give them your name, date of birth and National Insurance number.

☐ Contact your local tax office quoting your tax number, shown on your P60 or a payslip.

☐ If you've a driving licence or car you will need to get both your licence and your car registration papers updated with your new address (failure to do so is against the law). Complete the appropriate section on your car registration document and send to DVLA, Swansea, SA99 1AR (☎ 0870-2400010, 💻 www.dvla.gov.uk). Complete section 1 of your paper Counterpart Driving Licence (D740) and send it with your photocard licence and the fee to DVLA, Swansea, SA99 1BN (☎ 0870-2400009). Note that the DVLA no longer issues paper licences and if you have one you must obtain a photocard application pack from a post office or the DVLA.

☐ If you've got a TV licence, contact TV licensing (☎ 0870-850 1202) and give them your licence number and new address. If you've cable or satellite TV (or special aerials), contact your provider with your new address or to cancel your agreement (you can compare the cost of digital TV from different providers at 💻 www.uswitch.com). If you've a satellite system you will need to arrange for the dish to be moved to you new house or for a new one to be installed if you aren't taking it with you. This also applies to your television aerial.

☐ Contact your Internet Service Provider (ISP). If you've a broadband connection in your old home, you may need to make arrangements to have this service in your new home.

☐ Inform your children's current schools of the leaving date if known or warn them that you will be moving **as far in advance as possible**. This also applies to colleges, universities and local educational institutions where any members of your family are studying or plan to study. Obtain a copy of any relevant school reports or records from schools and arrange to visit schools in the area where you're moving to if you haven't already done so.

- [ ] If you're taking your carpets, appliances (such as a cooker or dishwasher) or anything requiring specialist removal and installation, arrange for someone to remove or disconnect them and reconnect/refit them in your new home. Some removal companies will do this or will arrange for someone to do it. If you need to buy new carpets or curtains for your new home, arrange a visit to take measurements and order them well in advance.
- [ ] Notify your stockbroker, share accounts, company registrars and other financial institutions.
- [ ] Make arrangements for cleaning your old home or furniture disassembling and assembling if you won't be doing it yourself. You may also wish to arrange for your new home to be professionally cleaned after the seller has moved out (few people leave a home spotless and the best time to spring clean is when it's empty).
- [ ] Arrange for any work to be done on your new home that needs doing before you move in. This not only includes essential work – such as fixing a hole in the roof – but also such things as changing the locks, installing an alarm system, or special electrical or plumbing installations.
- [ ] Start running down food stocks, particularly frozen foods. If your fridge and freezer are going into storage, they will need to be thoroughly cleaned and dried in order to prevent mould developing (or store them with their doors ajar).
- [ ] Make a list of all the major items that you plan to leave behind in your old home and give it to your solicitor. It's important that this is accurate as it will be appended to the contract and every item must be left when you move.
- [ ] Start sorting through your belongings in cupboards, loft, garden shed, workshop, garage, annexe, etc. and discard, sell or give away anything you don't plan to take with you. Investigate local car boot sales (or Ebay?) and charity shops.

- [ ] Make a list of all the major items you're taking with you for insurance purposes, including the cost, and date and place of purchase.
- [ ] Go through all your papers and copy any important documents – store the originals in a safe or safety deposit box. These may include birth certificates; driving licences; marriage certificate, divorce papers or death certificate (if a widow or widower); educational diplomas and professional certificates; employment references and curricula vitae; school records and student ID cards; medical and dental records; bank account and credit card details; insurance policies (plus records of no-claims' allowances); and receipts for valuables.

Two Weeks Before Moving

By now you should have finished sorting your cupboards, loft, garage, cellar, etc. and have discarded, sold or given away anything you don't plan to take with you. You should also have accumulated packing materials ready to start packing items you won't need in the next few weeks. Other jobs to do in the next week include:

- [ ] Start packing anything you won't need until after your move.
- [ ] Cut the lawns short so that you won't have to do them again. Drain any fuel from garden equipment such as lawnmowers, clean your BBQ, and ensure that all outdoor equipment is clean enough to transport. Make a list of plants and shrubs that you're taking with you and ensure that you've proper pots and tubs to transport them. Make a note of any garden ornaments and other items (shed?) that you're taking with you and dismantle any children's play equipment such as swings or climbing frames (keep all the nuts and bolts together in a plastic bag).
- [ ] If you haven't already done so, start running down the contents of your freezer. This is necessary if you need to defrost it – either to clean and leave or to take with you.

- [ ] Sort through your kitchen cupboards and start packing any equipment, tinned food, crockery and cutlery that you won't need before you go. Dispose of anything you don't want.
- [ ] Make a backup copy of any important data on your computer to floppy disks, a zip drive or a CD-ROM. (After making a backup, check that you can read the backup files – there's nothing worse than a backup file you cannot read!) **Bear in mind that computer hardware doesn't always travel well and the last thing you want to find is that you've lost vital data due to a hard disk crash and you don't have a backup!**
- [ ] Obtain written instructions from the vendors of your new home regarding: the operation of appliances and heating and air-conditioning systems; the maintenance of grounds, gardens and lawns (the name of their gardener); care of special surfaces such as slate, wooden or tiled floors; and the names of reliable local maintenance men who know the property and are familiar with its quirks.
- [ ] Arrange to do a final check or inventory of the new property a few weeks before you moving.
- [ ] Contact banks, building societies, post office, credit union, stores and other institutions where you have accounts. If you're staying with the same bank, arrange to transfer your account to the nearest branch to your new home or workplace. If you've a safety deposit box or documents in safe keeping at your bank, you will need to collect them and make alternative arrangements at your new bank. Arrange for any direct debits or standing orders for your old home to be cancelled at the appropriate time. If you change your bank account you will need to ensure that all your direct debits or standing orders are switched to the new account or cancelled.
- [ ] Contact credit, charge and store card companies and give them your new address and bank account details (if applicable). Also notify your card protection insurer if you've one.
- [ ] Contact insurance companies such as mortgage payment protection, permanent health insurance, pet insurance, travel

insurance, income insurance, life insurance, private health or dental insurance, etc.

☐ Make arrangements with gas, electricity and water companies to read meters and transfer your account to your new address. Although most companies officially require only a few days notice, it's advisable to contact them one or two weeks in advance and confirm the meter reading appointment a few days before. You may wish to take the opportunity to save money by changing your electricity or gas supplier. You can compare rates via Uswitch (💻 www.uswitch.com) or the Energy Helpline (💻 www.energyhelpline.com).

☐ Contact your telephone companies, both fixed and mobile. If you're moving locally you may be able to retain your existing phone number. You can compare the rates of the main phone companies at 💻 www.uswitch.com.

☐ Contact your local post office if you've got a pension book, as they will need to arrange for you to collect your pension from a post office close to your new home.

☐ If you've got some premium bonds you will need to notify the Bonds and Stock office (the form is available at post offices).

☐ Give your new address to your private pension companies, accountant, solicitor, and professional or regulatory bodies.

☐ Contact hire purchase and loan companies, and local businesses where you have accounts.

☐ Give your family doctor, dentist, optician and other health practitioners your new address. If you have regular prescriptions, ensure that you've adequate medicines to last until you've registered with a new doctor. If you're moving to a new area you will need to register with a new (NHS) doctor and dentist and arrange to have your records transferred (if possible, take them yourself). If you're undergoing hospital out-treatment, notify a new doctor as soon as possible and arrange to continue treatment in the new area.

- [ ] Notify any private clinics or health practitioners such as a chiropodist, chiropractor, optometrist, osteopath, physiotherapist, etc.
- [ ] Contact anyone necessary to tell them that you're moving. These may include your accountant, alarm company (home), babysitter, car breakdown service (AA, Green Flag, RAC), car washer, catalogue shopping companies, charities, cleaner, chiropodist, football pools coupon collector, gardener, gym or leisure centre, hairdresser, library, masseur, milkman, national savings/premium bonds, newsagent, nursery or playgroup, online shopping accounts (e.g. Amazon or Ebay), pension provider, religious organisations, store cards, trade unions, tutors, vet, website hosting companies and window cleaner. It's unnecessary to give everyone you new address, but it will save time to have a 'change of address' sheet printed to distribute to your family, friends and those listed above.

One Week Before Moving

One week before moving day you should have completed most of your packing and should only have minor items to pack such as food and clothes.

- [ ] Check that you haven't forgotten anything that you didn't agree to leave such as bathroom cabinets, shelving, mirrors, pictures and light fittings. If you haven't already done so, now is a good time to dismantle any furniture that cannot be moved in one piece (keep all the nuts and bolts in a labelled bag).
- [ ] Have your post redirected at the local post office. Redirection costs £6 per month, £13 for three months, £20 for six months and £30 to transfer all post addressed to one surname for a year. The post office requires one week's notice. Alternatively you can have post held for you if you're moving locally or arrange for a friend or your buyer to forward post (not that some post may get through even if it's redirected by the post office).

- [ ] Contact the local authority and inform them of the day you're moving. You may be entitled to a refund of part of your council tax.
- [ ] Arrange to drop off your keys with your estate agent and collect the keys to your new home at the earliest opportunity.
- [ ] Give the kitchen a thorough spring clean.
- [ ] Start finalising your 'survival rations' (see page 163).
- [ ] Make lots of copies of the map and instructions (see page 159) how to find your new home and give them to any workmen or friends who will be involved in you move. You will also need to give instructions to anyone who's delivering anything if your new home is difficult to find.
- [ ] Check (again) that the removers have all the instructions and information necessary – including maps and instructions how to find your old and new homes and the colour-coded floor plan (see page 162) of your new home – and confirm the moving date and time.
- [ ] Apply to the local council to suspend a parking bay (or two) or get the police to cone off a parking area on moving day.
- [ ] Obtain your pets' records from your vet.
- [ ] Give friends, relatives and business associates the address and telephone number of your new home or, if you're moving into temporary accommodation, an address (plus email) and telephone number (mobile?) where you can be contacted.
- [ ] Return any library books and videos or anything borrowed.
- [ ] Give your new address to all regular correspondents such as newspaper and magazine subscriptions, book clubs, social and sports clubs, and professional and trade journals. You can do this earlier, but it's advisable not to do so before the exchange of contracts, as your purchase could fall through.
- [ ] If you operate a business from home, arrange for the printing of new headed notepaper and business cards.
- [ ] Collect any dry cleaning, repairs or anything on loan.
- [ ] Obtain the forwarding address and telephone number of your sellers.

- [ ] Make sure that you've got a telephone number on the removal day where you can be contacted by the removers, your partner and anyone else who may need to contact you urgently. This could be your own or a borrowed mobile phone, or that of a friend who can relay messages.

Three Days Before Moving

By now you will be wondering whether you will ever get everything done in time, although you should be well on track if you've been following these guidelines!

- [ ] Before completion day it's important to check the general condition of the property you're buying and ensure that anything you purchased separately or which was included in the purchase price is present (see **Completion** on page 116). **Don't forget to do this in the chaos of moving.**
- [ ] Finish off cleaning the kitchen. Clear out the freezer if you're taking it empty, defrost the fridge and freezer and give them a thorough clean (make sure they're dry). If you're going to take your freezer full of food, turn it up to full power so that everything gets frozen solid over the next few days. Pack everything except your survival rations (see page 163).
- [ ] Prepare any plants that are you're taking with you; spray them with water, give them some nutrients if necessary and use canes to support them.
- [ ] Complete odd jobs such as finding and labelling spare keys, throwing away any junk you aren't taking with you, getting rid of sacks of rubbish, recycling bottles and newspapers, etc.
- [ ] Finish packing and labelling boxes and check that they're labelled correctly.
- [ ] Start cleaning the rest of the house.
- [ ] Confirm that meters will be read by utility companies before or soon after you move, and confirm that the meters will be read and services connected when you arrive at your new home.

- [ ] Do last minute laundry and pack any clothes you won't need before you move.
- [ ] Ensure that the keys for your new home are going to be available.
- [ ] Cancel any regular deliveries, e.g. milk, newspapers and magazines, and pay any outstanding bills.

The Day Before Moving

By now you should be almost finished and sitting around enjoying a well-earned rest, rather than running around like a headless chicken!

- [ ] If you haven't already done so, turn the fridge back on after it has been defrosted to keep your survival rations (see page 163) cool.
- [ ] Confirm that there's a parking area for the removal vehicle or hire van.
- [ ] Confirm that arrangement for your children and pets if they're being looked after by friends or relatives.
- [ ] Provide the shipping company with any last minute instructions regarding how to find your home from the nearest motorway or main road and how you can be contacted if they get lost.
- [ ] Make sure that you have all your survival rations (see page 163) – if not you may have to dash out and do a quick shop.
- [ ] Pack any remaining things that you've wanted to keep out until the last minute.
- [ ] Take down curtains and blinds if not done earlier.
- [ ] Check that you've the keys for your new home or when and where you can collect them.
- [ ] Finish cleaning the house.
- [ ] Disconnect the power and water from your washing machine and fit transit bolts if necessary.

- ☐ Disconnect your TV aerial or satellite dish if you're taking them with you.
- ☐ Have a final check over the home to see whether you've forgotten anything.
- ☐ Withdraw some cash from the bank to cover emergencies and out-of-pocket expenses.
- ☐ Get a good nights sleep – but don't forget to set the alarm (or two) if you're making an unusually early start!

Moving Out

There are certain unwritten rules when moving out:

- ☐ Don't remove door handles, light-bulbs or light fittings, fireplaces, fitted cupboards or anything planted in the garden or cemented down, unless it was specifically noted in the purchase contract.
- ☐ Leave a property in the condition in which the buyer first saw it, but cleared of items that weren't included in the purchase price or were purchased separately by the new owner.
- ☐ Do as you would be done by – clean the property and dispose of all rubbish and unwanted belongings.
- ☐ Don't forget to take everything with you, as the new owner could claim that any items you leave behind are now his and they could be hard to recover.

Moving Day

Hurrah – it's moving day at last! However, before you break open the champagne you've a long, exhausting day ahead of you, where anything and everything could go wrong. The following list assumes that you will be there to supervise the move at both ends. If this isn't the case, you must ensure that someone will be at the collection and delivery addresses to supervise the loading and unloading.

- [ ] Show the removal team's foreman around the house and give him any final instructions regarding the removal or packing of any special items.
- [ ] Ensure that the movers have the floor plan and colour-coded guide (see page 162) of your new home so that they know where to put items.
- [ ] Take the children and pets to their carers for the day or if they're staying with you, set aside a room with food, drink, toys, TV or computer.
- [ ] Provide ample tea, coffee and biscuits!
- [ ] Sedate the dog if you haven't found someone to look after it.
- [ ] Strip the beds and put the bedding into plastic bags for use that night.
- [ ] Pack up your toiletries and make a last check of bathroom cabinets.
- [ ] Check that wardrobes and cupboards are empty.
- [ ] Check that nothing is being taken that shouldn't be and that the packing inventory is accurate. This is the list that the remover will ask you to sign on departure and again after delivery.
- [ ] Check that all rooms are empty and the lights switched off.
- [ ] Switch off the fridge and boiler and disconnect any appliances that you're leaving. Ensure that the water, gas and electricity supplies are turned off at the mains and make a note of the final readings.
- [ ] Empty rubbish bins and leave rubbish bags for collection (or drop them off at the local rubbish dump).
- [ ] Close and lock all windows and doors. Leave all keys to internal doors, windows, garage, shed and other outbuildings (which should be clearly labelled).
- [ ] Once the van is loaded, check the complete house, garden and outbuildings with the foreman to ensure that all items to be moved have been loaded.
- [ ] Say goodbye to your old home, wipe away the tears and drive off into the sunset (taking one last backward glance in the mirror!).
- [ ] Drop the front door keys off at your solicitor.

On Arrival

On arrival at your new home you will need to do the following:

- ☐ Unload your survival rations and organise the children and pets. Pets should be kept in a quiet room from which they cannot escape.
- ☐ Make sure that you've protected the carpet in the hall and other rooms where it will get a lot of use from the removers, particularly if it's a wet day or the carpet is new or has just been cleaned.
- ☐ Ensure that everything is unloaded and stored in the appropriate rooms in your new home (and unpacked and unwrapped by the removers if applicable).
- ☐ Once you're satisfied that everything has been delivered (check them off against your inventory) and positioned in the appropriate place, you will be asked to acknowledge this by signing the delivery sheet. If you find that anything is damaged or missing later, contact the removal company immediately and make a claim.
- ☐ Make sure that your keys are returned by the removers.
- ☐ Have something to eat and drink (not forgetting to offer the removers a drink).
- ☐ Make the beds with the bed linen that you've brought with you.
- ☐ Plug in your fixed-line phone and any appliances that were left by the previous owners.
- ☐ If the house hasn't already been cleaned, start cleaning before you unpack and put everything away. This particularly applies to kitchen cupboards, fridge and freezer.
- ☐ Make a note of the meter readings and check that you aren't over-charged on your first utility bills.

After Moving

In the few days following your move you will need (or may wish) to do the following (some things will have been done already):

- [ ] Arrange to change the external locks (including the garage) as you've no idea how many keys are floating around. You may also wish to have an alarm system installed or the general security checked, e.g. are there locks on the windows?
- [ ] Photograph, measure and record the details of all period features and have them included in your household insurance.
- [ ] Contact the local council offices and organisations (e.g. CAB, tourist office) to obtain information about local amenities, sports facilities, clubs, educational establishments, etc.
- [ ] Make courtesy calls on your neighbours. This is particularly important in villages and rural areas if you want to become part of the local community.
- [ ] Register with the local council for council tax and the electoral roll.
- [ ] Register with a local National Health Service doctor and dentist.
- [ ] If you've oil or gas-fired central heating, you may need to order a delivery of oil or have the gas installation checked. You may also need to order logs or coal for open fires or boilers.
- [ ] Check with your local town hall regarding local regulations about such things as rubbish collection, recycling and on-road parking (you may need to obtain a resident's permit).
- [ ] If you've changed your bank account, you will need to ensure that all your direct debits or standing orders are switched to the new account or cancelled.
- [ ] Check that you've given everyone necessary your new address and telephone number.
- [ ] Make sure that you're receiving your post if it's being forwarded by the post office.
- [ ] Organise your house-warming party and invite your neighbours to it!

DUN SEARCHING

Appendix E: Glossary

Words in italics have their own entry in the glossary.

Acceptance: Agreeing to accept an *offer* on a property, which constitutes a contract.

Acceptance fee: See *Mortgage application* fee.

Agency sales' fee: A fixed percentage of the sale price that's payable to the selling estate agent.

Agent: Someone who acts on behalf of another, such as an estate or letting agent.

Agreement in principle: A document provided by a lender showing that a prospective buyer is eligible for a *mortgage,* subject to the valuation of a property.

Air brick: A perforated brick that aids ventilation in enclosed spaces.

Amortisation: The gradual process of systematically reducing debt in equal payments (as in a *mortgage*) comprising both *principal* and interest, until the debt is paid in full.

Annuity mortgage: A *mortgage* in which both the *capital* and the interest are repaid over a fixed or variable *term.* Also called a *repayment mortgage.*

Appraisal: The current market value of a property as assessed by a prospective selling agent.

APR (Annual Percentage Rate): Everything financed in a loan package (interest, loan fees and other charges), expressed as an annual percentage (APR) of the loan amount. The APR must be quoted when a *mortgage* rate is advertised.

ARLA: Association of Residential Letting Agents.

Arrangement fee: See *Mortgage application fee.*

Arrears: Overdue payments, e.g. for a *mortgage,* rent, ground rent, etc.

Asking price: The price a vendor hopes to get for a property.

Assignment: The transfer of ownership of some kinds of property to another person, such as a lease or an insurance policy that's protecting a loan.

Assured shorthold tenancy: The normal tenancy agreement for domestic lets whereby the landlord can repossess the property after six months, provided he has given the notice required by law.

Assured tenancy: A tenancy agreement whereby the landlord doesn't have the right to repossess a property after six months

ASU: Accident Sickness and Unemployment insurance. Covers your *mortgage* payments should you fall ill or be made redundant.

Auction: The process whereby prospective buyers bid against one another for a property.

Balance outstanding: The amount of a loan owed at any given time.

BAR: The British Association of Removers.

Base rate: The interest rate set by the Bank of England which is used as the basis for setting *mortgage* and savings rates by banks and building societies.

Bedsit: A studio flat with one room for both living and sleeping.

Blind bids: Sealed bid offers made in Scotland after estimates and surveys have been conducted.

Booking fee: A charge paid on application to secure funds, usually required for special deals such as capped and discounted rates.

Boundaries: The limits of a property or its land.

Bridging loan: A short-term loan designed to allow you to buy a new home before you have sold your existing home.

Broker: An independent agency through which you can seek the most appropriate or economical financial service or product (e.g. insurance, *mortgage*).

Buildings insurance: An insurance policy that protects homeowners from damage to their home. Mandatory when a property has a *mortgage*. See also *Household insurance*.

Building survey: See *Survey*.

Buildmark: A structural guarantee from the *NHBC* provided on most new homes.

Bungalow: A single-storey detached or semi-detached house.

Buy-to-let mortgage: A *mortgage* for investors wishing to buy property to let out.

Buyer's market: A falling property market when sellers may be willing to reduce the price to sell a property.

Cap and collar mortgage: A *mortgage* with maximum and minimum interest rates.

Capital: The *mortgage* loan (also *principal*).

Capital gains tax (CGT): Tax payable on the profits made from the sale of certain assets, including second homes and investment property.

Capital and interest: Another name for a *repayment mortgage*.

Capital reducing mortgage: A *repayment mortgage*.

Capped-rate mortgage: A *variable rate mortgage* with a maximum interest rate, either for a set period of months or years, annually or over the whole *term* of the *mortgage*.

Cashback mortgage: A payment you may receive when you take out a *mortgage*, which can be a fixed amount or a percentage of the mortgage sum.

Cash buyer: A buyer who doesn't have to sell a property before buying.

Cavity wall: Modern building method whereby two walls are built with a small gap between them for insulation.

CH: Central heating (fitted in all modern homes). GCH is gas central heating.

Chain: Where a number of people are dependent on the sale or purchase of another property before they can complete on their own.

Charge: Any right or interest, subject to which freehold or leasehold property may be held, especially a *mortgage*.

Clear title: The title of a property that's unencumbered by legal charges regarding its ownership.

Cloakroom: A small room or closet with a toilet and hand basin (called a half bathroom in some countries).

Closing: The final procedure in a property transaction when documents are executed and recorded, funds are disbursed and the *title* transferred from the *vendor* to the buyer. Also called *completion* or settlement.

Closing costs: Costs the buyer must pay at the time of *closing* in addition to the *deposit*, including solicitor's fees, *mortgage indemnity guarantee* fee and *buildings insurance*.

Closing statement: A statement prepared by a solicitor detailing the closing costs for both the seller and the buyer.

CML: The Council of Mortgage Lenders, which has devised the Mortgage Code to ensure that lenders treat customers fairly.

Collar: A collar is the term for when a lenders sets a rate below which interest rates cannot fall, irrespective of how low the *base rate* falls.

Collateral: Anything that's pledged as *security* against the repayment of a loan, such as the *title deeds* of a property.

Commission: The percentage of the selling price of a property received by the selling agent(s).

Common elements: The parts of a property (e.g. an apartment or flat) that aren't individually owned.

Completion: The final legal transfer of ownership of a property. See also *Closing*.

Completion date: The date on which a transaction is finalised, the money is paid, the *deeds* are handed over and the keys are given to the new owner.

Conclusion of missives: The point at which a property sale in Scotland becomes binding.

Conditions of sale: The standard terms governing the rights and duties of both parties as laid down in the sales contract.

Contents insurance: An insurance policy protecting a homeowner from loss or damage to personal belongings or home contents. See also *Household insurance*.

Contract: The agreement to buy and sell a property, which isn't binding in England, Wales or N. Ireland until the *exchange of contracts*.

Conveyance: The act of transferring the *title* of a property and also the document (such as a *deed*) used to transfer ownership.

Conveyancer: The person (e.g. a solicitor or licensed conveyancer) who undertakes *conveyance*.

Conveyancing: The legal and administrative process involved in transferring the ownership of land and buildings from one person to another.

Cottage: Traditionally a pretty, quaint house in the country, perhaps with a thatched roof (although the name is often stretched nowadays to encompass almost anything except an apartment). Can be a *detached* or *terraced house*.

County development plan: A plan drawn up by a county council for the use of land over a period of five years. See also *Zoning*.

Covenant: A promise in a *deed* to undertake (if the covenant is positive) or abstain from (if the covenant is negative) doing specified things such as building on land or prohibiting business use.

CRA: Credit Reference Agency.

Credit check/score: A lender's method of assessing the risk of lending to you, based on your financial record.

Current account mortgage (CAM): A *mortgage* that's combined with a current account and credit card offering all or some of the advantages of a *flexible mortgage*.

Deed(s): A written legal document that conveys *title* to property and provides evidence of ownership. Also called *title deeds*.

Deed of assignment: A *deed* used to transfer *leasehold unregistered land*.

Deed of mortgage: A *deed* used to transfer *title* in a property to the *mortgagee*.

Deed of transfer: A *deed* used to transfer *registered land*.

Deed restrictions: A clause in a *deed* that restricts the use of land.

Deferred start mortgage: A type of *mortgage* where no repayments are made for the first one to three months of the *term*. Only available with a *repayment mortgage.*

Deposit: The amount that needs to be paid in cash in order to obtain a *mortgage*, e.g. if you have an 80 per cent mortgage, you must make a 20 per cent deposit. It also usual to pay a deposit (e.g. 10 per cent) on the *exchange of contracts.*

Detached house: A single-family house that stands alone, usually with its own garden (possibly front and rear) and garage.

Differentials: When a lender operates a 'banding system', under which extra interest is charged on larger loans, the 'bands' are called differentials.

Direct mortgage: A home loan sold exclusively over the phone or the Internet.

Disbursements: Costs such as *stamp duty*, *Land Registry* and *search* fees that are payable to the *conveyancer* when a sale is completed.

Discharge fee: A fee charged by a lender for releasing its charge over a property once you have paid off your loan. You may also incur this fee when switching to another lender (remortgaging).

Discount period: The period of reduced rate payments at the start of a *discounted rate* mortgage.

Discounted rate: A guaranteed reduction in the standard variable *mortgage* rate, usually over an agreed term.

Disposition: The legal document that transfers ownership of property in Scotland.

Draft contract: A legal document containing the terms of a sale used by solicitors as a starting point for negotiation.

Drawdown facility: The ability to borrow through your *mortgage* at a later date.

Early redemption: Paying off a loan before the end of the *mortgage term*. There's usually a penalty charge for doing this.

Earnest money: Funds paid with an offer to show good faith to complete a purchase.

Easement: The interest, privilege or right that a party has in the land of another party, e.g. a right of way.

Encumbrance: Any right or interest in a property that affects its value such as outstanding loans, unpaid taxes, *easements* and *deed* restrictions.

Endowment insurance (or policy): Life insurance policy incorporating investments that pays out a specified sum (or more) on a specified date or an agreed sum in life insurance if the holder dies before the end of the term.

Endowment mortgage: A type of *mortgage* loan on which only interest is paid. Repayments are combined with savings through a life assurance policy. By the end of the mortgage *term*, the value of the endowment policy should have grown sufficiently to repay the mortgage and (hopefully) leave the *mortgagor* with a surplus. See also *Interest only.*

Engrossment: The final executed deed.

Equity: The amount of value an owner has in a property after the deductions of any outstanding *liens* such as a *mortgage*, e.g. if a property is valued at £100,000 and the amount outstanding on a mortgage is £50,000, the owner has £50,000 equity.

Equity loan: A second *mortgage* where the owner borrows against his *equity* in a property.

Escrow: A procedure in which documents of cash and property are put in the care of a third party, other than the buyer or seller, pending completion of agreed conditions and terms in sales' contracts.

Estate agent: A person or company selling property on commission. Called real estate agents, realtors and brokers in some countries (e.g. the USA).

Exchange of contracts: The process of making an agreement to buy and sell a house legally binding in England, Wales and N. Ireland.

Extended redemption penalty: When the redemption penalty extends beyond the period of a capped or fixed rate period.

First charge: The legal charge that a lender has over your home, i.e. it has first call on any funds available from the sale of the property to cover your loan.

Fixed-rate mortgage: A *mortgage* with a fixed *interest rate* for an agreed period of months, years or the whole term.

Fixtures & fittings (F&F): A fixture is generally something attached to a property as part of it, e.g. the bathroom fittings or the kitchen units. A fitting generally usually refers to something that can be removed, e.g. carpets and curtains.

Flexible month mortgage: A type of *mortgage* whereby no repayments are made in one or two months of a year.

Flexible mortgage: A *mortgage* that offers maximum flexibility by allowing over payments, payment holidays, a cheque book and borrow back facilities. See also *Current account mortgage*.

Foreclosure: Legal proceedings instigated by a lender to deprive a person of ownership rights when *mortgage* payments haven't been maintained. Also called repossession.

Freehold: The highest interest in a property that can be held by an individual. In theory the owner is free to do with the property what he wishes, although in practice various restrictions (e.g. *planning permission*) are placed on this right.

Freeholder: One who owns the *freehold* of a property.

FSBO: An abbreviation for 'For Sale By Owner', when a home is being sold privately without the assistance of an *estate agent*.

Full status loan: A loan where complete checks are made on your credit history and income.

Full structural survey: See *Structural survey*.

Funding fee: A fee incurred by the *mortgagor* when switching from a *fixed rate* to a *variable rate mortgage* before the end of the fixed rate period.

Gazumping: When a *vendor* accepts a higher offer after a previous offer has already been accepted (but contracts haven't been exchanged). The person who made the previous offer is said to have been gazumped.

Gazundering: The term for when a buyer lowers the price agreed for a property just before the planned exchange of contracts, in an attempt to force the vendor to reduce the price.

Ground rent: An annual fee payable by the *leaseholder* of an apartment to the *freeholder*.

Guarantor: Someone who agrees to guarantee your loan and is fully liable for its repayment should you default.

Guide price: The estimated selling price, e.g. at an auction.

Homebuy schemes: Schemes run by *housing associations* to sell their property.

Homebuyer's report: A *survey* (inspection) of a property that is more detailed than a *valuation*, but less comprehensive than a *structural survey*.

Homesearch agency: An agency that will search for a property meeting specific criteria.

Home seller's pack: See *Seller's pack*.

Household insurance: An insurance policy that combines building and contents policies.

Housing association: Non-profit organisation established to improve the provision of housing in a particular area through rental and ownership schemes.

IFA: Independent Financial Advisor. A regulated advisor who can recommend the best *mortgage* for you.

Improvement grant: A grant made by the local authority (council) towards the cost of repairing or improving property.

Income multiplier: How a *mortgage* lender works out how much you can borrow, usually by multiplying your gross annual salary.

Index map search: A search to discover whether the ownership of a property is registered at the *Land Registry*.

Index tracker mortgage: See *Tracker mortgage*.

Individual savings account (ISA): A tax-free savings scheme.

Individual savings account (ISA) mortgage: An interest-only, investment *mortgage* linked to an *individual savings account*.

Instruction: The term used when an estate agent is formally instructed by a property owner to market a property.

Insulation: Material used (in walls and the roof space) to retain warmth in the structure of a property.

Interest-only mortgage: Your monthly payments to your lender comprise interest only and you don't pay off the *mortgage* during the life of the loan. This is accomplished by the proceeds from a savings policy such as an endowment. See also *Endowment mortgage*.

Interest rate: A percentage that when multiplied by the *principal* determines the amount of money that the *principal* earns over a period of time (usually one year).

Inventory: A list of items included in the sale price of a property or provided by the landlord in a rented property.

Investment-linked mortgage: A *mortgage* linked to an *Individual Savings Account (ISA)* or *Personal Equity Plan (PEP)* or other tax-free savings scheme.

ISA: Individual Savings Account. See *Investment-linked mortgage* above.

ISA mortgage: An *investment-linked mortgage* that is repaid via an *ISA*.

ISVA: The Incorporated Society of Valuers and Auctioneers.

Joint mortgage A *mortgage* involving more than one person.

Joint (sole) agency: When two estate agents agree to market a property together and share the commission.

Joint tenancy: Property ownership by two (e.g. a married couple) or more people with an undivided interest and the right of survivorship, where if one owner dies the property automatically passes to the joint owner(s).

Land certificate: A certificate issued by the *Land Registry* as proof of ownership.

(Her Majesty's) Land Registry: A government office where the ownership of all property in England and Wales (with registered *titles*) is registered. It has its head office in London and district offices in various other towns.

Land Registry fee: The charge payable to the *Land Registry* to enter your details into its records when you have finalised a home purchase or changed your *mortgage* lender.

Lease: Permission to own or rent property for a limited period.

Leasehold: Ownership of property but not the land on which it stands. Leasehold ownership is restricted to a number of years (e.g. 99 to 999) and creates a landlord-tenant relationship between the *lessor* (*freeholder*) and the *lessee*.

Leaseholder: One who owns a *leasehold* property.

Legal charge: To all intents and purposes, the same as a *mortgage*.

Lender's reference: An endorsement from a previous lender to say that you have maintained your *mortgage* repayments (often required by a new lender when you *remortgage* your home).

Lessee: The person to whom a *lease* is granted.

Lessor: The person who grants a *lease*.

LIBOR: London Interbank Offered Rate, the rate at which banks nominally buy and sell money to each other. LIBOR-linked *mortgage* are susceptible to a change in interest rate every three months.

Licensed conveyancer: A person licensed to perform property *conveyancing*.

Lien: A charge against property making it *security* for a debt such as a *mortgage*.

Loan to value (LTV): The size of the *mortgage* as a percentage of the value of the property or the price to be paid. A £160,000 mortgage on a house worth £200,000 is equal to an LTV of 80 per cent.

Local authority search: An application made to the local authority for a certificate providing information about a property and the surrounding area.

Lock-in: A *mortgage* with a *fixed*, *discounted* or *capped rate*, where the borrower is locked-in to the standard *variable rate* for a number of years during which a high *redemption penalty* applies if you want to change your lender or pay off your mortgage early.

Lock-out agreement: An agreement whereby a seller takes a property off the market for a period during which contracts must be exchanged.

Low-start mortgage: A *mortgage* where repayments start low and increase by a certain percentage each year until the full level is reached.

LTV: See *Loan-to-value*.

Maisonette: Part of a house or apartment block forming separate living accommodation, usually on two floors with its own outside entrance.

Management company: A company, such as an estate agent, that manages a property which is let. Also a company that manages a leasehold property.

Market value: The current value of a property compared with similar properties, generally accepted to be the highest price a buyer will pay and the lowest price a vendor will accept. The value calculated by a selling agent when he does an *appraisal*.

Mews house: A house that's converted from old stables or servants' lodgings (usually 17th to 19th century) and is the town equivalent of a genuine cottage.

MIG: See *Mortgage indemnity guarantee.*

Missives: The letters exchanged between solicitors in Scotland agreeing acceptance of an offer on a property (similar to the *exchange of contracts* in the rest of the UK). Once the missives have been exchanged the deal is legally binding.

Mobile (park) home: A pre-fabricated timber-framed home that can be moved to a new site, although most are permanently located on a 'home park'.

Mortgage: A loan for which a house is the security or collateral. A written instrument that creates a *lien* against a property as *security* against the repayment of a loan. Gives the lender the right to sell the property if payments aren't made.

Mortgage application fee: A fee charged by the lender for evaluating, preparing and submitting a proposed *mortgage* loan. Also called an *acceptance* or *arrangement fee.*

Mortgage deed: The document containing the conditions of a loan secured on a property. Also called a *legal charge.*

Mortgage indemnity guarantee (MIG): A compulsory insurance policy that's required by a lender for a loan that's greater than a certain percentage (usually 90 per cent) of the value of a property. Also known as mortgage guarantee insurance (MGI).

Mortgage protection policy (MPP): Insurance that pays a *mortgage* and protects the *mortgagor* against *foreclosure* in the event of job loss, major accident, illness or death.

Mortgage term: See *Term.*

Mortgagee: The company or organisation that lends the money for a *mortgage.*

Mortgagor: The person taking out a *mortgage.*

Multiple agency: An agreement whereby a number of *estate agents* market a property and the one that sells it receives the commission.

NAEA: The National Association of Estate Agents.

Negative equity: The situation when the market value of a property is less than the *mortgage* outstanding on it.

New instruction: A new property for sale that has been added to an agent's list.

NHBC: The National Home Building Council, which provides warranties for new homes.

Non-profit endowment: A *mortgage* that's guaranteed to repay the loan but provides no benefit other than life cover.

Non-status mortgage: A loan where the borrower isn't required to provide employment or income references. Also known as special status.

Offer: A bid to buy a property at a specific price.

Off-plan: The process of buying a property from the brochures and floor plan (and possibly a show house), before it's built.

Open market value: The price a property fetches when there's a willing buyer and a willing seller.

Overhang: When the *early repayment* penalty extends beyond the fixed or *capped-rate* period.

Park home: See *Mobile home.*

Pay rate: The rate of interest you pay on your *mortgage.*

Payment method: The way you repay your *mortgage,* such as *pension, ISA, endowment* or capital and interest (*repayment mortgage*) payments.

Payment protection insurance (PPI): See *Mortgage protection policy*.

Pension mortgage: A type of *mortgage* in which the repayments cover only the interest on the loan, while separate payments are made into a personal pension plan. They are usually available only to those who are self-employed or whose employer doesn't offer an occupational pension scheme.

Period property: A loosely used term for a property usually built before 1914 and named after the period in which it was built, e.g. Georgian, Victorian or Edwardian.

Permitted development rights: The right to carry out certain alterations to a property without planning permission.

Personal equity plan (PEP): A tax-free savings scheme.

Planning permission: Permission granted by a local planning authority to erect or alter a building.

Power of attorney: The legal authority to act on behalf of another.

Preliminary enquiries: The questions asked about a property before *exchange of contracts*.

Premium: Payment in respect of a *mortgage* or insurance policy. Can be a one-off payment or periodical.

Principal: The amount of money borrowed to buy a property and the amount still owed.

Principal and interest payment: A periodic (usually monthly) *mortgage* repayment which includes interest charges plus an amount applied to the *amortisation* of the *principal* balance.

Private treaty sale: A method of selling a property by agreement between the vendor and the purchaser, either directly or through an *estate agent*.

Provisional loan approval: A service offered by lenders whereby they provide provisional approval of a loan (for a maximum sum) thus establishing a buyer's price range, strengthening his buying position and shortening the loan approval period.

Quotation: A document detailing all the costs involved in taking out a particular *mortgage* deal.

Redemption: Full repayment of a *mortgage* loan.

Redemption fee/penalty: A fee or penalty incurred by the *mortgagor* when redeeming a loan (or part of it) before the end of the *term*.

Re-finance: To replace an old *mortgage* with a new one, either to reduce the *interest rate*, secure better terms or increase the amount borrowed. Also called a *remortgage*.

Registration fee: A fee payable by a purchaser to have *title deeds* registered at the *Land Registry*.

Registered land: Land, the title to which is recorded at *HM Land Registry*.

Remortgage: To take out an additional or new *mortgage* against a property. See also *Re-finance*.

Repayment mortgage: A loan on which part of the capital plus interest is paid back throughout the loan *term*.

Repossession: See *Foreclosure*.

Reserve price: The minimum price acceptable to the vendor when selling a property at auction.

Retention: Holding back part of a *mortgage* until certain repairs or improvements to a property have been completed satisfactorily.

RIBA: The Royal Institute of British Architects.

RICS: The Royal Institute of Chartered Surveyors.

Right of way: An individual's legal right of way to use a particular part of a property in order to gain access to his own land or property.

Rising damp: Where damp rises up a wall leading to wood rot and plaster decay.

Sealed bids: Where prospective buyers make bids in writing and the highest bid wins.

Sealing fee: A charge made by lenders when you repay a *mortgage*.

Search: An enquiry made by or on behalf of a purchaser to ensure proper *title* to a property, e.g. a local authority search.

Security: Assets such as house *deeds* pledged in support of a loan.

Self-build mortgage: A *mortgage* on a property that you manage and build yourself or by employing others. The loan is paid in stages as building work progresses.

Self-certification mortgage: Where you declare your income to a lender, which is generally accepted with the minimum of checks.

Seller's market: When demand is high and sellers can command top prices.

Seller's pack: A government initiative whereby sellers may in future be required to provide a seller's pack (including a survey) for their home before putting it on the market. No date has been set for the introduction of the seller's pack.

Seller's property information form: A form completed by the seller and his solicitor after an offer has been accepted giving relevant information to the buyer.

Semi-detached house: A detached building containing two separate homes joined in the middle by a common wall.

Service charges: The annual fees payable by leaseholders to the maintenance and repair of an apartment building.

Settlement: See *Closing*.

Settlement day: In Scotland, the point at which the legal ownership of a property transfers from seller to buyer.

Show home: A model home built on the site of a new development to show the sort of property on offer.

Sink(ing) fund: A fund financed from *service charges* to pay for one-off major repairs.

Sitting tenant: Someone who has a legal right of occupation, even if a property is sold to someone else, and can apply to the local authority to set a fair rent.

Sole agency: An agreement giving an *estate agent* the exclusive right to sell a property during the term of the agreement (but the owner can retain the right to sell it privately).

Sole selling rights: Where one agent has the exclusive rights to sell a property and is entitled to a fee however the property is sold (even if it's sold privately by the owner).

Solicitor: A legal professional similar to a lawyer who traditionally carried out all property conveyancing (now also done by *licensed conveyancers*).

Stakeholder: One who holds a deposit as an intermediary between the buyer and seller, pending *completion*.

Stamp duty: A tax payable by the buyer when a property is purchased for over £60,000.

Standard variable rate (SVR): The basic rate of interest a lender charges on a straight *variable rate mortgage*.

Structural survey: The most in-depth *survey* of a property usually encompassing all structures and systems. See also *Homebuyer's report*.

Studio flat: A one-room dwelling plus a bathroom, possibly with a separate kitchen.

Subject to contract: The words that should be contained in every letter to a seller (or his agent or *solicitor*) before contracts are exchanged.

Superior: In Scotland, the original owner of feudal tenure who's able to impose conditions on the use of the land or property in perpetuity.

Survey: An examination of the condition of a property before purchase, performed by a professional surveyor. See also *Homebuyer's report* and *structural survey*.

Tenant: The person in possession of a property, usually by way of a *lease*.

Tenants in common: Two or more people who hold property in such a way that, when one dies, his or her share doesn't pass automatically to the survivor but under his will or intestacy.

Tenancy in common: A form of ownership in which two or more people buy a property jointly, but with no right of survivorship. Owners are free to will their share to anyone they choose, which is the main difference between this and *joint tenancy*. Often used by friends or relatives buying together.

(For sale by) Tender: A property offered 'for sale by tender' has no asking price and offers are invited (usually in excess of a minimum sum) by a specified date. The vendor isn't obliged to accept an offer, but if he does it constitutes an immediate contract. This is the standard procedure in Scotland.

Tenure: Whether a property is *freehold* or *leasehold*. The ownership of property in Scotland is by 'feudal tenure'.

Term (of a mortgage): The number of years over which a *mortgage* is to be repaid, which can be either fixed (e.g. 15 or 25 years) or variable according to the rate of repayment.

Terraced house: Houses built in a row of three or more usually two to five storeys high.

Time is of the essence: A legal term where if either party is late for completion, the contract can be enforced only by serving a notice to complete setting a time limit to finalise the transaction. This step has serious legal consequences.

Title: The right of ownership of property.

Title deeds: The documents that confer ownership of land or property.

Title number: The unique number allocated to each property by the *Land Registry*.

Title search: A professional scrutiny of public records to establish the chain of ownership of a property and record any outstanding *liens*, *mortgage*, *encumbrances* or other factors that may restrict clear *title*.

Top-up mortgage: An additional loan from another lender when the first lender doesn't provide sufficient finance to buy a house.

Townhouse: Similar to a terraced house but more modern and larger, often with an integral garage.

Tracker mortgage: A home loan where the *interest rate* 'tracks' the *base rate* and rises and falls in line with it.

Transaction period: A procedure drawn up by the Law Society intended to speed up the process of preparing the contract.

Transfer: The *Land Registry* document transferring the ownership of property from the seller to the buyer.

Under offer: The term used when an offer on a property has been accepted. This isn't legally binding in England, Wales and N. Ireland, where sellers can still accept a higher offer until the *exchange of contracts*.

Unregistered land: Land which isn't recorded in the *Land Registry*.

Upset price: The minimum advertised price for a property in Scotland. Offers should be made above this price.

Vacant possession: Where the previous occupants must vacate the property before you move in or complete, including any tenants.

Vacation fee: A fee charged by the lender for sealing the deeds following repayment of a *mortgage*.

Valuation: The professional examination of a property to determine its *market value*. A fee is usually charged by the lender for a valuation.

Variable rate mortgage: A *mortgage* loan whose *interest rate* changes in accordance with prevailing interest rates.

Vendor: The owner or person selling a property.

With-profits policy: A policy often used with an *endowment mortgage* where the bonuses from a life insurance policy are added to the original sum assured that is paid when the policy matures.

Zoning: The procedure that classifies land and property according to usage, e.g. residential, commercial or industrial, in accordance with a *county development plan*.

FOR SALE
ALL MOD CONS
-A SNIP AT-
£250,000

INDEX

A

B

C

D

E

F

G

H

N

O

P

R

S

T

U

V

W

Y

ARIEL
COTTAGE

BUYING A HOME SERIES

Buying a Home books are essential reading for anyone planning to purchase property abroad and are designed to guide you through the jungle and make it a pleasant and enjoyable experience. Most importantly, they're packed with vital information to help you **avoid the sort of disasters that can turn your dream home into a nightmare!** Topics covered include:

- Avoiding problems
- Choosing the region
- Finding the right home and location
- Estate agents
- Finance, mortgages and taxes
- Home security
- Utilities, heating and air-conditioning
- Moving house and settling in
- Renting and letting
- Permits and visas
- Travelling and communications
- Health and insurance
- Renting a car and driving
- Retirement and starting a business
- And much, much more!

Buying a Home books are the most comprehensive and up-to-date source of information available about buying property abroad. Whether you want a detached house, townhouse or apartment, a holiday or a permanent home, these books will help make your dreams come true.

Save yourself time, trouble and money!

Order your copies today by phone, fax, mail or e-mail from: Survival Books, PO Box 146, Wetherby, West Yorks. LS23 6XZ, United Kingdom (☎/📠 +44 (0)1937-843523, ✉ orders@ survivalbooks.net, 💻 www.survivalbooks.net).

ORDER FORM

ALIEN'S GUIDES / BEST PLACES / BUYING A HOME / DISASTERS / WINES

Qty.	Title	Price (incl. p&p)*			Total
		UK	Europe	World	
	The Alien's Guide to Britain	£5.95	£6.95	£8.45	
	The Alien's Guide to France	£5.95	£6.95	£8.45	
	The Best Places to Buy a Home in France	£13.95	£15.95	£19.45	
	The Best Places to Buy a Home in Spain	£13.45	£14.95	£16.95	
	Buying a Home Abroad	£13.45	£14.95	£16.95	
	Buying a Home in Britain	£11.45	£12.95	£14.95	
	Buying a Home in Florida	£13.45	£14.95	£16.95	
	Buying a Home in France	£13.45	£14.95	£16.95	
	Buying a Home in Greece & Cyprus	£13.45	£14.95	£16.95	
	Buying a Home in Ireland	£11.45	£12.95	£14.95	
	Buying a Home in Italy	£13.45	£14.95	£16.95	
	Buying a Home in Portugal	£13.45	£14.95	£16.95	
	Buying a Home in Spain	£13.45	£14.95	£16.95	
	How to Avoid Holiday & Travel Disasters	£13.45	£14.95	£16.95	
	Renovating & Maintaining Your French Home	Autumn 2003			
	Rioja and its Wines	£11.45	£12.95	£14.95	
	The Wines of Spain	£15.95	£18.45	£21.95	
				Total	

Order your copies today by phone, fax, mail or e-mail from: Survival Books, PO Box 146, Wetherby, West Yorks. LS23 6XZ, UK (☎/🖷 +44 (0)1937-843523, ✉ orders@survivalbooks.net, 💻 www.survivalbooks.net). If you aren't entirely satisfied, simply return them to us within 14 days for a full and unconditional refund.

Cheque enclosed/please charge my Amex/Delta/MasterCard/Switch/Visa* card

Card No. _ _ _ _ _ _ _ _ _ _ _ _ _ _ _ _

Expiry date ____________ Issue number (Switch only) ____________

Signature ____________ Tel. No. ____________

NAME ____________

ADDRESS ____________

____

____

* Delete as applicable (price includes postage – airmail for Europe/world).

ORDER FORM

LIVING & WORKING SERIES / RETIRING ABROAD

Qty.	Title	Price (incl. p&p)*			Total
		UK	Europe	World	
	Living & Working Abroad	£16.95	£18.95	£22.45	
	Living & Working in America	£14.95	£16.95	£20.45	
	Living & Working in Australia	£14.95	£16.95	£20.45	
	Living & Working in Britain	£14.95	£16.95	£20.45	
	Living & Working in Canada	£16.95	£18.95	£22.45	
	Living & Working in the Far East	Winter 2003			
	Living & Working in France	£14.95	£16.95	£20.45	
	Living & Working in Germany	£16.95	£18.95	£22.45	
	Living & Working in the Gulf States & Saudi Arabia	£16.95	£18.95	£22.45	
	Living & Working in Holland, Belgium & Luxembourg	£14.95	£16.95	£20.45	
	Living & Working in Ireland	£14.95	£16.95	£20.45	
	Living & Working in Italy	£16.95	£18.95	£22.45	
	Living & Working in London	£11.45	£12.95	£14.95	
	Living & Working in New Zealand	£14.95	£16.95	£20.45	
	Living & Working in Spain	£14.95	£16.95	£20.45	
	Living & Working in Switzerland	£16.95	£18.95	£22.45	
	Retiring Abroad	£14.95	£16.95	£20.45	
				Total	

Order your copies today by phone, fax, mail or e-mail from: Survival Books, PO Box 146, Wetherby, West Yorks. LS23 6XZ, UK (☎/📠 +44 (0)1937-843523, ✉ orders@survivalbooks.net, 💻 www.survivalbooks.net). If you aren't entirely satisfied, simply return them to us within 14 days for a full and unconditional refund.

Cheque enclosed/please charge my Amex/Delta/MasterCard/Switch/Visa* card

Card No. __ __ __ __   __ __ __ __   __ __ __ __   __ __ __ __

Expiry date ____________ Issue number (Switch only) ____________________

Signature ______________________ Tel. No. ____________________

NAME ____

ADDRESS ____

____

____

* Delete as applicable (price includes postage – airmail for Europe/world).

OTHER SURVIVAL BOOKS

Survival Books publishes a variety of books in addition to the *Living and Working* and *Buying a Home* series (see previous pages). These include:

The Alien's Guides: *The Alien's Guides to Britain* and *France* provide an 'alternative' look at life in these popular countries and will help you to avoid the most serious gaffes and to appreciate more fully the peculiarities (in both senses) of the British and French.

The Best Places to Buy a Home: The *Best Places to Buy a Home in France* and *Spain* are the most comprehensive and up-to-date sources of information available for anyone wanting to research the property market in France and Spain and will save you endless hours choosing the best place for your home.

How to Avoid Holiday and Travel Disasters: This book is essential reading for anyone planning a trip abroad and will help you to make the right decisions regarding every aspect of your travel arrangements and to avoid costly mistakes and the sort of disasters that can turn a trip into a nightmare.

Renovating & Maintaining Your French Home: New for 2003 is the ultimate guide to renovating and maintaining your dream home in France, including essential information, contacts and vocabulary and time and cost-saving tips.

Retiring Abroad: This is the most comprehensive and up-to-date source of practical information available about retiring to a foreign country and will help to smooth your path to successful retirement abroad and save you time, trouble and money.

Wine Guides: *Rioja and its Wines* and *The Wines of Spain* are required reading for lovers of fine wines and are the most comprehensive and up-to-date sources of information available on the wines of Spain and of its most famous wine-producing region.

Broaden your horizons with Survival Books!

Order your copies today by phone, fax, mail or e-mail from: Survival Books, PO Box 146, Wetherby, West Yorks. LS23 6XZ, United Kingdom (☎/🖷 +44 (0)1937-843523, ✉ orders@ survivalbooks.net, 💻 www.survivalbooks.net).

NOTES

Notes

NOTES

NOTES

Notes

NOTES

NOTES

NOTES

Notes

NOTES